EDUCATION, POLITICS, AND PUBLIC LIFE

Series Editors:
Henry A. Giroux, McMaster University
Susan Searls Giroux, McMaster University

Within the last three decades, education as a political, moral, and ideological practice has become central to rethinking not only the role of public
and higher education, but also the emergence of pedagogical sites outside
of the schools—which include but are not limited to the Internet, television, film, magazines, and the media of print culture. Education as both a
form of schooling and public pedagogy reaches into every aspect of political, economic, and social life. What is particularly important in this highly
interdisciplinary and politically nuanced view of education are a number of
issues that now connect learning to social change, the operations of democratic public life, and the formation of critically engaged individual and
social agents. At the center of this series will be questions regarding what
young people, adults, academics, artists, and cultural workers need to know
to be able to live in an inclusive and just democracy and what it would mean
to develop institutional capacities to reintroduce politics and public commitment into everyday life. Books in this series aim to play a vital role in rethinking the entire project of the related themes of politics, democratic struggles,
and critical education within the global public sphere.

SERIES EDITORS:

HENRY A. GIROUX holds the Global TV Network Chair in English
and Cultural Studies at McMaster University in Canada. He is on the edi-
torial and advisory boards of numerous national and international scholarly journals. Professor Giroux was selected as a Kappa Delta Pi Laureate
in 1998 and was the recipient of a Getty Research Institute Visiting
Scholar Award in 1999. He was the recipient of the Hooker Distinguished
Professor Award for 2001. He received an Honorary Doctorate of Letters
from Memorial University of Newfoundland in 2005. His most recent
books include *Take Back Higher Education* (co-authored with Susan
Searls Giroux, 2006), *America on the Edge* (2006), *Beyond the Spectacle of
Terrorism* (2006), *Stormy Weather: Katrina and the Politics of Disposability*
(2006), *The University in Chains: Confronting the Military-Industrial-
Academic Complex* (2007) and *Against the T~~~~~ ~N~~~~ralism: Politics
Beyond the Age of Greed*

SUSAN SEARLS GIROUX is Associate Professor of English and Cultural Studies at McMaster University. Her most recent books include *The Theory Toolbox* (co-authored with Jeff Nealon, 2004), *Take Back Higher Education* (co-authored with Henry A. Giroux, 2006), and *Between Race and Reason: Violence, Intellectual Responsibility, and the University to Come* (2010). Professor Giroux is also the Managing Editor of *The Review of Education, Pedagogy, and Cultural Studies.*

Critical Pedagogy in Uncertain Times: Hope and Possibilities
Edited by Sheila L. Macrine

The Gift of Education: Public Education and Venture Philanthropy
Kenneth J. Saltman

Feminist Theory in Pursuit of the Public: Women and the "Re-Privatization" of Labor
Robin Truth Goodman

Hollywood's Exploited: Public Pedagogy, Corporate Movies, and Cultural Crisis
Edited by Benjamin Frymer, Tony Kashani, Anthony J. Nocella, II, and Richard Van Heertum; Foreword by Lawrence Grossberg

Education out of Bounds: Reimagining Cultural Studies for a Posthuman Age
Tyson E. Lewis and Richard Kahn

Academic Freedom in the Post-9/11 Era
Edited by Edward J. Carvalho and David B. Downing

Educating Youth for a World beyond Violence: A Pedagogy for Peace
H. Svi Shapiro

Rituals and Student Identity in Education: Ritual Critique for a New Pedagogy
Richard A. Quantz with Terry O'Connor and Peter Magolda

Citizen Youth: Culture, Activism, and Agency in a Neoliberal Era
Jacqueline Kennelly

Conflicts in Curriculum Theory: Challenging Hegemonic Epistemologies
João M. Paraskeva; Foreword by Donaldo Macedo

Sport, Spectacle, and NASCAR Nation: Consumption and the Cultural Politics of Neoliberalism
Joshua I. Newman and Michael D. Giardina

America According to Colbert: Satire as Public Pedagogy
Sophia A. McClennen

FEMINIST THEORY IN PURSUIT OF THE PUBLIC

WOMEN AND THE "RE-PRIVATIZATION" OF LABOR

Robin Truth Goodman

First published in hardcover in 2010 by
PALGRAVE MACMILLAN®
in the United States—a division of St. Martin's Press LLC,
175 Fifth Avenue, New York, NY 10010.

Where this book is distributed in the UK, Europe and the rest of the world,
this is by Palgrave Macmillan, a division of Macmillan Publishers Limited,
registered in England, company number 785998, of Houndmills,
Basingstoke, Hampshire RG21 6XS.

Palgrave Macmillan is the global academic imprint of the above companies
and has companies and representatives throughout the world.

Palgrave® and Macmillan® are registered trademarks in the United States,
the United Kingdom, Europe and other countries.

ISBN: 978–0–230–61641–7

Library of Congress Cataloging-in-Publication Data

Goodman, Robin Truth, 1966–
     Feminist theory in pursuit of the public : women and the
"re-privatization" of labor / by Robin Truth Goodman.
          p. cm.—(Education, politics, and public life)
          ISBN 978–0–230–61640–0 (alk. paper)
          1. Feminist theory. 2. Sex role. 3. Power (Social sciences) I. Title.

HQ1190.G66 2010
305.4201—dc22   2010003049

A catalogue record for this book is available from the British Library.

Design by Newgen Imaging Systems (P) Ltd., Chennai, India.

First PALGRAVE MACMILLAN paperback edition: October 2011

Transferred to Digital Printing in 2011

Contents

ACKNOWLEDGMENTS

This book owes its very life to Henry and Susan Giroux, who not only continue to be intellectual inspirations, but who also have kept faith in the project from its inception. I also am greatly indebted to Kenneth J. Saltman, who went through every page of the manuscript with a fine-toothed comb and subjected each idea to his muscular scrutiny. Ralph M. Berry provided untold support and rigorous challenges. I wish also to thank Daniel Vitkus for his conversations in a course on Middle Eastern literature that we co-taught in 2008 and that led to many of the ideas in two of these chapters. I wish to thank Deborah Hall and the English department at Valdosta State University for providing a forum where many of these ideas first were aired, and John Marx for his valuable comments that helped with chapter 3. Barry J. Faulk, Elizabeth Spiller, and Scott Kopel were my muses who kept me supplied with food for thought. I also owe deep gratitude to Florida State University, both the English department and the Office of Research, for giving me the support and the time necessary to complete this project. And lastly, to my family and Mona, for everything.

INTRODUCTION

Feminist Theory in Pursuit of the Public argues that feminism needs to devise a theory of the public. Remarking on feminist theory's traditional adherence to an industrial division of labor—where women are closer to the private sphere, socialization and reproductive processes than other categories of action and identity—I start out by questioning why and how contemporary representations of femininity in literature, theory, and popular rhetoric make it seem incompatible with the public sphere. I argue that on an ideological plane, the incompatibility of femininity and a politics of the public sphere is creating economic zones of regulative nonintervention, beyond state control, by symbolically relegating them as provinces of women's work. The tools developed by feminist theory can unravel such representations to show how women's work can be realigned within a theory of the public.

What's known as the "Second Wave" of feminist theory developed predominantly as a theory of private life, assessing private life as the predominant form of women's inequality and oppression. As Juliet Mitchell, for one, put forward, "[F]eminist theory has isolated the family as the place in which the inferiorized psychology of femininity is produced and the social and economic exploitation of women (as wives and mothers without legal or economic independence) is legitimated" (xviii). This focus left a huge gap in feminist theory's political thinking on the public. It also tended to project an ideal of women's emancipation from the home as what would count as women's equality or women's freedom, not foreseeing that the private would take another form. Instead of disappearing as some women rejected the relegation of their work to the work of reproduction, or as technological advances eased up the demands of domestic work tied to reproduction, sites of the private multiplied. Presently, the private has become a substitution for the public and the state, no longer just a barrier to the state and public life defined through domestic women's work. I am calling "re-privatization" the current corporate and financial practice of avoiding the regulatory state by directly capitalizing on a type of labor that resembles women's work of the industrial era in its legal status, tasks, and definitional traits. Such labor is often called "enterprise" or "entrepreneur" and is configured in business lingo as "empowering" because it allows for "freedom" outside of liberal codes, controls, conventions, associations, taxes (often), and the protective status of the traditional "worker: That is, "freedom" in market terms. Currently, women's work is being "re-privatized" within rising forms of corporate exploitation, dispossession, and debt financing. That is, neoliberalism's transfer of public functions to private controls is partly happening through such a "re-privatization" of women's work. As Randy Martin has warned, "Perhaps the most mundane effect of the war on terror is to make clear how much we have to fear from the advance of the private itself" (61).

Rather than a rejection of the private/public divide, what need to be worked out are the different intertwining ways that the private sphere is called into being; that is, whether as (1) the disappearing private sphere of the industrial division of labor; (2) the persistent private sphere of neoliberal modes of exploitation and ownership, from outsourcing to microfinance, that bank on the appropriation and commodification of traits and work regimes traditionally recognized as "feminine"; (3) the understanding of the human individual as having an inner core of the self that precedes entry into the social, like a soul, a personality, desire, sex, suffering, sentiment, or freedom, particularly manifest in formulations of human rights and civil rights; and (4) the place of critique, consciousness, autonomy, and reflection. This last category of the private is needed to challenge market philosophies and the privatization of everything through preserving ideals of social and political improvement and public participation that are not necessarily just an extension of private power. All of these different modes of the private are being mixed together and confused in discourse, political rhetoric, and popular culture. The confusion leads to the values inherent through one such system of the private ends up emergent in another without any acknowledgment that the registers have been switched.

In literary studies of the 1980s, new feminist writing by scholars like Nancy Armstrong and Mary Poovey argued that in the eighteenth and nineteenth centuries, respectively, women's work in the private domestic sphere was "crucial to the consolidation of bourgeois power" (10).[1] In other words, women's activities in the domestic sphere aligned seamlessly into the dominant culture as the process of socialization produced its subjective adherents. The domestic sphere, Poovey continues, was depoliticized through its abstraction "both rhetorically and, to a certain extent materially—from the so-called public sphere of competition, self-interest, and economic aggression" (10). This rhetorical and material separation carried with it ideological functions, mostly in turning the effects of class struggle and structural economic hierarchization into naturalized qualities of gender and gendered values, like virtue. Similar questions need to be raised today about the symbolic work that the private, domestic sphere does to set in place an ideological justification for economic inequalities, as well as about the symbolic work that gender ought to and could do to offset its ideological confiscation.

Feminist Theory in Pursuit of the Public points out that the private, domestic sphere of industrial production is currently disappearing as a form of economic organization, but that it persists as a referent for various political intentions, value orientations, and justificatory arguments for economic liberalization. Mostly, by showing that the private sphere serves to normalize and consolidate the privatization of markets (i.e., labor, finance, etc.), I indicate here that the symbolism of the private sphere still is set in opposition to a public sphere, in the form of the state, educational, and public institutions of regulation and deliberation, but that this rhetorical and material separation carries different values and ideas than did its predecessors. On the one hand, I argue that such a symbolism of the private sphere is necessary in order to think through what a public sphere of participatory involvement, deliberative reason, civic independence, and autonomous critique might imply in an era of globalized production. On the other hand, I maintain that with the demise of industrialized labor, the form of private, domestic sphere has been filled with new content. Framed as it is within a romantically overemphatic deification of civil liberties as the uninhibited natural state of human activity, the new, still-woman-inhabited private sphere often takes on the categorical dressing of market deregulation; that is, the sense of a sphere of naturally moral economic activity that is, by definition, outside of or before public regulation. Whereas Poovey believes that exceptional women can step out of the ideology that encases them, and overcome it, surpass it, or rearrange it,[2] *Feminist Theory in Pursuit of the Public* remarks that the false collapse of the private, domestic sphere into this model of individualized civil liberties—in the figure of the rational economic actor—needs to be displaced by another model that it also currently includes: the private, domestic sphere as the material and rhetorical materialization of sovereign public communication.

The status of the private sphere, along with its public counterpart, is not only essential to reassess in light of thinking about transformations in the controls of economic power during an age of neoliberalism, but also this transformation has philosophical implications. The historical status of the private sphere has repercussions within philosophical discussions about autonomy, critique, and freedom, and their relationship to the structures of power that constitute their agency, or that they must transcend. Feminists like Poovey and Armstrong might read the private domestic sphere as embedded in power, the site of socialization where immanent critique develops, or otherwise as a site for the transcendence of power, an outside or a radical difference. I am thinking here of the debate between Seyla Benhabib and Judith Butler, most clearly articulated in the 1995 collection *Feminist Contentions*. Seyla Benhabib notes that in denying that there can be any autonomous position that transcends power, poststructuralism also "undermines the feminist commitment to women's agency and sense of selfhood" (1995: 29). She calls this "feminist commitment" the "ethical impulse" that comes from "articulating the normative principles of democratic action and organization in the present" (1995: 30). Butler, on the other hand, states that "power pervades the very conceptual apparatus that seeks to negotiate its terms, including the subject position of the critic" (1995: 39). Labeled as a conflict between Foucaultians and Habermasians, the debate has been taken up by subsequent feminist analyses. Without promoting a position that would elide or compromise the two, Amanda Anderson, for example, contends that Benhabib needs to take into account the denaturalization of identity that Butler privileges, and this would give her "an enlarged conception of public dialogue" (41), while Butler needs to develop an explanation for intersubjectivity rather than for just intrasubjectivity as well as a recognition of normative principles and justifications as the basis for critique. "For Benhabib," Anderson summarizes, "politics involves consolidating autonomy for the greatest collectivity; for Butler, politics involves deconstructing autonomy as the basis of any individual or collective life" (30). Amy Allen has also written about this debate as seeming "to turn primarily on the capacity for a reasoned critique of power and the possibility of disentangling the subject's capacity for critique from the power relations that constitute it" (10). Contingently, *Feminist Theory in Pursuit of the Public* is concerned with demonstrating that the feminist debates between critical theory and poststructuralism play out in response to historical changes in the status of the private/public division that is implemented with the neoliberal revision of economic organization. Autonomy is historically linked to the thinking of the private sphere.

Feminist Theory in Pursuit of the Public remarks on feminist theory's traditional adherence to an industrial division of labor, where women are closer to the private sphere and socialization processes than other categories of identity, or, as Michael Warner puts it, where feminism seems to be "embracing the system in which male is to public as female is to private" (58). I start out in the introduction by questioning why and how representations of femininity in Hillary Clinton's 2008 bid for U.S. president make it seem incompatible with the public sphere, and then follow up in the first chapter by looking at multiple cultural sites that similarly show how women and their labor are symbolically disconnected from public life as they are made to represent the privatization of public life: from liberalism and neoliberalism to self-help, psychoanalysis, queer theory, militarism, and global "women's empowerment" philanthropic schemes. I argue that the representational use of the private, domestic sphere of industrial production as performing what were formerly conceived as state or public functions is a ruse for placing those state and public functions in private, corporate control. The structural space of women's private labor in the liberalism of the industrial age—where domestic work is separated from politics and the state, serving as a refuge where subjectivities and class positions get socialized—is currently being reproduced as again a limit to outside interventions, now in the form of taxation, regulation, and oversight. While feminist theory repeatedly declares that the private/public divide is no longer operative, having disappeared from the organization of labor and culture as a result of modern technologies and bureaucracies and that therefore the era of gender can be declared over, global exploitation and its ideologies continue to privatize the state by re-privatizing women's work.

Something crucial is at stake: the takeover of state and public functions by private corporate interests (privatization)—which Italian Marxist thinker Antonio Gramsci (as well as his nemesis, Benito Mussolini) identified as fascism—is appearing before the public as women's liberation. What needs to be done is to break the symbolic interconnection between the private sphere of women's work and the private interests of the free economic actor as the main character in a civil liberties drama: Women's work in the private sphere has a more compelling association with the work of socialization; that is, an intersubjective communication based in a pedagogical relationship where agreement can be reached through shared understanding. The neoliberal economy employs the private sphere still as the site for the reproduction of the class inequalities that come out of the industrial age, even when today's private sphere appears as a replacement of the public sphere of the state more often than as its outside or its alternative. This study uses as its examples Middle Eastern literatures written in English by women—what I call "experimental war memoirs"—like Jean Said Makdisi's *Beirut Fragments* and Riverbend's *Baghdad Burning*. These documentary reports reveal how the radical destruction of the public has envisioned formations of women's labor that are newly privatized, symbolically repeating the industrial division of labor within a completely different historically grounded organization of labor and production. What becomes evident in these readings is that even in the most extreme crises in the public sphere of the state and its institutions, public life takes shape, and mostly in the form of women's work. I also discuss how some foundational texts of critical theory—Habermas, Adorno, and Marcuse in particular—formulate the private/public split persisting also as the backbone of critique. Such foundational critical theory forms a working notion of education, Enlightenment, and critique out of the unraveling of the industrial division of labor, and therefore connects the end of the privatization of women's labor to the development of the public sphere rather than to its "re-privatization."

Feminism's focus on the private sphere is most frequently justified on the basis that private life can explain the origins of inequality, and therefore it would be impossible to understand or contest such inequality starting from the position of abstract equality on which is founded democratic civil society. What often happens is that the language of private life takes over completely, and a language for analyzing public life is lost. This is echoed in the movement of global production increasingly into privatized forms, from homework and sweatshops to microenterprise and minibanks, where—often because of structural adjustments or other agreements—the state's interventions in the production process are limited by international protocols or the demands of financing bodies, and the governance of private and for-profit interests has taken hold. Though Marxism understood economic power under capitalism to reside in the state, it is now increasingly spoken of as against the state and as threatened by it, while references to state action increasingly take on the appearance of an unjust attack on private wealth and therefore freedom. The rejection of a consideration of the private/public divide in feminism often means the loss of a certain viable form of feminist agency that could be found in the public, and the loss of this agency means an inability on the part of feminism to confront or oppose—or even at times to notice—a change in the relationships and codings of public and private that are formative for emergent social ideologies of economy and state that are creating new forms of inequality: neoliberalism and militarism in particular.

In the first volume of *Capital*, Marx predicted that the historical project of what he called "primitive accumulation" would render obsolete and eventually obliterate domestic forms of private life. Starting in the sixteenth and seventeenth centuries, concentrated forms of production led to a confiscation of small-scale private land holdings, driving peasants off the land and forcing them into vagabondage.[3] Marx sees this as original alienation. Eventually, says Marx, domestic enterprise would end as the last real tie between the laborer and his labor, clearing the way for capitalism to evolve (and then for communism to take hold.[4]) "Thus, hand in hand with the expropriation of the self-supporting peasants, with their separation from the means of production, goes the destruction of rural domestic industry, the process of separation between manufacture and agriculture. And only the destruction of rural domestic industry can give the internal market of a country that extension and consistence with the capitalist mode of production requires" (699–700). Marx, we see now, was wrong about this. Domestic industry has returned with a vengeance; it is a hegemonic lever by which the new stages of capital manage dispossession. The globalization of capitalism is orchestrated not by the "divorce" of the laborer from his domestic forms of production, but rather by the increasing restriction of labor to privatized appropriations. Rather than her violent removal from the means of private subsistence, the laborer is dispossessed of her public. Neoliberalism, I argue, gains ideological footing by declaring an end to the state, the public, and the private/public divide, and then reasserts now emptied-out features of the private/public divide of industrial labor within its logics of privatization and deregulation. Feminist inattention to the public is therefore particularly worrisome now when the nation-state and its public seem to have diminishing power and compromised democratic agency. The waning of power attributed to the public sphere diminishes the influence that citizens can have in deciding on the conditions of life, and therefore minimizes the changes that feminists can envision or enact in the social field to work toward equality, access, deliberation, participation, just distribution, rights, and authority for women.

The private/public divide is mostly addressed as a determination of the organization of gendered labor and governance in industrial capitalism. In descriptions of industrial capitalism, as Gayle Rubin observes, "a 'wife' is among the necessities of a worker, [...]women rather than men do housework, and [...]capitalism is heir to a long tradition in which women do not inherit, in which women do not lead, and in which women do not talk to god" (164). Simone de Beauvoir also described the era of industrialization as when "the bourgeoisie clung to the old morality that found the guarantee of private property in the solidity of the family. Woman was ordered back into the home the more harshly as her emancipation became a real menace" (xxix). *Feminist Theory in Pursuit of the Public* studies not only how the privacy of political liberalism is rhetorically managed through gender, often to protect private economic power. It not only inspects how feminist analyses of private life often leave very little room for a public imaginary. The book also investigates how the uses of privacy in the industrial division of gendered labor are now being recycled in the new global economy to frame narratives about the minimizing of state and public power in favor of free market autonomy both in the "first" and "third" worlds. As industrialism's housewife figure gets inserted as a limit to postindustrialism's regulatory policies, legal abstractions, citizenship identities, and political inclusions, the symbolic relationship between privacy and women continues to determine, to a certain degree, a broader economic structuring—often contradictory—between private interests and public interests moving from industrialism through welfarism and now to neoliberalism.

According to Nancy Fraser, public and private have a spectrum of possible meanings that vary in emphasis over time: "There are several different senses of 'private' and 'public' in play here. 'Public,' for example, can mean (1) state-related, (2) accessible to everyone, (3) of concern to everyone, and (4) pertaining to a common good or shared interest. Each of these corresponds to a contrasting sense of 'private.' In addition, there are two other senses of 'private' hovering just below the surface here: (5) pertaining to private property in a market economy and (6) pertaining to intimate domestic or personal life including sexual life." (1992: 128). The two senses of "public" I might add would be: (7) of or pertaining to audiences created by mass culture, publicity, and public opinion; and (8) a sphere of citizen action, like civil society, that exceeds the state, as in public protest or, sometimes, public interest. This last meaning (8) sometimes—like the word "citizen"—bridges "public" with "private," while both the meanings (7) and (8) have, like Fraser's, corresponding definitions for "private." My contention is that these meanings easily flood into each other and confuse things, often through politically and ideologically purposeful manipulations. The sense of "public" that I see as particularly illegible at the current moment is this sense (8), a sense of the "public" as being related to the state, national culture, and national territory, but not identical to any of them, which implies on some level a prospective on collective action, or the sense that politics, as a human social practice, is not by its nature out of reach. Often, the other meanings of "private" and "public" obscure or distort this important one in particular as a possible referent.

Feminism's focus on thinking through the private meant that it relinquished some of the critical tools necessary for it to confront a mainstream attack on all things public that was promoting interests contrary to feminism, its egalitarian impulses, and its emancipatory potential. What such framings preclude is the possibility of making legible in political terms certain concepts of public consciousness that are fundamental to drawing out public citizenship as a form of participatory political agency—such concepts, for example, as contemplation, judgment, discussion, action, and autonomy (these were taken up in some Marxist, revisionist, phenomenological, and poststructuralist accounts of the political that I discuss in subsequent chapters). In parallel, feminism's focus on the private led to making demands on the state based demands to recognize private identities, rather than demands to restructure value in the workplace and the economy at large, or demands to redistribute powers over the production powers in more gender equitable ways. The loss of the imagination of the public has had repercussions in many social and political areas, especially areas where the line between public and private life has been discursively embattled, like education, health care, workers' rights, policing, childcare, safety, sexuality—in other words, the most prevalent core issues currently setting domestic political agendas in the United States. The private/public divide symptomatically becomes disputed in places where the meanings of citizenship are conflicted, and in a neoliberal moment where the nation-state and its institutions are losing representational authority and access for citizens, citizenship has become a troubled concept. The centrality of such issues makes clear that feminist politics has a necessary role to play that generally goes unacknowledged, if not openly disparaged.

Contingent to the crisis of citizenship identity and entwined in the citizenry's diminishing power to act as citizens, one of the casualties of the loss of the imagination of the public is turning out to be feminism. In this regard, it is not at all surprising that the past twenty years, which have witnessed the growing obsolescence of state and public power in the face of growing corporate transnationalism, have also been afflicted with a subsiding of feminism in the forms of backlash, less curricular emphasis,[5] fewer scholarly contributions and innovations, and a growing popular distrust in feminism's efficacy, particularly when faced with current crises and needs: common knowledge seems to have judged that feminist interests no longer articulate with the most pressing issues or possibilities that pervade contemporary life. Feminism seems completely obvious and so not important to teach or learn about, completely failed and so better to ignore, archaic and so either cute or irrelevant, finished and successfully completed, or completely unnecessary. Wendy Brown attributes this archaism or "past-ness" of feminism—which she identifies in theoretical movements that define themselves as "beyond sex and gender"—to the end of modernist discourses of revolution:

> I want to [...] ask not whether feminism and feminist scholarship can live without sex or gender, but how it lives, and will continue to live, without a revolutionary horizon. Not how we may thrive in the aftermath of the dissemination of our analytical objects, but *what are we* in the wake of a dream in which those objects were consigned to history? What does it mean for feminist scholars to be working in a time after revolution, after the loss of belief in the possibility and the viability of a radical overthrow of existing social relations? What kind of lost object is this? Revolution belongs to modernity and whatever our respective orientations toward the value of modern versus postmodern *thought*, there is little question that *the time* of modernity is no longer securely ours, that key elements of modernity are waning. (2005: 99)

Whether or not the time of modernity is so decidedly over as Brown claims, the "past-ness" of feminism overlaps with the "past-ness" of concern over civics and the category of citizenship; i.e., whether its inclusions can be universally expanded through abstraction, or whether it inherently operates through setting its own limits. Such a "past-ness" clearly does expose the projected end of the agency of the present—or of the possibility of being in the present as a feminist or a citizen, most notably as those categories carry with them a promised projection of the universal. The resultant embattlement of the public is a further sign of the loss in the active value of the utopian thinking that pervaded the texts of modernity, including feminist ones. With the end of revolutionary discourse as either a metaphor or a prophecy comes a fading of social alternatives and of the imagination of a radical difference to be called the future.

HILLARY CLINTON AS "FEMINISM'S LAST STAND"

Bringing into play a narrative of feminism's final gasp for air, the 2008 U.S. presidential campaigns ushered in a new phase in the dynamic between women and the state. In mainstream coverage, a referendum on feminism got encoded as what was at stake in Hillary Clinton's presidential future. At the beginning of the campaign, remarks Kate Zernike in a *New York Times* article called "Postfeminism and Other Fairy Tales," "it was Mr. Obama who seemed to transcend the identity politics that many young women in particular found tiresome and anachronistic" (8). Zernike observes of a generation of women who mistakenly concluded that feminism had reached a threshold. The media's reaction to Hillary Clinton's candidacy, commenting on her as "shrill, strident, angry, ranting, unattractive" (8), however, Zernike resumes, made such women understand that feminism could still provide a necessary counter to gender bias. "[T]he 'sulfurous emanations' about Mrs. Clinton"—Zernike cites, for example, *The Nation* correspondent Katha Pollitt—"made [me] want to write a check to her campaign, knock on doors, vote for her twice—even though [I'd] probably choose another candidate on policy grounds" (8). Zernike poses Clinton's campaign as a historical moment when even women who espoused "post-feminism" and believed in a "post-gender" politics suddenly realized that "it has proved harder to move the country beyond stereotypes" (8) and revived their feminist commitments. The very idea of feminism, for Zernike, was reduced to representational recognition.

The main clue that made her informants realize the need for feminism, explains Zernike, is that the story of Hillary Clinton's campaign dovetails with the concurrent drama of the Eliot Spitzer scandal.[6] For Zernike, the lessons learned in the opposition between these two stories play out in the idea that the private sphere, as a place inhabited by women and their suffering, has no chance of contesting patriarchal domination: "I'm not saying I'm for Hillary now," confesses one of Zernike's young post-feminist-identified interviewees, "and I'm not saying that Hillary's history with sexual peccadilloes is uncomplicated, but it certainly makes me appreciate the fact that she's learned other ways of manipulating power" (8). Hillary's entry into the public translates into the possibility of her escape from her sexual, particularized body and, contingently, from all women's womanly suffering. It also falls back into a hierarchy that values public life as a form of strong agency and devalues private life as the specific sphere of women, their work, and their subordination. As private life can only be a source of pain and victimization for women, Zernike celebrates the escape from private life itself as enough for characterizing agency for women. In the end, the association between women and the private sphere seems to be more indelible than before, making most women disempowered, dominated, objectified, inferior, and therefore unfit for life in public, even prerational, with few uncertain and temporary exceptions.

Zernike restricts feminism (and thereby politics) strictly to battles over images in the media, while reducing what counts as feminism's success to a woman from an elite class (or a self-proclaimed feminist) being seated in an elected political office that represents the corporate state indiscriminately. There is no engagement at all with Clinton's policies, perspectives, or political alliances. Not only does Zernike avoid any kind of critical analysis of what constitutes the private/public split, its symbolic functioning, and its naturalized hierarchies, but also the assumption of a preconstituted private/public split turns an exclusive state into the only possible form of public participation for women. The logic goes like this: Women's connection to the private sphere is what causes their oppression, and the best way to resist women's oppression is therefore not for all women to dismiss, upset, transcend, or leave behind the gendering form of privacy, but for some women, if possible, to enter the world of public maleness, leaving privacy in place still as the source of (women's) oppression in general. Zernike's logic means: Even as "women"—as identities or concepts—can be constructed or subject to temporal or other types of manipulations, the private sphere cannot, so the essentialization of the oppressed in the private sphere persists over and above the de-essentialization of gender as representation. The "private" has replaced the "sex" of before-poststructuralism—the category of naturalization, determinism, or of metaphysical foundations. Privacy cannot enter an alternative historical stage as can the different manifestations of the public sphere. As Julia Kristeva has aptly warned, however, "That women have assumed commercial, industrial, and cultural power has not changed the nature of this power [...] The women who have been promoted to positions of leadership and who have suddenly obtained economic [...] advantages that have been refused to them for thousands of years are the same women who become the strongest supporters of the current regimes, the guardians of the status quo, and the most fervent protectors of the established order" (192) (unfortunately, as I discuss below, Kristeva would agree with Zernike that electing women to public office serves as the only possible manifestation of a feminist politics of the public).

Moreover, Zernike is not only blind to the material structure and effects of gender—that is, to how equating gender equality to a broader inclusion within existing practices and hierarchies reaffirms those practices and hierarchies, making unequal distributions of economic and political power seem inevitable—but this formulation of feminism as an image-battle also limits the future of feminism to Clinton's career. However, the same election cycle saw the electorate's choice for the first legislative body with more women than men in New Hampshire's state senate. This story barely received mainstream coverage even though it was of possibly greater importance for feminism than a figurehead candidacy for the White House. Most notably, the effort behind this electoral victory was by Planned Parenthood, whose members went door-to-door promoting pro-choice platforms, most of which happened to be supported by women candidates. Though the pro-choice legislature certainly has the potential of triggering greater public life for women as well as a reconceived struggle over the meanings and practices of private life, the mobilization of Planned Parenthood volunteers canvassing their issues and educating their neighbors throughout the state shows that feminist public participation does not need to be confined to state electoral politics, elected office, big money interests, or centrist compromise. Rather, public sphere involvement can include principled discussions on issues relating to rights, access, and citizenship, and the structural, ideological, and economic changes that would be necessary to bring this about.

The unfolding of subsequent event confirms that the private/public hierarchies were not vitally reconsidered or undermined as a result of her presidential run, and that the endurance of this hierarchy distorts the feminist project and postpones the liberation of women. In the wake of Clinton's bid for the presidency, a broad disappointment in feminism's political future lodged itself into John McCain's choice of a running mate, Alaska governor Sarah Palin, who appealed to her constituents on the basis that she could do politics because she could do motherhood, even with troubled children, that in fact politics was nothing more than motherhood. This rhetorical strategy made her "real," at least according to her proponents. As women were "re-privatized," feminism itself seemed unamenable to—even illegible within—the politics of the present, and along with it was lost the effectuality of public process to change the symbolic coding that naturalizes material distributions as the "real."

The ideal of relegating women's work to a separate sphere of pure privacy was an organizational ruse of industrial capitalism that could not exist except for in ideological terms, was never materially dominant, and certainly now—in an era of postindustrial, service, or neoliberal labor forms combined with a culture of consumption—is unrecognizable as a structure of economic activity at any level. The private/public split is a symbolic formation that, as a form of social organization, has very real effects that have more to do with the formal opposition between the two terms than with any real contents or solid referentiality. Yet, as Mary Douglas writes,

> Any institution that is going to keep its shape needs to gain legitimacy by distinctive grounding in nature and in reason: then it affords to its members a set of analogies with which to explore the world and with which to justify the naturalness and reasonableness of the instituted rules, and it can keep its identifiable continuing form. Any institution then starts to control the memory of its members; it causes them to forget experiences incompatible with its righteous image, and it brings to their minds events which sustain the view of nature that is complementary to itself. It provides the categories of their thought, sets the terms for self-knowledge, and fixes identities. (112)

For Douglas, the primary legitimating tool or instituted rule is the law of gender produced in the division of labor, where "the division of labor supplies authority to an analogy that locates a structured social situation firmly in nature" (65). Gender naturalizes and grounds both institutions and knowledge. The idea that women's labor could be attributable to some kind of autonomous private life, natural and domestic, has become malleable as a symbolic tool to naturalize labor organization and material distributions as well as to justify power distributions, even when it cannot reference any sort of recognizable structural content within production or social systems. As Susan Gal has similarly pointed out, despite repeated debunkings of the private/public distinction as ideological, the division persists as ideological structure in both politics and language: "[H]istorical changes in the 'content' of what is legally or conventionally considered public and private have not undermined the distinction in normative discourse and social theory any more than has evidence about the inseparability of principles" (262). This book investigates how the current rule of gender underlies an attack on public authority and entrenches the privatization of public life into the seemingly natural.

1

FEMINISM AND THE RETREAT FROM THE PUBLIC

LIBERALISM, OR PRIVACY AND THE LIMITS OF THE PUBLIC

Second-wave feminism had very good reason to interrogate critically the politics of privacy. The private as a female domestic space could be used to create differential values in categories of work, space, thinking, and activity, often to the detriment of women. In her introduction to a collection of feminist writings on the public/private divide, Joan Landes situates the private sphere "as a site of sexual inequality, unremunerated work, and seething discontent," as well as "problems accompanying woman's multiple roles as wife, mother, sexual companion, worker, and political subject," leading to "private despair" and "private isolation" (1998: 1), which feminism was to address. As Michelle Zimbalist Rosaldo pointed out in her theoretical introduction to the inaugural volume of academic feminism, *Woman Culture & Society*, "[A]s long as the domestic sphere remains female, women's societies, however powerful, will never be the political equivalents of men's; and, as in the past, sovereignty can be a metaphor for only a female elite" (42). As Michael Warner describes it: "Private labor is unpaid, is done at home, and has long been women's work. Far from being symmetrical or complementary, this sexual division of labor[...] is unequal. Public work, for example, is understood to be productive, forming vocational identity, and fulfilling men as individuals' private labor is understood as the general reproduction of society, lacking the vocational distinction of a grade or a profession, and displaying women's selflessness" (37). The category of the private that recognizes certain work as female work and therefore as "lacking," "unproductive," nonremunerative, or "nonprofessional" also inflects inside the increasingly feminized, increasingly privatized sphere of "third world" labor as functionally distinct from its control and management apparatuses located mostly in the industrialized and financialized economies of the "first world."

This chapter asks if this private sphere that feminist theory has described so disparagingly (and rightfully so) is not currently where the values, practices, configurations, and identities of a public sphere could develop. That is, feminist analysis has already exposed the private sphere of the industrial age as producing inequalities; as these same inequalities are currently wielded to give the public sphere the symbolic qualities and structural placements of the formerly private sphere, this chapter challenges feminism to apply its criticisms more broadly. After visiting various cultural and theoretical sites where feminism has identified the hierarchical codings of the private sphere—its ideological separation from the law, for example, or its economic devaluations and social marginalizations—this chapter goes on to present a neoliberal world picture where these same narrative appraisals and judgments have been harnessed and transferred into justifications for privatizing public life. In this, I show the tendencies of a "re-privatization" of women's labor within current formations of capitalism: That is, I show how the current organization of corporate power seeks to bypass the regulatory state by reframing labor according to the conventions of work in the industrialized home, and then directly capitalizing on this type of work, for example, a status of legal exceptionalism, of existing beyond the law and public interventions, as submissive, as under-remunerated and unprotected, and the like. As feminists predicted that the end of privacy would usher in the end of gender with all of its oppressions, privacy actually turned out to be more resilient than anyone foretold, and in actuality, privacy was where the deepest and most insurmountable essentialisms seemed to lie, because the private could shift its meanings as fast as capitalism demanded, to defend its structures. In other words, the private could be emptied of content and shift its meanings, but it would still connect symbolically to women, their spaces, and their work, lowering their value. Instead of being the same private that second-wave feminists critiqued for its ideological separation from the state under liberalism or for its false autonomies, this private of "re-privatization" now is a cover for an undermining, a fracturing, and a selling-off of public power, and as such, carries inside of it some of the features of the dismantled public sphere.

FEMINISM AND LIBERALISM

Feminist critiques of the private sphere get to the heart of liberalism. What was at stake in the feminist analysis of privacy was the question of what place "freedom" would hold as a concept in emergent political imaginaries, particularly in relation to feminism. The manipulation of privacy does not stop at creating hierarchies of value in work. As well, the connection of privacy to women's work often blurs with privacy as protection against social infraction promised in the governance-through-rights organization of liberalism. As Beate Rössler warns, "[B]oth things, the dimensions of life in which the freedoms of individuals can be manifested and women's sphere of caring for the family, are covered by one and the same concept: privacy" (55). Lamenting how discourses of equality are often at odds with discourses of liberty, Rössler goes on to advocate nonprescriptively for a critique of the concept of privacy and a redescription of the private sphere that could and would separate civil protections from the naturalization of the domestication of women. In the end, however, she wonders how "the conventions governing the protection of privacy are able to reproduce power relations and inequalities in the freedoms available to women and men" (64); that is, why the current order of gender conflated into the liberal private/public distinction is so resistant to change. What her analysis does not consider, and what might actually explain her conundrum and the stability of gender coding in private/public terms, is how the order of gender has stayed the same by redeploying these old ideologies to different settings and economic arrangements. In an age of neoliberalism, the concept of "privacy," both as the space protected against state actions and the place of refuge and women's care, is symbolically appropriated by economic interests that use it to attack state regulatory policies, families, and the equalizing functions promoted in domestic welfare practices.

The concept of privacy bridges economic value with the identity of the citizen under liberalism: This citizen's identity is divided between a public life of social involvement and a private life of protected civil rights and individual freedoms. Definitionally and structurally positioned by liberalism as the outside of the public and as its limit,[1] the private could be considered or ideologically manipulated to mean the reverse of politics. As John Stuart Mill remarks, trying to work out a productive negotiation between Individual initiative and social control in *On Liberty* (1859), "But neither one person, nor any number of persons, is warranted in saying to another human creature of ripe years, that he shall not do with his life for his own benefit what he chooses to do with it" (76). Invoking a zone where interest, impulse, and independent judgment would be protected against social encroachments, liberalism conceptualized privacy as a naturalized and essentially human antecedent to customs, contracts, and association, a necessary component of national citizenship in a democracy.

The second wave's suspicions about the construction of autonomous privacy in legal terms were, at least in part, based in the conviction that privacy was an ideological term borrowed from liberalism
and misapplied to maintain the sexual division of labor that creates, in
economic terms, structural inequalities and exploitation at women's
expense. John Stuart Mill's defense of the private as a space for the
practice of freedom continually falls back into constructions of the
private/public distinction as distinguishing different economic roles
on the basis of gender, particularly in the modern age: "When the
support of the family depends, not on property, but on earnings,
the common arrangement, by which the man earns the income and
the wife superintends the domestic expenditure, seems to me in general the most suitable division of labour between two persons" (164).
Mill goes on in *The Subjection of Women* (1869) to talk about this
gendered division of labor as an indispensable complement to liberalism's construction of citizenship though outside of citizenship
proper: "Citizenship, in free countries, is partly a school of society
in equality; but citizenship fills only a small place in modern life, and
does not come near the daily habits or inmost sentiments. The family,
justly constituted, would be the real school of the virtues of freedom"
(160). Though Mill confesses that privacy often takes the form of a
"school of tyranny" (160) in its current occurrences, privacy—recognized through its materialization in domestic life—is necessary to
citizenship because it has the capacity to educate citizen virtues and
habits, but it stands outside the abstract disembodiment and protections of public action by definition.[2] When the abuses inherent in
its legal and social character and the inequalities of its unfair property distributions finally get cleared up, Mill says, most women will
choose marriage and family life as the career style best suited to their
talents, and (women's) privacy will be preserved as the foundational
bedrock of liberal governance.

The liberal idea that the private is a sphere protected against the
arbitrary actions of states or the social therefore connects foundation-
ally to the idea that the private is a sphere related to women in their
domestic roles: The private home could serve as the symbolic limit to
legal action. Carole Pateman rereads the history of liberalism to show
that the private sphere stood for the state of nature; that is, as prior
to civil association and as the basis of freedom through which contracts of association could be formed, but which got left behind with
the contractual alliance. Freedom had to be assumed as the natural
foundation that was traded off by will to the regulatory state for its
protections. Explains Pateman: "[W]hat is 'natural' excludes what is

'civil' and vice versa [...] Women are incorporated into a sphere that both is and is not in civil society. The private sphere is part of civil society but is separated from the 'civil' sphere" (1988: 11). For feminism, this disjuncture meant that the home could be a site of illegal or extralegal abuses beyond state interventions, or economic neglect outside of standard wage and other protections. Feminism had two responses to the legacy of privacy in the liberal tradition: Either it could reappropriate the private/public distinction but demand their equalization—this strategy would entail remuneration of domestic work but would also remarginalize women in separate spheres; or it could abandon the private/public distinction, with women entering positions that were traditionally designated to men, producing a deeper stigma and lower wages for those—most likely racial, ethnic, and national minorities—who take on the formerly feminized and privatized tasks, while revaluing the superiority of work rituals that favored men. Some feminists argued that the private was "always already" infused with power structures and state principles of all sorts, or that the private had to be abandoned completely, and women needed to redefine identity, in opposition to privacy, as assimilated within the technologies of public life. Betty Friedan, for example, famously argued that women were imprisoned and suffering in their homes, and that only by exiting the home into professional labor would this social wound of women's domestic unhappiness finally be cauterized. Radical feminist Shulamith Firestone went further in suggesting that all domestic functions, including reproduction, could be outsourced to laboratories or socialist state agencies—what she called "cybernetic communism." "In a world out of control," she inveighs, "the only institutions that grant the individual an *illusion* of control, that seem to offer any safety, shelter or warmth, are the 'private' institutions: religion, marriage/family, and, most recently, psychoanalytic therapy. But, as we have seen, the family is neither private nor a refuge, but is directly connected to—is even the cause of—the ills of the larger society which the individual is no longer able to confront" (201). Firestone's only hope is in seeing how marriage and the family are becoming increasingly defunct because technology would replace them—babies would be farmed in test tubes ("so that pregnancy, now freely acknowledged as clumsy, inefficient, and painful, would be indulged in, if at all, only as a tongue-in-cheek archaism" [216]). Under the disinterested reign of modern technology, a postpolitical future would magically usher in the radical end of inequality.

This critique of privacy placed privacy at the source of the politics of inequality. In actuality, it replicated the liberal structuring of privacy that assumed privacy, because it was feminized, to be the absolute opposite of the abstract disembodiment that constituted the public. With the private sphere steeped in everything that is painful and socially regressive, the public could be without attributes, without power, without differentiation, and self-functioning, valueless, without a consciousness at its controls. With the private sphere exemplary of a victimizing and afflictive wielding of power, the public could be an escape from its implementation, an objectivity without hierarchies.

The feminist attack on private life had a counterpoint in the dystopias of popular culture. *The Cinderella Complex* (1981), for example, a less than radical self-help guide, based its advice on the premise that women were brought up to remain mired forever in private life and not to feel comfortable with independence: women's connection to private life made them totally incapable of existing as part of a public culture. Independence here assumed the form of a total separation from any reliance on others that private life demanded. Colette Dowling begins her book with a confessional about the level of anxiety she used to feel, when she was still married, about the threat of aloneness: She is lying on the floor with a bout of the flu when she realizes how horrible, strange, and disturbed her life would be if she were disconnected from family care. She notes that this fear is the reason that women are passive and insecure, unable to take that leap toward self-sufficiency, initiative, and professional success. This leads to the conclusion that any attachment to others is a sign of feminine social illness. When she moves with her kids to the Hudson Valley, where there is a community of other recently divorced women: "We lent money to one another and met on street corners in the early New York mornings. Sometimes we would stand right out on the street and put our heads on one another's shoulders and cry" (25). Dowling cites this moment as evidence of her fear of adulthood and her inability to shed her need for dependency. This dependency affects the kinds of jobs that women can get, as they accept employment at the bottom of the ladder, in low-paid positions, and often part-time: "This need for, and attachment to, 'the other' inhibits in all kinds of ways women's capacity to work productively—to be original, zestful, and committed" (47). Public associations—like "joining a union or fighting for women's rights" (57) or "being terrifically responsible" (69)—are just further signs that she cannot leave behind the illness of femininity or resolve her dependency conflicts.[3] Dowling finds the only outlet for social trust in professionalized therapy. As private life repeatedly appears as oppressive, stultifying, and the cause of phobias and depressions, public life again is thinned out into a vision of objectivized, dehumanized, disinterested, technological, valueless, self-operative, scientific disengagement.

Feminism does have investments in liberalism, and particularly in the idea of civil autonomy that structures the relationship between the state and its citizens in liberal philosophy from Hobbes on. Yet, at the same time, feminism must be wary of that same liberalism and its structured relationships, because it connects the privacy of civil autonomy to the private of property in ways that have historically disadvantaged women, if not totally excluded them. Liberalism, then, is caught in a contradiction between liberalism's rights and civil protections (which seem worth defending) on the one hand, and on the other, the home as the pure space of women and intimacy, of care giving and refuge from economic and political turmoil, of property as the origin of autonomy, freedom, and self. Jean L. Cohen has argued that posing the political choice as between either one (promoting privacy as pure autonomy representing freedom in liberalism) or the other (the relinquishing of privacy as a concept because it is entrenched in gender and class inequality) presupposes a false division. These scenarios each presuppose a different power structure: The first presupposes a solipsistic self facing off against repressive power; the second presupposes power as productive, where women as agents can voluntarily claim equality by resignifying meanings that are not, then, predetermined by repressive power. "To both," Cohen concludes, "where state sovereignty stops, individual liberty begins" (2004: 86). Her solution is to reconceive privacy as socialized through its inception: What the legal category of privacy under liberalism can do is to set off what she calls "domains of decisional autonomy" (1996: 198): "Decisional privacy rights designate the individual as the locus of decision-making when certain kinds of moral or ethical dilemmas or existential concerns are involved" (1996: 199). These rights would protect certain, partial areas of ethical choice, where individual needs and collective definitions of the common good might not coincide, and would balance shared community values against individual self-realization. Cohen, however, does not specify on what basis the "ethical" of autonomous decision rights might be distinguished from community rights or rights of the public good.

Yet, Cohen's critique makes clear that within the liberal tradition that opposes privacy and the social absolutely, privacy exists as a social relation, and that the shaping and forming of privacy within a certain social paradigm has to do with envisioning a corresponding configuration of power. To see how autonomy is distributed across social categories, what is needed is an analysis of the interlacing of abstract concepts of autonomy and collective force on the one hand with, on the other, economic positioning, its objectifications, and its reproduction of inequalities that comfortably hide behind the equalities premised in liberal legal ideals and ideologies of market freedom. Large and powerful interests have a stake in keeping privacy associated with women, their work, and their civil protection against arbitrary infractions of a "public good" consensus. These associations make privatization seem natural so that any enforcement of this "public good" consensus appears as an act against freedom. Though liberal interests have not been motivated to end the impoverishment and privatization of women's work or to ensure the liberties that connect the citizen to the state, the liberal wielding of the term "privacy" to conflate women and their work with the idea of freedom from the public does not seem as though it is disappearing anytime soon.

PSYCHOANALYSIS

The focus on private life in second-wave feminist theory results in part from a turn to psychoanalysis in the early seventies. Before then, feminists such as Beauvoir and Friedan understood Freudian psychoanalysis as part of the problem, punishing women who deviated from the norms of bourgeois behavior by declaring them ill, or talking about sexual oppression as a natural or inevitable outcome of anatomical differences. In the seventies, Lacanian psychoanalysis started to challenge some of these interpretations by reading the Unconscious like a language, opening up a debate on how to read Freud. Psychoanalysis would then offer a structural linguistic claim to the body's fluidity, to the ungroundedness of identity in the body, as well as a quasi-coherent terminology and an overarching explanation for understanding the social implications of the issues of most concern to feminist cultural researchers. As Juliet Mitchell elaborates, "[P]sychoanalysis gives us the concepts with which we can comprehend how ideology functions; closely connected with this, it further offers an analysis of the place and meaning of sexuality and of gender differences within society" (xxii). As an analytic of the nuclear family that revealed how individuals suffered into the identities that the family structure opened for them and often forced them to inhabit, psychoanalysis offered a causal accounting of patriarchy as well as a narrative of gender development that was replete with opportunities for gender to go completely wrong.[4]

Importantly, Lacanian psychoanalysis also pointed to avenues along which French theory could be imported into U.S. academic discourse. It created a commonality through the construal of patriarchy as a linguistic rather than historical effect. This linguistification meant that inequality could be seen in the operations of language, but also led to developing an understanding that inequality could be uprooted along with its seemingly entrenched meanings assigned to seemingly entrenched identities. Furthermore, psychoanalysis could "fill in" to leftist discourses certain ideas to which Marxism was traditionally inattentive, at the expense of accounting for women and sexuality: (1) the persistence of the private, domestic sphere of reproduction and socialization (which Marx predicted that capitalism would transcend); and (2) the role, place, and development of consciousness, subjectivity, and the manipulation of desire as factors in historical transformation between the different stages of material production.

The suggestion, in the psychoanalytic story of gender, that gender was a constructed category that fulfilled certain social and symbolic functions, and that its relation to biology was circumspect at best, allowed feminists to think about alternatives for gender reconstruction, to de-essentialize gender. Psychoanalysis pointed to a necessary role for such imagining of the body that was irreconcilable with biological essentialism. In fact, psychoanalytic feminist theory was particularly concerned with avoiding biological essentialism because it was seen as the reason that (1) the private sphere was constructed through its relationship to women; and that (2) women's work was defined in relation to the private sphere. As Juliet Mitchell foregrounds, psychoanalysis develops an analytic of the Unconscious and of sexuality that resists any easy causal reductionism of normality to the body.[5]

Yet, the iterability and abstractability of bodies and identities that importing structural linguistics allowed did not necessarily fulfill the promise of overcoming a basic and essential causality engrained through industrialism's separate spheres, and particularly through the private. The concepts that psychoanalytic theory used—sexuality, the Unconscious, and then language—allowed an abstraction of the developing subject beyond the structure of the family. Yet, psychoanalysis as a theory also contextualized the original appearance of such concepts within localized familial dramas. That is, even with the advent of linguistic principles at its core, psychoanalysis situated the family, rather than a diversified, mobile, and updated division of labor, as the primary apparatus calling gendered identities into being.

Whereas the first wave of feminism saw the "tyranny of the private" as an obstacle to developing a morality of the civic, and sought to open up the civic—including property ownership, education, and suffrage—to women, the second wave, coming on the heels of the sexual revolution and the civil rights movement, focused on questions of subjectivity. These questions intersected at various levels with psychoanalysis, especially since psychoanalysis also provided methodologies for unraveling standard interpretations of sexuality, identity, language, and the body with which subjectivity was tightly bound. Feminist theorists saw these areas as the legacy of women's subordination in the symbolic and material forms of private space. Psychoanalysis supplied a grounding narrative in which to locate such conventions of gender and, as well, a set of conflicting codes that would help to foreground the splits, creases, and distortions in the constructions of these core components of gender's psyche. Psychoanalysis translated the first wave's private tyrannies into the troubled interiority of the modern subject.

At the same time, partly because of its inheritance in psychoanalysis, the categories around which feminist debates were oriented shared, often inadvertently, the first wave's structured dichotomy of private and civic life. For example, in U.S. feminist theorist Jane Gallop's examinations of seduction and domination, interpersonal relations disclose a field in which power plays out through the symbolic, though not necessarily biological, gendering of people. Taking up Lacan's reading of the phallus that, like the Unconscious, operates as the "difference" that structures language, Gallop argues that the phallus is not attached to the male body, but rather is a grand signifier that floats, taking on a plethora of context-contingent meanings and reversals of meanings, and so is endlessly "up for grabs." "As a pro-sex feminist," she writes in *Anecdotal Theory*, "I had assumed that [having relationships with students in which they were understood as human rather than as knowledge-receptacles] involved recognizing—and when pedagogically useful, commenting upon—the sexual as part of the relation between people. By sexual here, I do not of course mean sex acts but rather the erotic dynamics which intertwine with other aspects of human interaction" (65). The struggle for control of this grand signifier of difference affects all relationships where power is negotiated: between father and daughter, between critic and text, between therapist and patient, between teacher and student. All of these relationships, for Gallop, are subject to gender symbolization and its hierarchies, and through the negotiations of desire in such interactions, through symbols, the power differentials invested in these symbols can invert or change course: The text can criticize the critic, or the seduced can turn into the seducer. The relationships are still embedded in gendered hierarchies, where masculinity has the upper hand, but you do not need a male body to take control of the master signifier, nor can the control ever be permanent, ontologized, or assumed.

Gallop acknowledges that the symbolic coding of power that is variously claimed and lost is engaged with socially decided and sometimes institutionalized readings of gender. Nevertheless, any change in these readings is necessarily already predicted within the institutions themselves that are saturated with the shifting symbolics of desire. There cannot, then, be such a thing as an overturning. Rather, without determined or fixed referents, symbols of power are struggled over in zones of sexual and intimate life: Power becomes visible in private encounters and can therefore only be confronted there. The main example that Gallop gives is in sexual harassment policy, which refuses to consider students as sexual agents with the choice to play or comply, and defines sex as always inherently coercive. It thereby fixes the position of "student"—like the position of "woman," or the nonphallic—as always its vulnerable object.

> [T]he preliminary battle and the fantasy repetitions that insistently frame that experience [of sexual harassment] are hyper-gendered. Whether in my idealistic utopian mode or in my bad-girl fantasies, I would like to separate and choose one of these erotics and discard the other. But to my embarrassment I find I cannot disentangle an erotic which I believe to be gender-irrelevant from hypergendered scenarios. I thus find myself in the apparently contradictory position of claiming this scene generally representative of pedagogical relations, regardless of gender, while at the same time emphasizing the particular gendering of female teacher and male student. (107–9)

Personal interactions reveal the sexuality embedded in institutions, despite institutional attempts at repressing it. In personal and sexually charged interactions between individuals, the challenges that are already immanent in social and pedagogical institutions and their symbols reveal themselves, and those symbols and institutions appear now as inherently unfixed and nonreferential on the level of the personal. Replete with desire, private life represents the inherent semiotic play in the attempts of institutions to set down their law and ground their self-definitions and rules. Individuals can represent certain institutional positions provisionally, but the changes in power relations only happen as individuals, in private interactions and seductions, exchange positions with each other. With public life and public struggles funneled as symbols through private encounters, with social power thereby made immanently unstable and negotiable, there is no way for individuals to interact directly with the institutions that produce the symbols nor intentionally and purposively participate in them, through them, or against them. "Play" is only a possible strategy within individual and private encounters that happen inside of already established institutions and congealed symbolic forms.

As in Gallop, feminist psychoanalytic employment of psychoanalysis often has the effect of privatizing the social. French feminist theorist Julia Kristeva, for example, equates the phallic language of the Symbolic to the nation-state, and argues that the memorialization that the nation-state represents through exclusion is being seriously challenged by new cyclical ideas of space related to the Semiotic, that is, the private language of women and reproduction, Kristeva borrows the castration narrative from psychoanalysis to mark feminist subjectivity through a differential linguistics, wherein the Semiotic, as the type of multiply referential sounds that the infant shares with its mother,[6] is divided from the Symbolic, or the type of language acquisition, subjective certainty, sign, syntax, singularity, and centered referentiality characteristic of the maturing child's access to the social (what Lacan calls the "mirror stage"). The private language of the Semiotic is what survives for her once the Symbolic temporality of the nation-state—and its sedimented history—can no longer account for experience and memory.

In her 1979 essay "Women's Time," Kristeva critiques the social movements that constitute public and political oppositional culture as products of the logic of the sacrifice, or of the reproduction of the Symbolic order through a separation, cut, or exclusion of otherness and difference. Most prominently in this essay, these social movements include two generations of the feminist movement. The first one rallies for women's access to make them equal to men ("abortion rights, contraception, equal pay, professional recognition, and others"[186]) under the banner of the singular "Universal Woman" that cuts out difference in a similar manner to the egalitarian ideal of both Enlightenment humanism and nation-state-oriented socialism. Kristeva concludes disapprovingly that this form of feminism has no mechanism for recognizing sexual difference and "has ignored the role of the human being in *reproduction* and the *symbolic order*" (188). The second generation is identified through "a quasi-universal rejection of linear temporality," as well as through a contingent "highly pronounced mistrust of political life" (186–187), based in "the specificity of feminine psychology and its symbolic manifestations" (186). This she links to Freudianism, and particularly to the phase of development before castration and the institution of Symbolic meaning, where "certain biological or familial conditions prompt some women [...] to deny this logical operation of separation [the Symbolic] and the language that ensues" (189).

For Kristeva, then, the future of feminism lies in its identification with maternity and its representations, and most notably in the pre-Symbolic (presocialized) Semiotic language structure that maternal relations entail, that understands maternity as "a true *creative act*" (196) and demonstrates, through its absorption into difference, "the utmost mobility within individual and sexual identity, and not through a rejection of the other" (197). In Kristeva's rendering, the social has even a completely different language than the feminized inarticulable language of private life that she understands as the truly resistant and universal, and she favors this inarticulable pre-Symbolic language of private life over direct but particular political demands for equal public recognition: thus she favors a transnational union based in spiritualism, which does not "reject the other" (198), over governance through or in relation to an exclusionary, territorially-bound nation-state which can account for production but not reproduction. She calls the future and radical potential of this other language "art" and "literature." In this, "art" and "literature" reflect the radicalism of the individual in private intimacies, where sexual difference "comes forth as an *interiorization*" (198). She sees this inarticulable language of private life as the foundation to reimagine subjectivity without resorting to the radical violence of exclusion and outsider-ness— even terrorism—that erupts from fixing identities inside the political demands of an older version of the temporally focused nation-state.

Kristeva divides public from private life in order to reject politics. She sees the state as the same as the Symbolic, something that happens after the cut, that represses or excludes a primordial connection to the mother, her language, her difference, and her body by assuming the subject/object split as primary. Kristeva then values the private as the possibility offered in language before the cut; that is, the possibility that meaning can wander and connect outside of the histories of identity named by the state. In particular, she rejects the politics of the nation that is based in the homogeneity of linear time and production, in favor of the politics of supra- or transnationalism that is based in what she calls the "monumental time" of Europe. In order to incorporate larger groupings, "monumental time" gives up on the unity of the subject and its violent exclusion of rejected objects that is a necessary action of nationalism. In other words, Kristeva wants to adopt a social understanding based in spatialization, linking the spatial idea of Europe's unification to the preSymbolic, the spatialization of pregnancy or maternity. In calling this "cosmopolitanism" or "globalization," Kristeva implies that the future of Europe rests on an a- or antipolitical redomestication of women for the purpose of establishing an unbounded, pan-nationalist, nonexclusionary consumerist vitality that wipes out historical and political identifications, particularly with the nation-state. Though the state does not constitute in itself the entirety of public life, Kristeva applies her reorganization of conceptual categories of the state to a critique of both feminism and socialism as social movements that made demands based on citizenship and its premises of equality. As in liberalism, the state and the social are interruptions, obstacles, and violent intrusions, a developmental block to the fullness of language and subjectivity. Kristeva's adoption of a psychoanalytic narrative leaves women's only political choice between the alienated, disembodied, violent, exclusionary form of the state on the one hand, and, on the other, the depoliticized but redemptive private sphere of women's bodies, their special languages, and their infantile intimacies.

QUEER THEORY

Starting in the late eighties/early nineties, and rooting itself in the newly hegemonizing theoretical methods of cultural studies, queer theory began to add vitality to scholarly discussions about the private/public divide. In the aftermath of the 1986 U.S. Supreme Court decision in *Bowers v. Hardwick*—upholding antisodomy laws, even for sexual practices between consenting adults in the privacy of their bedrooms—and in the midst of public outcries for AIDS funding for treatment and research, queer theory took up the psychoanalytic mantra that identified secrecy as the core of modern identity. Queer theory sought to elaborate on Foucault's critical thesis that "at the outer limit of every actual discourse [is] something akin to a secret whose discovery is imperative" (1978: 35). For Foucault, the hidden inner core of the self that is sexuality is a projection of public discourses that manage identities, producing them as a production of power: institutional networks, professionalized specialization, and the rise of scientific surveillance. Eve Sedgwick called this hidden core of a very public impetus to sexuality the "glass closet," "coming out," or the "open secret," insinuating homosexual identity into a paranoid narrative necessity that frames an instability in sexuality and discourse in general by blurring the categories of public and private that sexuality demands. "I want to argue," Sedgwick leads,

> that a lot of the energy of attention and demarcation that has swirled around issues of homosexuality since the end of the nineteenth century, in Europe and the United States, has been impelled by the distinctively indicative relation of homosexuality to wider mappings of secrecy and disclosure, and of the private and the public, that were and are critically problematical for the gender, sexual, and economic structures of the heterosexist culture at large, mappings whose enabling but dangerous incoherence has become oppressively, durably condensed in certain figures of homosexuality. (70–71)

In part, Sedgwick forms these assertions within her insightful analysis of the tension in modern sexualities between minoritizing and universalizing tendencies, or a basic unpredictability that affects a sexuality oscillating between what defines us as humans on the one hand, and, on the other, what divides us into identities based on object choice, conduct, lifestyles, experiences, and types of desire[7]: The minority identity always inhabits the majority one, threatening to expose that the majority identity is not exactly what it thinks it is, that it could in fact be no different on the inside from that which it fears on the outside. Sedgwick and her followers recognized the two sides of the private/public divide to be in constant play and frequently overlapping, in fact interchangeable. The best-concealed personality traits or self-defining experiences were often the most obvious, the most open to the public, and the reverse was also true.

The idea that the private/public divide would play out on the cultural level, rather than only defining degrees of autonomy from politics and commerce, perhaps was adopted from Habermas's theory of the public sphere. In the long list of uses of the understanding of "public" with which Habermas begins his text *The Structural Transformation of the Public Sphere*, "public" moves across many different settings of what we now call "society," orienting "[t]he relation between authorities and subjects" (18): from a collective of readers and salon culture to the press, the police, commerce, dress codes, publicity, celebrity, media and public relations. In queer theory, this insistence on the cultural backbone of the private/public divide was essential to advancing critiques of identity and formulating ideas about political engagement that did not necessarily coincide with particularized interests and limit themselves to demands of the body. Yet, the culturalization of the private/public divide meant that it could be conceptualized outside of political relations: That is, relations between citizens and states, struggles over public allocation, distributions of power, etc. Instead, the public could be divided from the private by its aesthetic content.

Lisa Duggan, for example, exposes and criticizes this tendency. She addresses how the private/public divide was created by liberalism and reaffirmed by neoliberalism, both political ideologies that defined privacy as the independent expression of culture and then used culture to divide constituencies by obscuring their potential of affiliation and association: "Inequalities are routinely assigned to 'private' life, understood as 'natural,' and bracketed away from consideration in the 'public' life of the state" (5).[8] Such an analysis performs two vital functions: (1) It shows how identity politics feeds into the oppressive distributions of power, access, and goods that neoliberalism depends on, marginalizing certain populations economically and politically, and alienating groups from each other through its designations of private life. (2) Culture becomes the root cause that explains economic inequalities, as when certain cultural practices and family forms are ideologically made to seem the root causes of impoverishment. It also reduces "public life" to the life of the state: "But the most public site of collective life under Liberalism is always the state, the 'proper' location of publicness, while the most private site is the family" (4). Duggan's criticism holds that because culturalism often separates the public life of the state from what it agrees to be the private life of the culture, it often misdiagnoses social and economic problems as problems of expression, aesthetics, and representation rather than as problems of economic distribution or political control of capital flows, institutions, and regulatory bodies.

To be sure, queer theory's and cultural studies' culturalization of both the public and the private meant that both public and private were aesthetic categories that could be understood as images and could replace one another with minor brushstrokes. If one could be the metaphor for the other as Foucault seemed to be saying (that secrecy was but an effect of power), differences between the two would not appear that would make the public, say, irreplaceable by the private or cause social disturbances, irrationality, or nonsense if the private should appear where the public was expected. Lauren Berlant, for example, boldly declared that "there is no public sphere in the contemporary United States" (3). She meant by this not that the state had suddenly dissolved, or that citizens had stopped advocating, protesting, and demanding, or that the United States had suddenly started basing all politics on executive authoritarian decisions and enforced consensus rather than deliberation, although these events might have been within her spectrum of expectations. Rather, what she meant was—as she explains—that the public sphere, as much as it could still be considered within the range of viable political grounds, was wrapped up in representations of private life: it had been sentimentalized in the TV family melodramas, cartoons, and sitcoms through which most people were currently filtering their identifications. Such infantilizing, she says, had as its aim the "privatization of U.S. citizenship" that is "rerouting the critical energies of the emerging political sphere into the sentimental spaces of an amorphous opinion culture, characterized by strong patriotic identification mixed with feelings of practical political powerlessness" (3). In other words, the public could now take the form of a representation, an aesthetic product for children, a narrative whose features borrowed from the child-focused conventions of storytelling and emotional manipulation found in mass media and popular culture. Liberalism's call to public deliberation over what kind of society we might construct, or of what kind of political logic might be the best for the most, or of how such decisions could be made and who would be involved in making them—these kinds of ideal functions of the public sphere were being crowded out by an idea of the public as a set of private commercial pictures, scripts, mise-en-scènes, narratives, or performances, designed by corporate experts, depicting citizenship as an encounter inside the family alienated from its social context, easing into dominance an identification with the powerlessness of citizens.

In the age of AIDS, she and Michael Warner later add, the relegation of sex and intimacy to liberalism's private sphere serves to privatize the politics of sexuality, which overlaps with other sites of politics more generally: e.g., the politics of space, urbanization, property, taxation, zoning, work, bequeathment, and the like. What they call the "privatization of citizenship and sex" (550) means that certain modern forms of lifeforms appear as the "private" so as to preclude their public recognition and thus their politicization.[9] This marks the end of their affinity to the public, the complete separation between their practices and a broader participatory dialogue about social conditions, and therefore the public is made inconsequential and marginalized: "Heteronormative forms of intimacy are supported [...] not only by overt referential discourse such as love plots and sentimentality but materially, in marriage and family law, in the architecture of the domestic, in the zoning of work and politics. Queer culture, by contrast, has almost no institutional matrix for its counterintimacies" (562). (Such an analysis occurred, quite obviously, before gay and lesbian politics started to define its dominant political initiatives around marriage.) In place of the privatization of sex, Berlant and Warren encourage "a world-making project" for queer culture, where both private and public would disappear.[10] This takes its most strident form in the sexualization of work and citizenship. Trying to rethink identity as other than a hidden core of sex à la Foucault, the article raises the question of how this divorcing of sex from domestic space might, in their own words, build into "the critical culture that might enable transformations of sex and other private relations" (559). Yet, the authors do not address how commercialization and consumerism would in all likelihood take hold of the public narrating of these private intimacies and sexual identities, especially where such private identities are all that is left of public expression. What might uphold a difference between public expression and practice, on the one hand, and, on the other, an engagement with a redistributional politics of rights, goods, power, justice, and access? Do "queer" and "culture" make the political only recognizable as spectacle? How might the increased diversification of commercial space to include sexual subcultures, which they describe as a claiming of the public, be anything but more commercialization, with the contingent privatization of identities that public commercialization and consumerism are constantly inflicting? How might the culturalization of the workplace through sex be different from an extension of privatization into the workplace and a further distancing of a public politics?

This pattern of culturalizing the private/public divide has continued in queer theory, and even intensified. For example, Martin F. Manalansan IV's contribution to a 2005 special issue of *Social Text* on queer studies starts out promising an ethnography of the effects of neoliberalism as it manipulates the private/public divide to police everyday sexual practices in urban spaces. It soon becomes clear, however, that the article's main concern is not to talk about the separation of public and private as a problem of a changing state, a growing sense that private business logic is reenvisioning the command structure and decision structure of governance, an elevated conquest of public and state powers by private business interests, or a structural method for further dispossessing the poor through a newly commandeered and more endemic division of labor. Rather, neoliberalism here is defined as an increase in the numbers of private businesses and police surveillance to "clean up" for them, an increase that was driving gay sex into secretive hideaways, darkened street corners, and hidden doorways in outlying New York City neighborhoods. "The Christopher Street piers no longer exist" (149), we learn. "The piers were [...] sites for Latino and African American queer youth who would prance around and practice their vogueing moves and conduct informal competitions and runway shows" (149). Now, "[s]urrounding the walkways are concrete plant holders" (150). The police have driven the prancing and vogueing into deepening privacies, while skating and biking have become the new public pastimes, and the decor has changed. Latino and African American youth have lost "a sense of ownership" (150) of the Christopher Street area. (Manalansan seems to have forgotten here that private ownership of public spaces was the problem to begin with.) Again, it is not easy to dismiss allegations that the public sphere has or might soon become simply the screening of a public cultural performance or expression rather than an invitation to a discussion of community values or what would count as social connectedness or uses of space or an evaluation of the present that would form the basis for thinking the future. Still, with "public relations" or "public opinion" as the model "public," the loss of even the ideal of a public as process—what Michael Warner calls "world making" (61)—implies a tragic translation of all politics into a self-expressive stage play or entertainment for kids. What is missing is any sense or aspect of the public that refuses to conflate into private narratives, any noncompliant or nonconforming, noncollapsible remainder of the public that, as I analyze in chapter 4, resists reconciliation or total identification with private individuation.

INDUSTRIALISM, WELFARISM, NEOLIBERALISM

Feminist Theory in Pursuit of the Public traces the symbolic formation of the division of labor through three stages of contemporary political history. These stages schematize differently though interrelated and evolving formations of the symbolic relationships between women, feminism, and the public. Such relationships enable narratives of power to seem preconceptual, natural, and prior to politics.

The first of these stages understands the modern state in accordance with the predominant division of industrial labor—the domestic sphere is depicted outside the disembodied, disinterested political sphere of the state and the citizen. The second phase is organized around the welfare state and its semiautonomous institutions of bureaucratic care, where public practices are represented through women's work[11]—the symbolic association of the state with women and their work entails a gradual sliding of public power away from its constructed centralization in state power, and a coterminous growing sense of the state as no longer the place where democratic actions and protections can be located. The third is where private, often corporate interests have taken over the exercise of power in the public's name, and women's newly privatized work typically indicates the recession of state power or its regulative marginalization. Women's work, still standing for the outside to state power as it did during the eras of industrial and welfare capitalism, is "re-privatized," indicating the public as failing. Women's work limits state and public power by instituting, at its edges, a regime of private interest. This sequence of stages implies, paradoxically, that the further inclusion of women and their work within representations of the public—the gradual inclusion of women and workers being one of the foremost representations of the democratization of state and public power—coincides with the gradual decline of representations of viable political power within the state and the public. Women's work provides a hegemonic symbolization for the new regimes of "re-privatization" under neoliberalism.

That is to say, the concept of privacy, as the limit to state and legal authority, once was understood as diminishing the value of everything associated with it, notably because of its connections to women and domesticity. Welfare, as Carole Pateman understands it, is patriarchal in that it mimes the family structure that it is supposed to be progressively overcoming by continuing to uphold men as both the heads of households and the main breadwinners, deserving of a "family wage," while situating women as dependents, and thus confirming that "the private sphere has been seen as women's proper place" (1998: 246). Nevertheless, welfare-state capitalism has often been seen as a substitute for the father's role, providing alternative avenues for support and therefore often allowing for the family's gradual dissolution as the primary mechanism for organizing the social. Feminists had various responses to welfare and its relation to a feminist agenda. As Iris Marion Young has chronicled, the initial reaction in the feminist movement was that welfare was but another form of patriarchal domination, where women's dependencies were shifting away from the family and toward patriarchal state agencies: "[P]ublic institutions have taken more direct control of women's productive and reproductive labor than in any previous society and have taken over primary control of children as well" (1990: 63). This assessment, however, was challenged by later analyses that understood "these institutions [...as] the main sources of the empowerment of women in contemporary society" (1990: 64), because they granted women opportunities for self-improvement and involvement outside of the family. Yet, as Nancy Fraser has shown,[12] the welfare state's associations with neediness, and particularly with needy women, coincided with a general perception of the welfare state as consumed in a perpetual fiscal crisis and as ineffectual. As the welfare state got glossed as the bloated "nanny state," or the bureaucratic state that took on some functions formerly assumed as affective or nurturing familial functions, the public sphere increasingly appeared within a metaphor of the private and the maternal, with its private caring functions as its specifically bankrupting functions.[13]

As the welfare state has waned, the dichotomy between public and private is again being redefined, articulated through vast webs of increasingly decentered, antistatist neoliberal corporate accumulation. The end of welfare, however, has not meant the end of representing the limits of the state in the privacy of women's work. As John Marx has aptly remarked, "For any number of scholars and critics, the novelty of globalization must be articulated to gender [... T]hese divergent uses of women to mark globalization's difference, herald its accomplishments, and figure its victims suffice to identify a critical trend that is also a bit of a puzzle: What do women mean to the scholarship of globalization?" (1–2). In a postwelfare political formation, the older symbolic connection between women and the domestic reappears: As women and their work still call into play the "private" as a symbolic limit to state intervention, the "private" refers formulaically to a corporate transcendence of state power and its laws. Women no longer signify a naturalized domestic, familial hierarchy predicated on domination and inequality as in industrialism, nor the weakening of state representational capacities and legalism as in welfarism, but rather the sense that the public and political functions of the state itself were being given over to private economic power. David Harvey defines neoliberalism as when "[t]he free mobility of capital between sectors, regions, and countries is regarded as crucial" (66), where a "suspicion of democracy" (76) leads to increased labor flexibilization and privatization,[14] and "[s]tate sovereignty over commodity and capital movements is willingly surrendered to the global market" (66), setting up a type of "accumulation by dispossession" for which women are hardest hit (129, 170). In the context of Europe, Pierre Bourdieu also laments neoliberalism as the shrinking of the "soft" or caring arm of the state in favor of its punitive arm, its policing function, in the service of defending the reign of commerce and its media.[15] This replacement of the political or nurturing sense of the state with an economic sense of "private power from without" contradicts the modern liberal state's ideologies of abstract equality in the public sphere. The shrinking of the caring arm of the state is coterminous with the "re-privatization" of functions associated with women, their work, and their symbolic function of linking the state to care for the public. As Saskia Sassen has noted, though women's employment in modern manufacturing and industrial sectors has decreased, new trends point to their higher participation in the workforce. "What emerges clearly is that a large share of women migrants constitute a certain kind of labor [...T]he employment of women migrants in domestic service in the Third World represents a vehicle for the reproduction of a labor reserve that can be seen as the equivalent of the welfare state in highly industrialized societies" (115). With women and their work outside of the state's embrace, the economic field that now accepts them is increasingly moving further outside the state's reach and into privatized enclaves of formerly public or ideally public services. In the wake of the welfare state, the public itself has been devalued and, often, deauthorized.

What ensues with the privatization of public life is a diminishing sense that the public can be a viable means of political agency or social change. The persistence of the symbolic welfarist connection between women and private life in the service of the public was accompanied by the creation of a sense of the public and the state as being over-extended or obsolete—as in the many proclamations of the demise of the era of "big government" or the implementation of limits to public economic controls and Keynesian spending in International Monetary Fund (IMF) and World Bank policy recommendations— and a growing common understanding of state action as being, at best, ineffective or, in the worst-case scenario, repressive to growth, accumulation, and freedom. Though in the Obama era, acceptance for Keynsian policies seem to be making, minimally, a tentative resurgence, the neoliberal demonization of the state and the public sector still seems to be thriving in, for example, allegations that a public health-care option would have been socialist (and therefore "bad" for undefined reasons), and widespread and naive perceptions that economic stimulus is just a burden to our kids (even when a severe economic downturn or natural disaster hurts the national budget more than social spending to relieve it through job creation, and many states have been strapped and even on the verge of bankruptcy).

One can see this scenario playing out in new "reconstruction" policies that stand in for the new imperialism. One can look, for example, at a November 13, 2009, *New York Times* article taking up the military's line that counterinsurgency is still possible in Afghanistan in the form of small-grants development projects investing directly in villages. The article answers to the malaise surrounding the war in U.S. public debate due to the obvious corruption in the Karzai administration that the U.S. supports—evidenced in the 2009 presidential elections, where polling stations were able to produce ballots even without voters and where a host of other indiscretions were on widespread display. The corruption in the Kabul administration does not really matter for U.S. efforts, the *New York Times* suggests, because money does not need to be filtered through the central government to reach the population of the needy or for development. Instead, money can find its way directly to village councils, where it can back projects that communities themselves decide through local governance, with a little bit of help from foreign private contractors and nonprofit groups. "Local residents contend that the councils work," writes reporter Sabrina Tavernise, "because they take development down to its most basic level with villagers directing the spending to improve their own lives, cutting out the middle men, local and foreign, as well as much of the overhead costs and corruption." The message here is that development can happen without the state, and that insurgencies are best put to rest through privatization. The outcome is the same one that we see endlessly offered in report after report about developmental success—namely, girls' schools were constructed. The idea is that schools (and therefore liberalism) can only appear in these backward, savage, warlord-torn regions with private foreign investment that does not need to pass through a regulatory, democratic body like a state. The fact that the state has been supported as a puppet of foreign interests that might not want the Afghan authorities to educate its public is not mentioned. That is, the reporter does not draw a connection between the election of a U.S.-supported government through a corrupt election and the absence of public schooling (often replaced by formal and informal religious teaching that excludes girls). This conclusion gets covered over by the conclusion that the Afghanis themselves are responsible for the production of backwardness and ignorance, and that only private capital can fix this. The once public project of educating the next generation is being handed over to foreign finance, to the *New York Times*' glowing approbation.

A tendency that one finds in much social science literature on globalization is to suggest that the current climate offers only two possible solutions to the problems of public and citizen agency ushered in by the seemingly uncontrollable advance of transnational capital. The choice that political actors can make, according to Suzanne Bergerson's account of neoliberal political economy in *Signs*, is between the all-powerful dominance of the market, which the writer wants to problematize, and the receding power of the nation as the site where collective identity gets wholly constituted (this includes both the Keynsian welfare state and state-powered politics of development), but which is in decline. In distrusting both these options equally—specifically the "'statecentric' discourse [...] based on a dichotomous state-market framework that implicitly assumes that the nation-state remains the primary site of women's political identity and agency in terms of resistance to global capitalism" (994)—the writer wants to propose a politics based in interest-based interventions and private associations. This solution acknowledges that economics works in a multiplicity of ways, some of which, on a local level, might challenge transnational capitalist dominance through a "renegotiation of boundaries, such as those dividing the global-local and the public-private" (994). Similarly, Gibson-Graham counters the inevitability and unquestioned dominance of transnational capitalism by building a concept of "noncapitalism" as a model of an alternative economics outside of states: "Noncapitalism is found in the household, the place of woman, related to capitalism through service and complementarity," and, as such, "appears as socialism" (7). The household is neither global nor extensive, does not tend toward dominance or expansion, and so "noncapitalism" can give a more positive and equalizing sense to "nomadic" economic identities formed at the limits of an "exaggerated and outlandish" (10) capitalism often described as history's hero. In the absence of developing a sense of a public except the one identical to the state, both of these neo-Marxist accounts fall back on the only remaining alternative to the unfettered maximization of capital, its hierarchies, and its exploitation as well as the homogeneity enforced by the state: "to discover or create a world of economic difference" (3)—the heterogeneity of the "social"—through a "re-privatization" of women's labor.

"Noncapitalism" in these accounts is just another name for informalization, and informalization has been used for the most part to dispossess the poor by allowing international finance directly into communities rather than promoting the state as an agent of development. This atomizes productive processes into isolated tasks that are disconnected from one another. Julia Elyachar has shown through her fieldwork how informalization and microfinance schemes are attempts on the part of international capital at "accumulation through dispossession." Such schemes allow financing to avoid the regulatory state by capturing the poor in debt systems. Much of this happens through capitalizing on the home as singular productive unit: "[T]rainers from the U.S. Agency for International Development (USAID), some on leave from their main work teaching America's poor to open up microenterprise in their homes, teach a group of Arab NGO leaders that the family is a microenterprise, the homeworker an entrepreneur,

and microenterprise the way forward to a strong civil society independent of the state [...] In that vision of society, finance channeled by
international financial organizations (IFOs) and bilateral development
institutions would directly engage 'the people' in relations of debt"
(26). For the most part, such arrangements do not lead to increasing
women's agency by giving them more control, but rather to demolishing more organic cultural structures and social organizations in
order to give foreign investors places to profit. Informalization generally gives credence to extralegal economic practices. It provides a way
for financers to get around the law.[16]

This symbolic link between women's work and state nonintervention persists. One need only look as far as 2008 initiatives by both
J.P. Morgan and Goldman Sachs to invest in business education for
women in the third world. Right at the same moment that these banks'
deregulatory practices were going to cause world financial markets to
come crumbling down, provoking worldwide havoc throughout the
systems they had created, Goldman Sachs was investing in the same
model of business and management education for 10,000 women in
sixteen countries over four continents, with the hope, their promo-
tional video announces, of global "economic and social growth";[17]
that is, translating their failed policies directly to third-world investments in women-run businesses by bypassing the regulatory state.
The video depicts such projects as a local caterer and a crafts man-
ufacturer, with women working in the home, maintaining domestic
gendered roles and the division of labor of the family as a productive
unit that has historically signaled the outside of state interventions.
The women in the video, extolling the virtues of the project, call
such practices "strategy" and "leveraging." Such forms of labor can
be feminized as, like the industrialized home, beyond oversight, and
often consolidate themselves through the practices of first-world corporate management in third-world labor-intensive settings.

During an age of neoliberalism, private life's ideal separation from
public life in liberalism resurfaces in the "free market's" ideologies
and justifications for its ideal detachment from public input. As it
was devalued in its association with women and their work, the private also could be wielded to create zones of weakened legal regulatory authority. For example, Filipina and Chinese garment workers on
the Mariana Islands are subcontracted to companies like Ann Taylor,
Ralph Lauren, Liz Claiborne, and Gap "in a unique exemption from
U.S. minimum-wage and immigration laws" (Clarren, 35). They are
often subject to substandard housing and work conditions, and are
close to indentured servitude due to recruitment fees and interest, no

overtime restrictions or reproductive controls, and frequently sexual abuse, all while employed in a U.S. territory that Congress has voted exempt from U.S. labor codes and that members of Congress have variously praised in their visits to the island. This is an ideal example of "non-state-centric discourse," where the nation-state in no way "remains the primary site of women's political identity and agency in terms of resistance to global capitalism." In this instance as in many others,[18] women represent a sphere of "domestic" privacy that marks the limit of the state regulatory authority of the old days of welfare-state capitalism, a limit to political intervention in the public sphere itself.

The form of privacy as a regulatory limit is still valued as a symbolic foundation of freedom, sovereignty, and power. Privacy has in many instances replaced the public and become indistinguishable from it. As Zygmunt Bauman has shown:

> The "public" has been emptied out of its own separate contents; it has been left with no agenda of its own—it is now but an agglomeration of private troubles, worries and problems. It is patched together of the individual cravings for assistance in making sense of the private, as yet inarticulate, emotions and states of mind, for instruction of how to talk about such emotions in a language which others would compre-hend, and for advice about how to deal with the flow of experience which the individuals find so difficult to cope with. The list of "public issues" is no different from that of "private affairs." (65)

This turnaround has not meant that women have been released from being mired in private life, as the early second-wave feminists aspired. Rather, in representing the failing protective power of the state, women project the "natural" limit of public power, and so often public power itself takes on the shape, appearance, value, and function of disempowered private life. For Bauman, this partly has to do with the increasing representation of public life through individ-ualized technologies and life stories, where spectators identify with spectacular, emotional histories that celebrities let them glimpse, or that, in Reality TV–like confessional moments, demand identifica-tion. As well, this disengagement with representations of the public-ness of the public, or the waning of the foundations for imagining it, has to do with the hardening conventions of describing the pub-lic in economic terms, defending its efficacy and necessity only by pointing to the private interests nested in it, and relinquishing any kind of prospects in or references to the public as universal. The symbolic division between public and private labor has evolved into a reconceptualization of the public as private, where private means "outside of controls" or "exceptional to the law," and a reconceptualization of politics as predominantly if not entirely a question of economics and private interests, particularly in imperialist and consolidated forms.

THE RE-PRIVATIZATION OF WOMEN'S WORK, OR CARE AND THE ER PUBLIC

Prevalent in many current developments in feminist discourse,[19] the idea of "care" implied in the privatization of the public takes over the public and its consciousness, now relegated to economic contracts, technological association, and mothering narratives, where the helpless citizenry is perennially represented through infantilism and injury. Agency is typically understood only through interest, and treated as a matter of affectivity, the body, interiority, family, particularity, and emotion. For example, in the September 2008 meeting of the United Faculty of Florida (UFF), the Florida State University System (FSUS) union senate, a motion was considered to change the policy in practice where the union represents all in-unit faculty in grievances, members as well as nonmembers.[20] In the discussion that followed, each side offered a metaphor to explain how a union should imagine itself as a public. Those arguing for offering representation in grievance cases only to dues-paying members suggested that the union should be thought of like an insurance company, where Geico does not help you if you call for insurance after you have rammed your car into a tree. Here, access to the public as "care" is framed through the actions of consumers and made available only through the profit motives of private interest. On the other hand, those advocating the continued union action on behalf of nonmembers—grievance chairs, for the most part—invoked an emergency room setting, where it might be true that some people need only Band-Aids, but others are burn victims and should not be abandoned in the face of serious injury. These perspectives echo on the national level, where someone like Warren Buffet describes the 2008 financial crisis as an accident victim in need of surgery. Such revealing narratives envision a sense of the public and social action as a crash scene. As what *M*A*S*H* character Hawkeye Pierce might have called "meatball surgeons," the public can only be understood as emergency first responders arriving a little too late to people who are helpless like children, on the verge of survival and writhing around in pain as a result of a catastrophic disaster that has torn their bodies apart or bashed in their skulls.

Wendy Brown (1995) has written about the theoretical conundrums brought to bear on thinking the public through personal injury. She criticizes the position of identity politics that makes demands on the state as a redress to injury, not only because the state often is the perpetrator of such injury, but also because it legitimizes the law as homogenous, egalitarian, and neutral: "I question the political *meaning* and *implications* of the turn toward law and other elements of the state for resolution of antidemocratic injury [...] I worry about the transformation of the instrumental function of law into a political end, and about bartering political freedom for legal protection" (1995: 28). In the union scenario mentioned above, the public is in a state of permanent injury, with "injury" being a code word for a state "failure" that has already taken place. Brown is concerned with a type of injury that makes demands of redress on a state that has the structural, antidemocratic features for perpetuating that injury, whereas the UFF organizers are projecting the absence or ineffectuality of the state and its public altogether, the certainty that the state cannot step in at all because it is not there or it does not regularly act on our behalf, and a resulting sense of permanent risk and unmitigated chaos. What goes along with the impossibility of imagining a role for the state or the public is a blockage to thinking any kind of public action in pursuit of universal projects, like justice or human emancipation. The result is a sense of fear and insecurity that cannot be resolved—better known as "terror."

This absorption of the public into metaphors of privatization or public ineffectualness takes shape against background assumptions that the gendered division of industrial labor constitutes a desired normalcy in public functions, or rather, that what is right and legitimate is a return to the habituation of everyday life that this division of labor in the private sphere implies. This does not usually mean a return to the domestication of women, but rather a reframing of women's work through domestication for the purposes of "re-privatizing" their labor, making it seem divorced from the state and available for corporate assimilation. For example, a 2008 CARE-sponsored feature-length documentary, Tom Copella's *A Powerful Noise*,[21] tells about three women's situations and empowerment within the globalized workforce: one from Mali, one from Bosnia, and an AIDS activist and victim from Vietnam. The purpose of the film is to tell the stories of women who make a difference to raise communities out of abject poverty. The main motivation in these empowerment narratives is to encourage investments in private charitable institutions of caring in order to restore women to employment at whatever the cost.

For example, in the Bosnia footage, the main informant is explaining to the filmmaker that when people returned to the community after the war, they could not find jobs, and therefore half the citizens are currently unemployed. "If we just had jobs," she concludes, "everything would be better." Calling on foreign assistance, she notes, "There are no factories here." Her project is to create localized craft cooperatives based on women's domestic talents and local materials in order to make products that would attract foreign investors and "factories"—meaning, privatized enterprises. During this exchange, the woman and the filmmaker speak in voice-over while the camera pans across a devastated landscape, showing images of bombed-out buildings, burned wreckage, broken glass, fallen brick, and the remnants of destruction—the visible signs of public annihilation. There is a compelling, discomforting contradiction between the voices and the images, which display a desperate scene that could not be remedied or improved with jobs, and could even be said to have been caused in the first place by the overextension of global surpluses and markets. To "keep my job"—working in the depths of a coal mine that is run on foreign capital—seems to be the best possibility for the future, even though such a resolution would not address the war fallout, the political turmoil, the negative environmental effects, and the remnants of ethnic and religious sectarianism that make jobs hard to come by in the first place. Later in the film, the Bosnian prime minister does make an appearance at a community picnic, and as he behaves buffoonishly in a suit and tie, he praises the women's craft cooperative for doing the government's work in stimulating the economy by restoring women to their work and possibly attracting foreign capital to purchase their labor.

Even more heart wrenching, the informant from Mali runs an employment agency to feed young women from the country into domestic service in the cities. Women come to the agency with bruise marks on their arms and legs, one with a small child whose face was severely burned, some who had been denied months' worth of salary payments. The informant was tasked with getting the women back into their employment situations by educating them, or often by training or by intervening in disputes. At one point, she asks one of the clients what she would want from her employer, and the client answers, "Only to eat." In the face of such unimaginable abuse that seems to endanger women's bodies and minds and put them at the edge of survival, "women's empowerment" appears to be about accommodating women back into the violent economic contract of domestic labor. The victims often return to their places of employment and abuse or others exactly like it, and the re-employment of such women after their retraining or other counseling is what the film considers its "success story." It is not only the absence of the state—also, of any expectation of the state—that is remarkable in scenes where traditionally one might imagine a state or legal role—policing abusive employers or enforcing salary commitments, for example. Also remarkable is the sense that the public is composed of powerless victims caught within the inevitability of current conditions, so that the only way to respond is to adapt to the division of labor and resort to mothers' work and abuse—only such adaptation can mean "women's empowerment."

In the film's Vietnam case study, the conclusion is much the same. The absence of jobs, particularly foreign-factory jobs, is creating the crisis because "[t]oo much time makes evil"; without work, it seems, the only recourse is illicit sex and lots of it. The informant's infant child has died, and the group of AIDS-afflicted patients she visits and cares for replaces the missing, as though the unrequited mothering instinct underlies her vocation. The informant's task is pedagogical, to raise awareness and offer family love in sanctuaries for the sick, and the film suggests that one person, standing alone in such a mothering role, can make a difference against global epidemics and economic devastation. A global situation of local disempowerment indicates that the only task remaining for politics is to fulfill the most basic needs of love, and that only the force of a great personality, religious calling, personal initiative, or family duty can solve such problems by restoring the norm of gender, one piece at a time. Instead of the state, the division of labor and the re-privatization of women's work appears. Instead of the state being seen as a macrolever of economic stability, mothering individualizes and sentimentalizes each injury by heroically micromanaging singularized problems, helplessness, and the pitfalls of nature. Though the public cannot be reduced to the state, the invisibility of the state in these scenarios makes evident the film's inability to envision the public's structural position of critique and to mobilize its ideal of universalism.

THE MILITARIZATION OF FEMININITY

Referring to the military, Cynthia Enloe demonstrates, "No other public or private institution comes so close to being the sine qua non of a state" (46). Enloe is here concerned with global political movements organized around broader acceptance of gays, lesbians, and women within the armed services, where gay, lesbian, and women soldiers "took on the status of paragons of citizenship" (18). In such rhetorical twists, the "solider as a public figure" (16) stands in for citizenship, and, as women have historically been relegated to the margins of citizenship, soldiering often seems as their only chance of entering public life, participating in a national activity, or engaging with public discussion: "[W]arfare has been imagined by many to be the quintessentially public and national activity" (11). For Enloe, this conflation between the soldier and the citizen leads to a basic contradiction; that is, sometimes the inclusion of women in the military could be seen as further democratizing the military, and other times it could be seen as further militarizing women.[22] This leads her to analyze the various situations that women engage with military service—as mothers, wives, prostitutes, rape victims, service providers, nurses, as well as noncombat soldiers—as caught between maneuvering, where gender is controlled for strategic ends on the part of power,[23] and empowerment, where the military accepts once-excluded minorities and is democratized by the acceptance.

What remains out of the scope of either of these options is to question the inevitable status of the military—an institution whose role in invasion, combat, and occupation is to de-democratize the public—as the only viable participatory public sphere. A third alternative to Enloe's maneuver/empower problematic can be found in current popular literature on combat, where the military, in its stubbornly masculinist ethos, remains the only viable recourse for public life, but now with women combatants in its ranks. The entry of women into this sphere becomes allowable only through a denial of gender difference in bodies and spaces. The absence of a substantive difference dividing female and male bodies in military service translates into the demolition of the line dividing soldier from civilian, or the disappearance of the "frontline" as the organizing principle of the laws and practices of populations in war. With gender no longer delineating the "homefront" as opposed to the "battlefield," privacy persists to define private military labor or contracting as civilian, performing the "feminized" tasks of support that women once did. In other words, contracting as "private" labor, often takes the structural position of civilian labor previously associated with the "homefront" and women, and therefore taking on features of submission and extra-legality. As contracted service labor, third world labor for the military ultimately fills the place formerly occupied by civilian and domestic service. In other words, the division of gendered labor gets maintained in the division between soldiers and private (often third world) contractors (now citizens)—that is, between the state and the private sector (or the market).

For example, the brigadier general in command of prisons in Iraq during the Abu Ghraib scandal, Janis Karpinski,[24] gives an account of her sense of her own mission in her memoir, *One Woman's Army: The Commanding General of Abu Ghraib Tells Her Story*. She elaborates how women's sameness with men makes them different from men. A self-defined feminist, Karpinski begins by talking about how her military career—including her pioneering role in creating and training the first Arab women's military division—would be an intrusion on "hallowed male turf" (43). "I...wanted to remain a woman," she insists, as though not remaining one was on offer or demand. "I wanted to be tough, but not to lose my femininity" (48). "You could become a master jumper and maintain your femininity, too," she later adds. Karpinski's attempts to define the content of that femininity do not give a clear sense of what specifically the coveted femininity entails. When she does make an attempt, gender difference often takes on surface forms like dress, style, softness, jewelry, hygienic needs, or hair length, but she dismisses all of these, along with childbirth and menstruation, as situations the army could and does easily overcome, creating a perfectly genderless society of warriors.

The area where Karpinski comes to be most at odds with army policy over gender is combat. For Karpinski, the restriction of women to noncombat roles is an arbitrary restriction on her career advancement that should be determined on the basis of her accomplishments, talent, and leadership—her enterprise. The army's rationale for keeping women out of combat is that women still have a protected place in American society and are not prepared for "the dirty work of warmaking" (47), so that if a woman got hit in a foxhole, the man with her would lose focus on the enemy in order to rescue her. Karpinski argues against this by citing her own extensive experience, where she has learned, she says, that the instinct that most determines conduct on the battlefield is not courtesy or chivalry but survival. Karpinski offers instead an alternative explanation for the army's preservation of an antiquated, even pretechnological idea of gender roles in work. In her reading, the underreported reason the army wants to maintain its policies that keep women out of combat can be found in the needs of the division of labor and the end of the draft. After Vietnam, men were volunteering for service wanting education and training marketable in civilian life, but were not so interested in combat, where acquired skills were less translatable to other professions. The extension of women personnel into the "noncombat" ranks was therefore designed to fill staff and combat-support positions so that male recruits would be forced to choose frontline jobs and lifetime career tracks. Karpinski criticizes this as too much regulation.

Like Enloe, Karpinski believes that accepting women into combat positions is the next necessary step for democratizing the public sphere, and like Enloe as well, Karpinski considers the military as the public figured large. The Iraq war, like feminism, proved for Karpinski the arbitrariness of the private/public divide: Places like Abu Ghraib were located outside of the combat zone, but shelling and insurgent attacks occurred regularly, so that even under fire, the troops there were not receiving necessary equipment or backup. With a woman general in command, Karpinski reasons, the prison was privatized: the army never saw fit to change the designation of the location of the prison to public combat status. This meant that the military did not come through in emergencies and did not supply adequate equipment—the prison did not fall under the codes and areas of military attention. As well, the prison had areas of labor that were not controlled by the army's command structure, personnel (often Iraqi) like military police, guards, or intelligence officers sent by private firms and so only answerable to private sector bosses, did not receive training, professionalization, equipment, and orders through conventional military channels. Much of the work force at Abu Ghraib existed outside of the usual legal regulations applied to the military. Yet, this replacement of women's work to designate, spatially, a "frontline" to limit combat areas meant that combat was privatized and could, like capital, extend indefinitely.

Karpinski's ideal shattering of gender with its private/public divide—or combat/noncombat divide—leads her to describe an alternative military structuring where large portions of those working in newly minted combat zones fell under private management. Like women in their formerly noncombat roles, paid security personnel would operate in Iraq as providers of "service" and support—like cooking and laundry, but also like protection, as well as "auxiliary duties" like security guards, military police, private intelligence gatherers, interrogators, and suppliers. She includes in this category the Iraqi national prison guards, who would, she imagines, easily cast off their citizenship, its state allegiances, and its sovereign loyalties for the much more appealing status of a low-level employee of a privately owned foreign company now protected from either Iraqi or U.S. law by its combat status. This means that the gendered division of labor was not relinquished so much as replicated within a division of labor that—under the provisions of combat—economically privatizes public services by "re-privatizing" women's work.

CONCLUSION

Feminist theory's early impulses were countercultural and even utopian. As Nancy Fraser has astutely observed, however: "[T]he cultural changes jump-started by the second wave, salutary in themselves, have served to legitimate a structural transformation of capitalist society that runs directly counter to feminist visions of a just society [...] In a fine instance of the cunning of history, utopian desires found a second life as feeling currents that legitimated the transition to a new form of capitalism: post-Fordist, transnational, neoliberal" (2009: 99). In particular, this book looks at how feminist theory's critique of the private/public divide has been appropriated and manipulated for purposes against its initial intentions. Feminism needed a theory of the public sphere that did not relegate women to its outside. Because "femininity" was thought of as incompatible with the public sphere, feminist theory, like neoliberalism, tended to focus on the private sphere as what needed to be changed in order to end structural inequalities and produce freedoms. Essentializing the connection between women and the private sphere, emphasizing that women's difference could be determined by their relations in the private sphere, feminist theory nevertheless did not adequately predict how the public sphere could be reconceptualized to take on the structural features that defined the private sphere. It also did not calculate the indelibility of capital's need for the private sphere as a cultural and symbolic zone of superexploitation and exceptions to the law. As well, it did not adequately prepare for the possibility that, instead of women leaving the private sphere and the private sphere disappearing as Marx foretold, the private sphere would become the model and the ideological excuse for a post-welfare character of work that eroded rights and protections.

This chapter has surveyed various settings where feminism's sense of its own identity and its investments in reformulating its relations to privacy make it unable to conceive a feminist politics of the public sphere. The next chapter turns to Jürgen Habermas's public sphere theory in order to discuss why feminist theory cannot identify with critical theory's thinking about the public sphere. Despite their deep differences and disagreements with Habermas, feminists continually turn to his writings. I suggest that this is not only because Habermas's analysis of modern rationalization processes—processes that feminists, too, need to criticize—provides a partial but lucid view of how such processes depend on a gender domination that often remains coded but ideologically available and habitually instituted. On another level,

Habermas's model of the public sphere is *educational* rather than empowering: It promises that modernity's self-reflection requires that human emancipation is always in the process of developing and expanding, meaning that the "human" side of universal emancipation, despite its pitfalls and prejudices, has to swell in excess of its own categorical placement and limitations. In fact, the feminist reading of Habermas's public sphere might even provide a set of procedures and norms against which to criticize not only public sphere theory itself, but also dominant trends in feminism—influenced by the equally patriarchal-dominant discourses of liberalism, militarism, neoliberalism, and psychoanalysis—that, maybe unconsciously, have absorbed and so assume the underlying structural inequalities in women's privatization. Feminist readings of Habermas—and critical theory in general—might offer feminism an accounting of a socialized public that does not resort to antifeminist ascriptions like disembodiment, objectification, degendering, depersonalization, statelessness, corporatism, consumerism, infantilism, combat, coercion, or terror. In this sense, this "public" might contribute, contra Habermas, to feminism's posing itself yet again as central to the discourses of revolution immanent in modernity's telling of its own history.

2

The Habermasian Public Sphere: Women's Work within the Critique of Instrumental Reason

As a tradition that understands public and private spheres as absolutely exclusive of one another, the liberal philosophical tradition relies on a metaphor of the social contract, where the strengthening of public decisions and collective life should happen at the expense of individual freedoms: Individuals trade a portion of their private liberties in exchange for public security protections to their person and property. Against such liberal tenets, however, the diminishing of powers in the public sector *has not* led to increased personal freedoms but rather the contrary. The privacy of citizens promised under liberalism—civil liberties and private expression, for example—has been compromised as much as the functionality and existence of the public sphere. The reduction of power, confidence, and investments in public regulatory and institutional bodies—for example, from welfare to education, from the overturning of the Glass-Steagull Act to the failure of the Federal Reserve system and the Security and Exchange Commission to enforce mechanisms of disclosure and accountability, from media consolidation to the squelching of public media sponsorship for minorities and local broadcasting on the public airwaves—*has not* led to the elevation of power in private initiative and responsibility. Rather, the moral elevation of private life in images of women's work analyzed in the last chapter forms an ideological cushion around new economies that exploit and colonize private life. Material and symbolic violence against women becomes more integral to production and profit regimes as public protections of labor, environment, bodily integrity, speech, civil rights, and mobility have been conceded. Constitutionalism, in the form of a public rule of law, and popular democracy, in the form of private sovereignty, seem to be equally at risk in ways that intersect. The "re-privatization" of women's work—as also the privatization of labor more generally—testifies to a global politics where the waning of the general will paces equally with the downward spiral of individuals' abilities to have a say in the conditions of life.

Early critical theory was concerned with giving a developmental story of modernity, and this story could be said to explain the desire to end privacy and its irrational social structures as an inaugural moment of the modern, rational public. Whether in the form of the disappearance of a Benjaminian "aura" that found its meanings in the family-focused religious rituals of peasant life, or in the form of the disappearance of the ethical community of Habermas's communicating society, or in the form of the disappearance of Adorno's particular, sensual, noncommodified, aesthetic individual (as I analyze in chapter 4), private life—and its associated women's work—would disappear beneath the social and administrative demands of modernity. Yet, private life would also dialectically rebound—as the Benjaminian "aura," though destroyed, frames the modern cinematic collectivity, or the communicating ethical community underlies and explains the intersubjective connections of Habermasian deliberation and action. While emphasizing that private forms of labor are always ready to resurface and take different forms within modernity's progress, foundational critical theory also forms a notion of critique out of the unraveling of the industrial division of labor, and therefore connects the end of the privatization of women's labor in industrialism to the development of the public sphere. "Re-privatization" means the disappearance of industrial domestic labor into different emergences of private labor, but it also shows that the disappearing private sphere continues to affect the non-instrumental moments of modernity's public.

In this chapter, I use social theorist Jürgen Habermas's public sphere theory to explore why liberalism overemphasizes the mutual exclusion between public and private spheres.[1] As can be read in Habermas's critique, the overlapping of public and private results from the placement of women and their work as the line of communication between them, in particular as a type of work that resists total instrumentalization. Habermasian public sphere theory does predict neoliberalism's appropriation of the private sphere into systems of money and power in its historical trends toward privatizing public life by "re-privatizing" women's work, but at the same time it posits the invention of the public sphere from within women's work in the private sphere. On the one hand, this means that thinking in the public sphere is always imminent alongside systems' regimes; on the other hand, the public sphere can be embedded and bound into private life and marginalized as outside of systems' dominant organizational force.[2]

The Habermasian public sphere's relation to women and their work brings to public sphere theory features that are necessary for imagining a public sphere that could resist the demonization of all things public that neoliberalism orchestrates. That is, the Habermasian public sphere theory relies on women's connections to the private sphere in order to explain its intersubjectivities, its antifoundationalism (its basis in rational argumentation and proceduralism), its contextualism (or ethos), its noninstrumentalism (particularly in its structural contingencies to aesthetic reason), its disinterestedness (in terms of its resistance to a predetermined interest, essential identity, or particularized or conceptual intention), and (in its relation to socialization) its formulation as the pedagogical process on which modernity depends for transcending the power that constitutes it.[3]

Habermas's idea of a just political future moves Rousseauian republicanism into line with democratic individualism. He develops a theory of communicative rationality precisely to think of power alternatively, rather than as divided up into competing public and private processes, a division that Habermas believes shares some of the fundamental mistakes of the philosophy of consciousness. As he observes, "The more modern legal systems actually redeem their claim to legitimacy in the currency of effective civil rights, the more the criteria for equal treatment come to depend on ever more inclusive processes of public communication" (1996: 76). I show here how Habermas's thinking on the public sphere depends on his doubled reading of women as simultaneously the particularity of traditional, concrete domestic-focused, ethical communities (relegated to the past) and the universality of future communicative abstraction. That is, under the influence of a Heideggerian temporality, women's work is represented in Habermas both as the public sphere's limited past and as the limitlessness of its future.[4] Habermas's public sphere suppresses and absorbs pedagogical socialization processes of intimate communication in its formation of argument and intersubjectivity, the backbone of his revision of the philosophical and political subject under modernity.

One of the points for which Habermas has been frequently criticized—and not least of all by feminist critics—is his treatment of community, ethos, and ethical validity. That is, his vision for the public sphere has to do with abandoning older forms of belonging and intimate association in favor of the more abstract, disembodied forms of disinterested communication in modernity. Not only do critics fault him for blocking out community and ethos from modernity's evolution, but also they point to the problem of transcendence: If the public sphere develops from within the context of private-sphere socialization processes, community interaction, and ethical life, then how does it transcend the context and become its own historical moment? Amanda Anderson, for example, insightfully claims that the culture of argument is its own ethos that transcends situatedness: "First, proceduralism as Habermas conceives it requires a specific ethos: the cultivated habit of refusing the comfort of a claimed collective identity (cultural, national, sexual and so forth). Second, [...] proceduralism offers one way of refusing the false option between reason and ethos precisely insofar as it affirms the possibility of argument as ethos" (173). On the other hand, Amy Allen is unconvinced by this reading: "The problem," she notes of Anderson's interpretation, "is not whether rationality or argument is instantiated as an ethos—Habermas never tires of pointing out that postconventional practices of argumentation and institutions must be anchored in a lifeworld that meets them halfway—the problem is whether they can possibly be thought to *transcend* their ethos in the way that Habermas's account requires" (9).[5] Unlike Anderson, Allen believes that communication specific to ethos, local and particular, the background understanding or lifeworld, does not necessarily disappear under the overarching claims of universalizing communicational reason.

For Allen, Habermas makes a mistake in order to distinguish the lifeworld from the systems, which are the modern, institutionalized forms and institutions in which power enters into the lifeworld from the outside (money and administrative power) and whose control the communicational public sphere is meant to check. This means that he tries to erase power from the lifeworld: "Habermas does not offer," Allen explains, "a satisfactory account of the ways in which power works through socialization processes to constitute individuals as subjects" (122). For Habermas, Allen notes, power is absent from the ethos and is only operative in modernity. Even though his account is rife with moments when the private sphere seems fundamental, he does not acknowledge outright socialization processes in the formation of the subject, covering them up under the dominant descriptions of public sphere linguistification.[6] This lack of acknowledgment of socialization processes, and the concomitant lack of an account of power in the lifeworld, are, for Allen, what makes it so difficult to understand the occurrence of transcendence in Habermas's account. As I explore in this chapter, I read the diffi-culty of reading the ethos in the varied temporality that Habermas's private sphere releases into his narrative of modernity: Habermas inserts Heideggerian temporalities into the private sphere; every-day practices uncover primordial relationships with the world that get called into the present by the future. The question of contex-tual transcendence, quasi-transcendence, or reflexivity—the vital question of how to think about autonomy without mystifying the past and social power—is less the aim and method of Habermas's argument than are the possibilities of world disclosure uncovered in socialization.[7] The private sphere's pastness, its repression by systems of money and administrative power, becomes the public sphere's future. This means that the public sphere by definition inherits and transforms the private sphere's learning process.

THE PUBLIC SPHERE, THE LIFEWORLD, THE AESTHETIC, AND THE DEMAND FOR FEMINISM

Habermas famously defined the public sphere as "the sphere of pri-vate people come together as a public [...] to engage them in a debate over the general rules governing relations in the basically privatized but publicly relevant sphere of commodity exchange and social labor" (1989: 27). Habermas describes this public sphere as evolving out of the Greek polis. As the heyday of classical Athens is usually seen as the birthplace of both philosophy and participatory politics, Heidegger understands Greece as the place where the question of Being was con-ceived, fulfilled, and lost: "[T]he question we are touching on is not just any question. It is one which provided a stimulus for the researches of Plato and Aristotle, only to subside from then on *as a theme for actual investigation*" (1962: 21). Yet, Being is always the question to which philosophy needs to return. In parallel, Habermas reconstructs Greece as where a coming together of public and private spheres first took form and began to disintegrate, to become discoverable only later in modernity through linguistification.[8] In this, Habermas is revis-ing Heidegger's unwillingness to take the question of Being into the question of the public. Heidegger instead places the public within the clutches of the present and its everydayness, where the question of Being is obscured. "The groundlessness of idle talk is no obstacle to its becoming public" (1962: 213), Heidegger begins, and then links publicness to the inauthenticity of the "they." In contrast, Habermas's project brings everydayness into existential historicity, the call from the future, or the Being-ahead-of-oneself, which is Being-in-the-world.[9]

Habermas's public sphere uses communicative reason to deliberate over the general standards and procedures for making claims to
validity in practical and expressive contexts as distinct from cognitive,
instrumental, strategic, and scientific contexts. As Peter Hohendahl
explains, Habermas "calls on communicative rationality in order to
undercut the power of the economic and administrative logic which
determined the historical process of modernization" (22). Language
itself provides the basis for the public sphere to be contextualized
within the modern culture where it develops, as at the same time
it is universalizing, referencing a context beyond its immediate and
instrumental embeddedness. Alongside the advent of a viable public
in language, gender vanishes with the subject, and this takes the form
of an incommunicability that persists between women and the public sphere within Habermas's version of universal communicability.
The private sphere of women's work remains privatized as the structural and temporal outside of modernity's communicating public.
As Johanna Meehan notes, in Habermas's account, "it is difficult to
explain the process of gender formation in a way that accounts for the
stubbornness of gender's hold on individuals and the culture" (45).
Yet, the privatization of women's work also bars it from complete
instrumentalization of the lifeworld or systems' coaptation, making it
a necessary component of Habermas's deinstrumentalization of reason within the modern emergence of public sphere communications.

Feminists for the most part focus on the initial stages of Habermas's
evolutionary accounting of modernity, where systems leave behind
the lifeworld. In this scenario, Habermas resorts to a scheme of privatizing the lifeworld outside of the developmental structure, and the
lifeworld comes to serve symbolically as the archaic. In these schemes,
Habermas preserves a division of labor based on women in the private sphere; that is, in particular, traditional, contextual, ethical, and
affective preindustrial forms of life that are then trapped in the historical past. With modernity, when systems of money and administrative power distort the linguistic material of everyday cultural
interaction through usurping private sphere functions in the family,
the school, and in ethical forms of communal life, the private sphere
that has been thrust out as nonsystematizable then comes—almost
nostalgically—to serve the preservation of cultural codes in procedures of argument and the model of communication through which
mutual understanding gets revealed and action gets coordinated.
With the advent of industrialization, then, the structural placement
of women and their work as the vehicle of symbolic reproduction
gets relegated to the aesthetic, which then carries forward the role of

cultural background to modern communicational processes, or the lifeworld. This might be criticized as Habermas's inability to include gender and women's work as a structure within modernity, and the consequent problem of how to oppose gender inequalities and exclusions situated within or resulting from modern life, as Nancy Fraser and Amy Allen have observed. However, Habermas also positions this private sphere as what gets called into the universalized development of a noninstrumentalized public communication that proves more fundamental than the division of labor.

One of the reasons that women's work seems structurally incompatible with Habermas's deinstrumentalized communicational public sphere is the traditional view of women's private sphere labor as instrumentalized labor. Though Habermas does instrumentalize traditional appearances of women's labor, he erases its instrumentalization with its absorption in the public sphere, thereby granting a way to understand women's work as outside of the instrumentalizations of modern life.[10] To be sure, feminist theory has been adamant in its critique of the instrumentalization of women's bodies and their work. As Simone de Beauvoir eloquently reasons in only one of many such instances, "Few tasks are more like the torture of Sisyphus than housework, with its endless repetition: the clean becomes soiled, the soiled is made clean, over and over, day after day [...] The battle against dust and dirt is never won" (451). Many such readings interpret women's connection to the instrumentalized private sphere as underlying their disconnection from subjectivity and autonomous reason. Contingently, in many interpretations of neoliberalism, labor has been thoroughly instrumentalized by systems of money and administrative power in many instances by taking on the autonomous form—that is, its seeming autonomy from systems—that determined women's industrial labor in the home. I refer, for example, to the regimes of what philosophers Michael Hardt and Antonio Negri have called "affective labor"[11] or what anthropologist Maria Mies has called the "housewification"[12] of the economy, where everyday communications and symbolic reproduction have been completely overtaken by the systems of money and administrative power, and where labor's compromise with the public and the state—in the form of labor unions, wage regulation, and rights protection—have been "colonized" by productive processes. Women's labor is also instrumentalized through the instrumentalization of the terms, symbols, and meanings through which the privatization of their labor enters into relationships with a broader economy. In her ethnographies of Mexican and Chinese women factory workers, feminist geographer Melissa Wright, for example, has illustrated how descriptors like "disloyal" and "licentious" have been attached to women's working bodies and their private sphere production to justify the cost crunch on labor in global production, particularly at the level of the "unskilled." Though Mexican women workers are "coveted" for such domestic-sphere aptitudes as "dexterity, attention to detail, and patience with tedious work," as well as "docility and submissiveness to patriarchal figures" (83), which are so exploitable for global corporate profits, these attributes also become the reasons for them to be kept in unskilled, high-turnover positions so that their value on the production circuit remains low. Contingently, feminist anthropologist Aihwa Ong has shown how Philippine and Indonesian women are trained in "flexibility and docility" (162) as well as servitude, traits that allow them to enter into contractual agreements for overseas domestic employment in other Southeast Asian nations. The production of these natural characteristics make such women viable for work as a foreign maid, often kept without being allowed to leave, without recourse, and at risk for their safety within the foreign home for what is claimed to be their own protection and well-being. Traits and aptitudes that are produced as natural aptitudes of the private sphere and of women have been made into a currency and capitalized upon. Femininity has been made into an instrumental value of capitalism.

Habermas's descriptions of the public sphere have much to offer a feminism that wants to think through a nonfoundational, noninstrumentalized political equality that dismantles philosophies of the subject based in domination.[13] Habermas's theory of the public sphere allows for the absorption of women's work into the public sphere as a deinstrumentalization. Habermas performs this deinstrumentalization, in part, by merging together women's work with the artwork, where, from its beginnings in religious and sacred traditions, the aesthetic gets absorbed into systems of exclusive expert interpretation and systems' rationalization, but resurfaces as a type of universally accessible and all-encompassing *"experience* of truth" (68), as David Ingram labels it, "capable of integrating and transforming cognitive significations, normative expectations, and aesthetic sensibilities" (68).[14] The aesthetic exceeds its context: It exposes the future in the present's pastness.[15] As Habermas himself elaborates:

> If aesthetic experience is incorporated into the context of individual life-histories, if it is utilized to illuminate a situation and to throw light on individual life-problems—if it communicates at all its impulses to a collective form of life—then art enters into a language game which is no longer that of aesthetic criticism, but belongs, rather to everyday

communicative practice [...I]t reaches into our cognitive interpretations and normative expectations and transforms the totality in which these moments are related to each other. In this respect, modern art harbors a utopia that becomes a reality to the degree that the mimetic powers sublimated in the work of art find resonance in the mimetic relations of a balanced and undistorted intersubjectivity of everyday life. (1984: 237)

Like women's work, aesthetics—as in Benjamin[16]—happens before modernity, gets shut down or instrumentalized in modernity or autonomized in a specific subsystem of reason, but then—also like women's work—mediates into the everyday life of modernity, getting unconcealed as the communicational processes of modernization. Though one might fault Habermas for aestheticizing the work of the private sphere, his linking of the aesthetic, its educational and communicational practices with women's work deinstrumentalizes the public sphere's foundation.

This chapter retrieves the side of the Habermasian prognostication where the communicational action connected to women and their work discloses the noninstrumentalizability of the public sphere. After presenting the relationship between systems and lifeworld that mobilizes Habermas's formulation of communicative reason, I start by looking at feminist responses to Habermas's theory of the public sphere. I then compare Kant's descriptions of the beautiful to Habermas's claims about communicative reason, and show that Kant separates the instrumentalized body from the intersubjective identification of the beautiful. I discuss how Habermas repeats Kant's rejection of instrumentalism in the work of women as an obstacle to the connection between subjects that underlies the public sphere's inevitable coming-to-be. Finally, I address how Habermas's embedding of the public sphere inside the learning process of the Kantian aesthetic suggests an alternative reading of the noninstrumentalization of women and their work as what builds into the constitutional moment of the public sphere.

WOMEN'S WORK, NONINSTRUMENTALIZATION, AND THE AESTHETIC

In Habermas's theory of communicational rationality, the private sphere invites incursions of money and power into the lifeworld, instrumentalizing the lifeworld. Yet, the deinstrumentalized lifeworld survives in truncated form within a private sphere now relegated to

the outside of systems. "[D]eformations of the lifeworld take the form
of a reification of communicative relations only in capitalist societies,
that is, only where the private household is the point of incursion
for the displacement of crises into the lifeworld" (1987: 386). This
crisis of the lifeworld distorts communicational practices, alienating
socially integrative symbols so that they no longer serve as the backdrop to agreement between actors; in fact, such lifeworld symbols no
longer have a defined function at all within the strategies of modern
systems. As Habermas reconciles the public and private spheres of
political action in constitutional democracies, the potential of non-
instrumentability in the private sphere preserves the noninstrumentalizability of public purpose and intersubjective association, but at
the expense of denying women their conjunction with modernity.
Habermas needs the public sphere to remain noninstrumentalizable
in order to safeguard its autonomy as well as its formation as a learning process steeped in intersubjective recognition.

Habermas's theory of communicative rationality provides a critique of what he reads as the assumption behind much Marxist and
post-Marxist philosophy that has declared that reason—e.g., in the
form of proletariat consciousness—has been absorbed into scientific
and cognitive reason and instrumentalized through capital.

> On the one hand, Marx, Weber, Horkheimer, and Adorno identify
> societal rationalization with expansion of the instrumental and stra-
> tegic rationality of action contexts; on the other hand, they all have a
> vague notion of association of free producers, in the historical model of
> an ethically rational conduct of life, or in the idea of fraternal relations
> with a resurrected nature—and it is against this that they measure the
> relative position of empirically described processes of rationalization.
> (1981: 144)

Habermas is here revisiting Adorno's critique of Lukács's equation of
proletariat consciousness with revolutionary action. The reason of the
proletariat has become suspect in this last phase of ideological critique.
As an initial stage questioned the interests involved in the truth-claims
through which relations of production were kept in place, the more
radical phase, as Peter Hohendahl indicates, "extends the suspicion to
the procedures of reason itself" (14): "Through instrumental reason,"
Hohendahl summarizes Habermas's reflections on Horkheimer and
Adorno, "the human race attained the domination of nature; but the
price it had to pay for this achievement was the repression of subjectivity" (13). Habermas, however, believes that Horkheimer and Adorno
still point to the fragments of fundamentals and norms indicating the

survival of a reflective process, but, having given up on reason as now totally instrumentalized, have lost the tools for reconstructing it.

Using the "ethically rational conduct of life" as a springboard, Habermas imagines the public sphere as outside processes of instrumentalization. In this, his public sphere borrows from sociological and anthropological perspectives on an everyday communication that has no end and no aim, but still, as cultural backdrop, coheres a community, making it possible for others to accept a validity claim. Habermas's public sphere of communication thus models itself on the communicational practices of those outside the instrumentalized systems of money and administrative power, what he calls the "lifeworld." This separation of everyday communication from organizational macrosystems, symbolic structures, and core technological processes makes it akin to the liberal coding of private life and women's work, and likens it to the idea of autonomy in art. Women's work has as its dominant concern the construction of noninstrumentalizable political life.

Some feminist theorists have remarked on the implication for women of a private sphere placed outside of the money and power contexts as the standard-bearer of noninstrumentalizability. Mostly this perspective still assumes the private sphere as domestic and women's privatization as relegating them to a place, outside of production and wages, where exclusion from the reach of politics and economics leaves them permanently in a state of inequality and subject to violence. Its solution, then, is that inequality can be assuaged by acknowledging the systems and their power structures already inherent in the lifeworld. For Nancy Fraser, for example, "it is not possible to insulate special discursive arenas from the effects of societal inequality," and "where societal inequality persists, deliberative processes in public spheres will tend to operate to the advantage of dominant groups and to the disadvantage of subordinates" (1992: 122–123). One of the issues here for Fraser is that the separation between systems and lifeworld can be ideological, and often leads to differential treatments, particularly when it comes to remunerative distributions within private economies, like paying housewives for their lifeworld labor. Habermas's absolute differentiation between systems and lifeworld, Fraser concludes,

> could be used to construct an ideological opposition that posits the family as the "negative," the complementary other, of the (official) economic sphere [...I]t directs attention away from the fact that the household, like the paid workplace, is a site of labor, albeit of unremunerated and often unrecognized labor. Likewise, it does not make visible the fact

that in the paid workplace, as in the household, women are assigned to, indeed ghettoized in, distinctively feminine, service-oriented, and often sexualized occupations. Finally, it fails to focalize the fact that in both spheres women are subordinated to men. (1989: 118–119)

Even when systems' incursions into the lifeworld have distorted life-world communication, women's connection to the lifeworld makes their systems' connection seem like they should be less systematiz-able, and so should be treated that way. Whereas neoliberalism instrumentalizes women by representing them as deinstrumental-ized, Habermas describes another possibility alongside modern sys-tematization: the private sphere of everyday communications—or the "lifeworld"—as also the place where intersubjective communication is ultimately set free.

Though dominant readings of public sphere theory tend to equate communicative reason to practical or moral reason, Habermas himself has noted that communicative rationality is an alternative to a prac-tical reason in that practical reason ascribes action "to the individual actor or to a macrosubject at the level of the state or the whole society" (1996: 3). Habermas thus likens communicative rationality to Kant's formulation of the beautiful, which also steps in when cognitive and practical reason reach their limits. Habermas's revisions of Kant are meant to deviate from the philosophy of the subject that developed from Enlightenment thinkers like Kant. Habermas's adoption of Kantian philosophy is meant to, contra Kant, break down any concep-tual contradiction between the "I" and the "we" as determinations of experience by positing that the distinction between "I" and "we" is developmentally phased in: "Complementary to the construction of the social world, there is a demarcation of a subjective world: the child develops its identity by becoming qualified to participate in norma-tively guided interactions" (1987: 28). The aesthetic stops short the reduction of all thinking to categorical thinking bound into instru-mentalism, intention, and private interest by socializing the subject. As the pivot that breaks down the division between universalism and particularism, between idealism and empiricism, between subject and object, between morality and ethics, between social (and state) struc-tures and individual freedoms, aesthetics can also be read as provid-ing the political reconfigurations that Habermas requires for bridging liberalism—with its basis in private autonomies—with republican-ism—with its public autonomies. As J.M. Bernstein remarks, "[T]he discourse of aesthetics is a proto-political discourse standing in for and marking the absence of a truly political domain in modern enlightened societies" (1992: 3). Like Habermas, Hannah Arendt appreciated that the judgment of the work of art was where Kant located the categorical rights of human sociability, political community, and perpetual peace: "[O]ne judges," she interprets Kant to mean, "as a member of a community" (*Lectures*, 72).

Habermas thus strategically selects the noninstrumentalized intersubjective moment of the Kantian aesthetic as the inspiration for public life. The beautiful postpones the private response to the beautiful object—the "I" that is saturated with gratification and interest—until after the collective agreement. One of Habermas's fundamental claims for communicational reason is that it provides a nonliberal way of thinking about language as explaining what makes people identify or integrate with their social collective in a noncoercive or cooperative manner.

As well, the Kantian aesthetic lends the public sphere its quality of fallibalism or antifoundationalism that allows Habermas to draw the conclusion that citizens must be the authors of the laws that govern them, or that argument in the end can never be determinate. In particular, Habermas's appropriation of the Kantian aesthetic promises that the pubic sphere cannot be turned into a tool of either money or administrative power—it is, by definition, noninstrumentalizable. This idea is key to Habermas's disagreement with the Frankfurt School, poststructuralist, and deconstructivist philosophies: These philosophies, says Habermas, have taken the Enlightenment's legacy to mean that reason has fallen completely into the service of technology, power, interest, and profit; that reason is unredeemable; and that the only possible alternative to a thoroughly corrupted reason is in aestheticism (Derrida), nihilism (Foucault), or irrationalism (Adorno).[17] Instead, Habermas believes that the Enlightenment tradition has not necessarily absorbed all reason into administrative controls, but rather splits reason, leaving a certain part of it available to not yet institutionalized everyday communicational exchanges.

The Kantian aesthetic that inhabits the Habermasian public sphere is based on an exclusion of the private sphere. Kant divides judgment into, on the one hand, a private or noncommunicable response of bodily gratification to an object, and, on the other hand, an intersubjective recognition based in a universalizing projection related to understanding. Because this process of intersubjective recognition cannot be subsumed in an already existing abstraction, generality, or concept, it resists being instrumentalized or foundationalized. In this division, the public gains its definition of noninstrumentalizability in opposition to a private, bodily feeling that then can assume, and often does assume, the position of instrumentalizability, or interest.

Habermas's public sphere is based on the idea that the public sphere cannot be instrumentalized. Whereas part of its resistance to instrumentalization has to do with its carrying the burden of autonomy and providing the symbolic material for cultural cohesion, another part has to do with its being modeled on an intersubjectivity and universalizability adapted partly from Kantian aesthetics. Habermas formulates this intersubjectivity through socialization—that is, as a learning process—and characterizes this learning process as the possibility of incorporating others' worldviews through shared understanding in a way that would bring them around to accepting my validity claims:

> For both parties the interpretive task consists in incorporating the other's interpretation of the situation into one's own in such a way that in the revised version, "his" external world and "my" external world can—against the background of "our" lifeworld—be relativized in relation to "the" world, and the divergent situation definitions can be brought to coincide sufficiently. (1981: 100)

As a learning process, communicational reason is a meeting between subjects that changes the subjects involved through a reference to an objective though historical relation, a shared world of meaning in language.

Beyond Instrumentalism: Freeing Up the Lifeworld

The intermeshing of the public sphere with women's work evolves out of Habermas's descriptions of public-sphere communications in the lifeworld as emanations of a socialization process. As well, the post-conventional intersubjectivities that form the basis of conversation and agreement in the public sphere initially grow out of developmental learning situations, where one learns by extending one's context into the context of the other until a third context forms, outside of the initial two, in which both can be recognized. Habermas developed his ideas of the transformation of the public sphere in the early 1960s, but by the early eighties, his emphasis had turned to communicative action in order to explore the path of reason within human speech acts that trigger human sociability, learning, and, then, modern community. Within secular modernity, communication takes the place of what once was a sacred function or received practice, supplying the symbolic codes necessary for social integration and imparting moral authority to both people and institutions.[18] This process of social integration through communicative reason is not functionally dependent on "the systemic imperatives of economic and administrative subsystems growing with dynamics of their own" (1987: 373).

For Habermas, communication is action, and the action it performs is reaching a mutual understanding or forming a public through argument. Speech acts, for Habermas, require standard normative conditions that make the speech acts' claims acceptable to and sharable among interlocutors. The rational basis of speech acts is disclosed contextually as they work to coordinate action through reaching a common understanding with others.[19] "We credit all subjects with rationality who are oriented to reaching understanding and thereby to universal validity claims, who base their interpretive accomplishments on an intersubjectively valid reference system of worlds, let us say, on a decentered understanding of the world" (1981: 134). Language reveals such a decentered rationality when subjects "broaden their horizon" in order to enter into the horizon of understanding of another, a practice that Habermas compares to both fiction and hermeneutics. Speech acts are antifoundational because they require learning, or identifying into another person's perspective and connecting it symbolically to one's own perspective; that is, like the beautiful in Kant, they require a projection of arguments that could claim validity within another person's symbolic context that then gets revealed as having something in common.

Like Heideggerian "thrownness," the lifeworld is the cultural background or traditions that make mutual understanding possible and without which communication could not happen: "The background, against which interaction scenes are played out and out of which, as it were, the situation of action oriented to mutual understanding issues, consists not only of cultural certainties, but equally [...] of individual *skills*—the intuitive *knowledge* of *how* to deal with a situation—and of customary social *practices*—the intuitive *knowledge* of *what* one can count on in a situation. The certainties of the lifeworld have not only the cognitive character of familiar cultural traditions, but also the, so to speak, psychic character of acquired and proven competences, as well as the social character of tried and true solidarities" (1987: 221). In everyday interactions, the lifeworld is not visible or knowable.[20] The lifeworld is coterminous with closed but familiar contexts of everyday interaction that people navigate without thinking, like domestic intimacy. Like Heidegger's equipment,[21] the action of communication opens the horizon to the total communicative world that we already know is there; learning to communicate reveals a social interrelatedness—a unity of reason—that precedes the individuation of the subject and the separation of the objective world.

Unlike Heidegger's question of Being,[22] the lifeworld is therefore language based.[23] The lifeworld allows meaning to be taken out of the particularization of context and abstracted into a different, now shared context. The postconventional manifestation of the lifeworld is the internalized generalized other:[24] "A can now *objectify* the reciprocal interconnection of participant perspectives from the perspective of an observer, that is to say, he can adopt an objectivating attitude toward his interaction with B and distinguish the system of intermeshed perspectives between himself and B from the particular situation in which he and B find themselves [...] Under these conditions the concept of a concrete pattern of behavior can be generalized into the concept of a norm or action" (1987: 36).[25] The lifeworld is also formative for what Habermas calls "forms of life" or "ethical life," that is, prereflexive communities bound together through common practices and traditions that are separated from one another by both concrete and expressive elements—language and culture. Habermas takes up the lifeworld as stabilizing a society that eventually is disrupted by modernity's systems.

Eventually, specialized functions begin to break off from within the lifeworld and become subject to technological appropriations or external controls. Systems come in to reorganize private life; monetary goals and bureaucratic decision set agendas from outside the lifeworld.

> In modern societies, action systems take shape in which specialized tasks of cultural transmission, social integration, and child rearing are dealt with professionally [...] Since the eighteenth century, there has been an increasingly pedagogical approach to child-rearing processes, which has made possible a formal system of education free from the imperative mandates of church and family. Formal education today reaches into early childhood socialization. As in the case of cultural systems of action and political processes of will-formation that have been converted to discursive forms, the formalization of education means not only a professional treatment of symbolic reproduction of the lifeworld, but its *reflective refraction* as well. (1981: 146–147)

Forms of social solidarity based in normative consensus, private-sphere interactions, and ethical forms of life become differentiated from social integration based in "functionally specified domains of action" (1981: 115). On the one hand, this process of differentiation leads to an expanded scope of possible social interaction, autonomous contexts, and disembodied consensus formation, as well as a "readiness to criticize" and an "ability to innovate" (1981: 146). On the other hand, functional specification and increasing rationalization of the lifeworld bring about the "phenomena of reification" (1981: 147), as well as "loss of meaning, anomie, and alienation" (1981: 148). The mechanisms and symbols of social integration are alienated from the everyday communicative contexts that anchor them.

The systems-building codes of the division of labor that are born from the lifeworld end up separating out of it. The separation of systems and lifeworld reveals, for Habermas, the possibility of a noninstrumentalizable form of rationality that can coexist with the increasing separation of systems.

> In fact, the point of departure for the whole critique of capitalism was the question of whether the transfer of prebourgeois, normatively organized labor relations over to the money medium—that is, whether the *monetarization of labor power*—constituted an intrusion into living conditions and interaction spheres that were not themselves integrated via media and that could be painlessly—that is, without sociopathological consequences—cut loose from structures of action oriented to mutual understanding [...] I want to argue against this—that in the areas of life that primarily fulfill functions of cultural reproduction, social integration, and socialization, mutual understanding cannot be replaced by media as the mechanism for coordinating action—that is, it *cannot be technicized*—though it can be expanded by technologies of communication and organizationally mediated—that is, it can be *rationalized*. (1987: 267)

Habermas interprets the new social movements—including the women's movement, but also environmentalism and youth movements—as lifestyle movements, or "resistance to tendencies toward a colonization of lifeworld" (1987: 394); that is, communicative registers that are rearing their heads against distortions and divisions imposed by the growth of systems, especially into lifeworlds. Once the state and capital extract what they need for their own reproduction, everything that remains is "the sphere of the private, which indeed can now only be characterized privately—by [...] the unfettering of the empirical needs of isolated subjects who compete for scarce resources according to the laws of the market" (1987: 358). The placement of the lifeworld outside of the systems that rationalize modern areas of action link it structurally to reproductive and private life functions.

Women's work is therefore not only the opening to systems colonization, but simultaneously the primary and most convincing
example that Habermas gives of a type of communicative action
and coordination that has been freed from systems and resisted
total technicization, yet is still rational. The economic system has
infiltrated into "the life-forms of private households and the life
conducts of consumers and employees," subjecting them to "its
imperatives, consumerism and possessive individualism, motives
of performance, and competition" (1987: 325). The feminizing of
work appears as both the point of juncture where the systems enter
the lifeworld, smothering the formation of public-sphere communicative practices, and also where the lifeworld gains freedom from the
systems' colonization and technologization, opening up possibilities
for the realization of mutual understanding and social integration
that modernity promised but has not yet delivered in the form of
the public sphere. The lifeworld that forms out of the private sphere
in the end destroys the private sphere.[26] In the process of finding
an agreement in the Habermasian public sphere, the world of noninstrumentalized relations that already existed in this private sphere
gets revealed through speaking, and this, we discover, is a world we
already know. The lifeworld as modernity's background is disclosed
as the public sphere's call from the future—its "potentiality-for-
Being."[27]

FEMINIST THEORY, HABERMAS, AND THE PUBLIC SPHERE

Feminist critical theory returns repeatedly to Habermas's theory
of the public sphere with both a flurry of optimism and intense
frustration. For the most part, this is because Habermas's theory of the public sphere is premised on the infinite expansiveness
of political participation and the universalizing potential in social
democracy, while at the same, it analyzes the structural and systematic development of the public sphere as inherently in opposition
to an older, other, or more primordial time when "the orienting
power of the private sphere would become weaker and weaker"
(1987: 324). In other words, the Habermasian public sphere is
constituted *and* disenchanted (or alienated) through the exclusion or loss of legitimacy in "a traditionally based lifeworld with
a subjectively produced and morally centered unity of private life"
(1987: 324). After presenting some of the recent feminist debates
and issues surrounding Habermas's work, I show how Habermas's

appropriation of the Kantian aesthetic within his theory of public-sphere transformation allows for this double interpretation, where the private sphere of women's work is excluded both temporally and symbolically from the public sphere even as the public sphere cannot really separate from its integral relation to the private sphere of the lifeworld.

For Habermas, the uncoupling of systems from the lifeworld leads to the rationalization of the lifeworld, its reification or instrumentalization, which is destructive to human association and meaning (Habermas, 1981: 359). As well, this uncoupling promises the emancipation premised in the Enlightenment's autonomy of reason. Habermas safeguards the lifeworld as a third path that is neither, on the one hand, the instrumentalizing subject of history that Adorno, for example, describes as having sucked up individual consciousness and life fulfillment, nor, on the other hand, the absence of reason that poststructural and post-Nietzschean philosophies describe.

For Habermas, the public sphere is ultimately a bridge where the private household (or *oikos*) and the public forum (or *agora*) are united in the forms and practices of collective household management that Habermas, following Hannah Arendt, calls "the social." Important to feminists, then, is not only Habermas's deep analysis of a developing ideal of equality in the public sphere. Feminists are also concerned with the ways that equality in the public sphere is premised on its assimilation of the private sphere as the residual of the lifeworld. The public sphere allows the set of linguistic and cultural intuitions and assumptions called the "lifeworld" to become universally and rationally accepted as they are taken up from their particularization in ethical forms of life. Habermas addresses the family and its form of life in four conflicting ways: (1) as an archaic mechanism of social integration that is eroded by modernity; (2) as a portal through which modernity starts to alienate itself from the integral interactions that cohere a community and reproduce its norms and values; (3) as a social organization based on systems' relationships of ownership and domination that gets bracketed out of discursive exchange; and (4) as an ideal and formative model for a type of public interaction based on feelings of "human closeness"[28] and the possibility of reaching an agreement based on the force of the better argument.

The private sphere that, in various distorted ways, defines the family serves also as the organizing principle that opens into deliberative processes that lead to intersubjective agreements. "If [...] we [...]

recognize in the structural transformation of the bourgeois family
the inherent rationalization of the lifeworld; if we see that, in egalitarian patterns of relationship, in individuated forms of intercourse,
and in liberalized child-rearing practices, some of the potential for
rationality ingrained in communicative action is *also* released; then
the changed conditions of socialization in the middle-class nuclear
family [...] suggest the growing autonomy of the nuclear family
in which socialization processes take place through the medium
of largely deinstitutionalized communicative action" (1987: 387).
Teaching (socialization) is what decontextualizes the nuclear family
from the systems that have absorbed it in parts, giving it a different communicational function based in an ideal of egalitarian recognition. Habermas is saying that power is modernized out of the
lifeworld, reserved to systems. Even though Habermas says that ethics are retrievable within a modern sense of belonging, returning to
ethical life seems only possible as a regressive measure. "Forms of
life," for example, are where Habermas locates "male monopolies"
and "male privilege" (1987: 393) of a patriarchal society that rational
lifeworlds have superceded.

Scholars of feminist theory have engaged with Habermasian theories of the public sphere in various ways, just as they have engaged with
theories of liberalism more generally, with various degrees of caution,
conditions, and qualifiers. The ensuing disagreement results in part
from the ambiguities in Habermas's account. Some claim the limitations of the universal in actually existing social discourse are essential to the public sphere's very construction,[29] where "the exclusion
of women had a structuring significance" (1992: 428), as Habermas
himself has acknowledged, while others adopt Habermas's sense that
modernity's ideal is yet to be realized, where class-based and other
types of identity-based specifications for rights of participation are
eventually overcome in the forward projection of the universal.[30]
Joan Landes, for example, argues that in the case of postrevolution-
ary France, the bourgeois public sphere was constructed as an ascetic
alternative to the women's literary salons[31] that extended the theatrics of court culture into urban society gatherings as a result of
the growth in print and literacy. Habermas's analysis, she concludes,
does not take into account the necessity of the rhetorical gesture that
restricts women to private domination in the bourgeois household
in order to institute a new order opposed to the frivolous and open
theatrics of the aristocracy. In addition, she remarks, "Habermas's
formulation fails to acknowledge the way the symbolic contents of the
bourgeois public sphere worked to rule out all interests that could not

or would not lay claim to their own universality" (1988: 44–45). On the other hand, Seyla Benhabib, with her focus on moral issues and her interest in "publicity in political life" (1992: 74), reads Habermas as improving on the liberal tradition by allowing for a plurality of publics to form. She writes, "The public sphere comes into existence whenever and wherever all affected by general society and political norms of action engage in a practical discourse, evaluating their validity. In effect, there may be as many publics as there are controversial general debates about the validity of norms. Democratization in contemporary societies can be viewed as the increase and growth of autonomous public spheres among participants" (87). Also, Mary Ryan sees Habermas's theory as an invitation to plurality, giving a foundation for feminists to start thinking beyond "gendered limits on participation in the public sphere" (259) because it "freed politics from the iron grasp of the state" (261). Instead of analyzing the structural features of the public sphere that exclude women constitutionally, Ryan is interested in providing a historical "counternarrative" in nineteenth-century U.S. literary public spheres—what Habermas calls "the literary precursor of the public sphere operative in the political domain" (1989: 29)—which reveals that women were always involved in modernity's public project of critique.

Feminists have also found disagreements with Habermas's account of the decentered subject. Marie Fleming, for example, has questioned Habermas's historicization of the subject, where its communicative basis in immanent reason is simultaneously both a product specific to modernity and, contradictorily, something Habermas assumes in every act of communication, with the Greeks furnishing his most basic example and the anthropological record offering a spectrum of proofs in developing "primitive" consciousness. Habermas needs to presuppose an inherent reason to communication in order to pose modernity's specific mode of cognitive-scientific rationalization as partial. "[T]he modern understanding of the world is indeed based on general structures of rationality but [...] modern Western societies promote a distorted understanding of rationality that is fixed on cognitive-instrumental aspects and is to that extent particularistic" (1981: 66). Fleming's critique of Habermas's wanting it both ways gives further impetus to her observations of irresolvable contradictions in Habermas's account of universalization that claims universal status only by assuming fundamental exclusions, and of women and the private sphere in particular.

In addition, Habermas sees the decolonization of the lifeworld from the systems of money and administrative power as a solution to social reification in ethical forms of life. Some feminist critics have read this as leading to the further marginalization of women and the private sphere or as a formula for exploiting women's labor further, possibly privatizing it into the future. Marie Fleming understands Habermas's decolonization thesis as resulting in the stifling of the family's role in reproduction and socialization under an institutional-legal framework: Family and school functions are transferred into systems' management. And yet, she continues, Habermas "is far from advocating regulation as a solution to problems in everyday life. He maintains that the most suitable arena for the 'struggle over needs' is not parliament, but the 'general public sphere,' and he observes that a lengthy process is generally needed before matters such as the question of spousal abuse or the demands of working parents for state-sponsored childcare facilities are even recognized as political themes" (1997: 95). This would coincide with Nancy Fraser's critique, where not only does Habermas depoliticize and legally marginalize women, but he also peripheralizes their work as economically irrelevant. At the same time, however, Habermas believes that a functional public sphere politics requires the freeing up of the private sphere from total systems' colonization. This would explain why the strengthening and consolidation of neoliberal ideologies and regimes of privatization gave rise to social movements and public concerns oriented around diversifying forms of family, sexuality, and reproduction, as well as around demands for greater access to literacy, communications, and equality of education.

HABERMAS AND THE AESTHETIC

Habermas interprets the Kantian aesthetic as the site where Kant theorizes the public. Like the beautiful, the Habermasian public sphere is the situation where human subjects come together to an agreement based on what they have in common: the ability to reason and to judge. Like the beautiful, the public sphere is always an action that forms itself through projecting an abstracted collectivity as an ideal or a future; it is a break from tradition, in fact, a formation that cannot be drawn from tradition since it requires agreement from a communicative situation. In effect, Kant uses the beautiful to describe intersubjectivity as qualitatively different from the contextual, private, concrete, and particular experience of the body.

The judgment of the beautiful implies that private pleasure or satisfaction cannot account for the recognition of the beautiful in the object as shared *as though* beauty were a property of that object,[32] or rather, as though beauty were separate from those judging, a third perspective. "It asserts only," Kant continues, "that we are justified in presupposing universally in every human being the same subjective conditions of the power of judgment that we find in ourselves" (*Critique*, 170–171). The beautiful therefore "does not produce an interest in the object" (*Critique*, 107); it cannot be privatized. The beautiful communicates through the "common sense," a "universal communicability of feelings" (*Critique*, 123), which Jacques Rancière has described as "the very manner in which something in common lends itself to participation and in what way various individuals have a part in this distribution" (12).[33] Because beauty projects the universal, but cannot, by definition, originate in the universal concepts that allow objects to be recognized and interpreted, the beautiful judgment proves the universal communicability of human subjectness. As Paul Guyer concludes, the beautiful "requires the existence and experience of society as its condition" (20).

The critics' dominant focus on Habermasian theory as moral theory or as a critique of scientific thinking has led to a marginalization of aesthetic considerations in the criticism. Martin Jay, however, does acknowledge the importance of aesthetics in Habermasian social theory: "[A]lthough Habermas must still be accounted a far less aesthetically inclined thinker than his mentors in the Frankfurt School, it will no longer do to claim that he gives no weight at all to the role of art in the process of emancipation" (133). For Jay, Habermas was criticizing Adorno's elevation of art as categorically underlying both "nonidentical thinking" and the resistance to the reification of instrumental rationality—that is, that art was the substance of the negation, the outside of reason. In opposition, Habermas's recourse to art and art theory supplied his communicative rationality both with the "theme of universal communicability" (129) and the possibility of access to "endangered meanings" (131). Albrecht Wellmer agrees that for Habermas as for Adorno, aesthetic experience was "the presence of a utopian perspective" (65). Unlike for Adorno, however, where art is the nonschematizable future projection of social redemption against the present of instrumental reason, for Habermas aesthetics, like women's work in socialization, furnished "an irreversible collective learning process which must be categorically distinguished from the learning processes in the dimension of science and technology" (51). The public sphere's adoption of the Kantian aesthetic is what makes it the part of the present that wrests itself from the present as a future development.

As well, the reception of the aesthetic connects with what critics read as the recognition of women and difference. Many critics interpret what they identify as Habermas's rejection of aesthetics as a rejection of difference and, particularly, of women. Lincoln Dahlberg, for example, explains, "The exclusion of aesthetic-affective modes of everyday communication, from what is defined as the legitimate rational form of democratic discourse, is seen by critics as privileging some groups' voices over others. More specifically, the public sphere conception is seen as systematically marginalizing the voices of women and non-Western persons" (114). The exclusion of the aesthetic is necessary, such critics claim, for Habermas to base the public sphere in rational, disembodied discourse that reaches agreement and consensus. As well, some critics have objected to Habermas's removal of the lifeworld—alongside its aesthetic, cultural, and linguistic qualities—into primordial space, where it takes on the guise of a "throwback" or "archaic anachronism" (Coole, 236). "It is the aesthetic," observes, for example, Diana Coole, "which is most downplayed by [Habermas] and whose rationality is the most problematic within his schema [...]. In considering Habermas's references to the aesthetic, my contentions are [...] that it is problematic for him precisely because of its association with alterity" (228).[34] On the contrary, Habermas's public sphere in effect projects itself as the disembodied and departicularized qualitative difference of the Kantian aesthetic and the possibility of decontextualizing transcendence.[35]

The beautiful, for Kant, like the public for Habermas, is a quality of subjects that have correspondence with each other, rather than with empirical objects or sensations: Beauty is the subjective experience of the common. The beautiful is necessary for conceiving the social,[36] as well as the basis for "the universal feeling of participation" and "the capacity for being able to communicate one's inmost self universally" (*Critique*, 229). Kant goes on to describe the subject's response: "For he must not call it beautiful if it pleases merely him [...] but if he pronounces that something is beautiful, then he expects the very same satisfaction of others; he judges not merely for himself, but for everyone, and speaks of beauty as if it were a property of things" (*Critique*, 98).[37] Defending the beautiful as non-instrumentalizable, Kant's explanation separates out sensuality, pleasure, interest, and the body as the agreeable[38] or "private feeling"[39]; in contrast to the beautiful, which has a "validity [that] for everyone can be presupposed" (97), the agreeable is described in relation to particularity, temporality, the physical, the empirical, the historical, and the contingent.

Habermas's reading of the universalizability of the beautiful, of its ability to separate out from its empirical context, is not the majoritarian one. For the most part, the Kantian aesthetic is read as not convincingly uprooted from the body and so not sufficiently universalizable or "disinterested." In other words, the beautiful, as the basis for the pubic sphere's universalism, is not a replacement for private, affective work but rather its entryway. As Jan Mieszkowski explains, "In this idiom of universalizability without universals, a judgment postulates the possibility of what it demands itself to be" (19). Kant needs to contrast the beautiful with the agreeable; that is, with sensual experience, "feeling," and private gratifications, particularly in bodies, in order to set up the beautiful as transcending subjectivity. "All satisfaction," he explains, "is itself sensation (of a pleasure). Hence everything that pleases, just because it pleases, is agreeable (and according to its different degrees or relations to other agreeable sensations, graceful, lovely, enchanting, enjoyable, etc.)" (*Critique*, 91). He continues, "With regard to the agreeable, everyone is content that his judgment, which he grounds on a private feeling, and in which he says of an object that it pleases him, be restricted merely to his own person" (*Critique*, 97). Also, Kant classifies the beautiful in distinction from charms and emotions, which he links to the agreeable and to judgments made "consulting only his own private sense" (*Critique*, 159), "the immediate feeling of our own well-being to our own sense, and not to that of others" (*Critique*, 159), egoistic and experienced ultimately only through a corporeality that is "merely consciousness of one's existence" (*Critique*, 159). These he calls "barbaric" (*Critique*, 108), because they are, he says, deprived of impartiality. Attributable to gratification, the agreeable involves intentions, a will toward a specific end, which Kant calls "interest" and opposes to the "disinterestedness," or absence of desire, that is the condition of possibility for the beautiful. Likewise, the satisfaction of the beautiful must be distinguished from the fulfillment of hunger because hunger is a private and interested sensation: "[P]eople with a healthy appetite relish everything that is edible at all [...] Only when the need is satisfied can one distinguish who among the many has taste and who does not" (*Critique*, 95–96). In other words, not amenable to scientific experimentation, nor the cause-and-effect logic of the conceptual, nor corporeal need, the beautiful cannot be instrumentalized. That is, the pleasures of intersubjectivity on which the beautiful is based cannot be equated to the pleasures of attaining personal aims or fulfilling needs or satisfied feelings or confirming a preexisting notion of "the good," but rather must be ascribed to the harmony of the understanding that results from the project of finding commonalities with others in recognition of the shared ability to communicate reasonably.

"Disinterestedness" is, then, that part of reason that Habermas adopts histories into his public sphere, because it cannot be ascribed solely within intersubjective will formation. As Bonnie Honig puts it in relation to Habermas's attempts to unify constitutionalism (government by rights) with popular democracy (government by participation), "disinterestedness" requires that "private and public rights are created simultaneously" (2001: 793) since laws and public procedure require agreement by the individuals they then address. Interest, on the other hand, "involve[s] the concept of an end, hence the relation of reason to (at least possible) willing, and consequently a satisfaction in the existence of an object or of an action, i.e., some sort of interest" (*Critique*, 93).

The difficulty of credibly establishing a sphere that would completely deny the role of interest—that is, the constant return of interest in any discursive or political attempt to declare its obsolescence or avoidability—serves to link the aesthetic to women's relations in the public sphere. In other words, the aesthetic provides the public sphere with its sense of a communicative, learning exchange that can crush, suppress, deny, or transcend its particularity inasmuch as it, paradoxically, needs its particularity for it to become different from its particularity. For Habermas, the public, like the Kantian aesthetic, does not live out a preconception, a particular interest, or a regulative principle. Like the beautiful, the public is groundless or, rather, a permanent process of displacement. "Disinterestedness" in the Kantian sense means not the absence of personal interest per se, not the opposite of interest, but the ability to communicate my own interest as other in such a way that everyone could sign on. Kantian "disinterestedness" translates into an "innerworldly transcendence"—an interiorization of the subjectivity of the other—that Habermas equates to "learning processes" (1996: 5). As such, "disinterestedness" turns the beautiful into the first communication, the nonfoundationalized opening to the social. As well, "disinterestedness," like primary socialization, provides the context for reproducing knowledge that others understand because it is made accessible within their own standards of validity.

DEBATING DISINTERESTEDNESS

Habermas's public sphere theory is an attempt to find an alternative to reason's tendencies toward strategic thinking, determinism, instrumentalism, or domination in the public sphere's contextual engagement with the private sphere's communicational ethos. "The challenge," however, as Amy Allen has points out, "is that the disentanglement of power from validity might not be possible, and the claim that it is possible might itself be an attempt to exercise power" (10). That is, the assumption of disinterestedness, decontextualization, or the possibility of transcendence implies that the power relations that enabled such movements toward autonomy are mystified. To be sure, critics of disinterestedness, like Pierre Bourdieu and Mary Wollstonecraft, have, in fact, understood it as embedded in socialization processes, where social relations of power mask power's interest in instrumentalizing of the body.

Yet, unlike Habermas, this critique of disinterestedness at the same time demands that women's private sphere work of socialization be instrumentalized. Poststructuralism and feminism have both adopted such positions. Whereas Bourdieu's aesthetic theory asserts that the private sphere and its socialization processes can only advance the broader context of power and domination in which they are embedded, Wollstonecraft believes that the private sphere's unenlightened power relations can be separated out from the broader civic community that centers on education. That is, whereas Bourdieu thinks that the private and public spheres cannot be separated and so the public sphere cannot be extricated from the power relations that compose it in the sphere of private property, Wollstonecraft advocates abandoning the private sphere to enter an autonomous civic sphere that, in its Enlightenment and its freedom, has shed itself of power. Whereas Bourdieu posits a public sphere that is saturated with the relations of domination that exclusively define socialization processes in the private sphere, Wollstonecraft idealizes a public sphere that, in its educational mission, is a pure release from power because it has locked out the private sphere's relations of power—its tyrannies—in its processes of socialization. In either case, in contrast to Habermas, whether the public sphere is totally transcendent and autonomous or totally contextually embedded, women's work in the private sphere, and particularly in the context of teaching in the private sphere, can only influence the public sphere as a mode of domination.[40]

In contrast to Habermas, Pierre Bourdieu, for example, sees Kant's aesthetic "disinterestedness" as articulated through class hierarchy. "Disinterestedness" is bound up in the divisions of social space and characterizing systems of learned bodily dispositions, or "habitus." "Disinterestedness" allows bourgeois class interests to be communicated as though they were not particular interests to the class, but rather seemingly universal or natural, as ideology. The universalism of "disinterestedness," for Bourdieu, allows Kant to create a case for categorizing aesthetic value as qualitatively different than the value of popular culture with its thirst for quick gratifications and vulgar pleasures of the body[41] as well as with need. Aesthetic value hides the class interests that are set in place through its construction. For Bourdieu, the aesthetic is first and foremost a question of taste, or a system for the reproduction of class hierarchy through the unequal distribution of social and cultural distinction, and therefore resides dominantly in the private experience of the body, socialized before consciousness, whereas for Habermas, the aesthetic works as a learning process—that is, it works socially, through recognition, interiorization, and intersubjective identification, and can always be challenged in an encounter with the other. In Habermas's logic, Bourdieu would be reducing socialization and its teaching processes essentially to a situation of domination, where the preconscious individual absorbs the class formation into his/her body, rather than as a working project of subjects coming to understanding through coming to agreement, that is, through projecting subjective consciousness into the context of the other. In the process, women who socialize subjects are constructed, by Bourdieu, as instruments, that is, as the carriers, disseminators, and transmitters of conservative cultural values and ideologies of private property. Habermas interprets readings like Bourdieu's—where the aesthetic is always doused in instrumentalized reason—as a product of rationality's disremption (that is, the splitting of realms of reason into specialized knowledge categories), where cognitive validity claims and scientific thinking have come to substitute for the representation of all thinking, while alternative procedures and validity claims and different normative structures have vanished on the margins.

On the flip side, feminism has explained the Kantian aesthetic as embedded in the ethos of subordination in the private sphere, freeing the public sphere for transcending these power relations. Feminism of Kant's time claimed that women's experience corresponded to sensibility (outside of reason), where their affections and their bodies seemed as interested, cunningly manipulated for achieving property, position, and protection. Unlike Habermas, who believes that the existence of the private sphere historically or structurally gives evidence of a division of reason that is redemptive in its refusal to be instrumentalized, Mary Wollstonecraft argues that the private sphere's bond to the aesthetic turns women into

machines of cunning, strategizing, and manipulation. "Taught
from their infancy that beauty is woman's sceptre," interjects Mary
Wollstonecraft in 1792, but two years after the first German pub-
lication of Kant's aesthetic critique, "the mind shapes itself to the
body, and, roaming around its gilt cage, only seeks to adorn its
prison" (44). Women affect sweetness so they can "gratify the
senses of man" (19), gentleness and childishness so they can give
him pleasure. For Wollstonecraft, women's absorption in frivolous
tricks of the body, display, and the pursuit of pleasure, motivated by
desire, block the development of their capacities for moral thought
as well as their knowledge of science; that is, they fail at learning
cognitive, abstract, practical, universalist, or conceptual thought:
"[I]n the education of women, the cultivation of the understanding is always subordinate to the acquirement of some corporeal
accomplishment" (23). In addition, women's obsessions with such
bodily affectations lock them out of the cultures of civic participation where learning occurs. "Confined then in cages like the feath-
ered race, they have nothing to do but to plume themselves, and
stalk with mock majesty from perch to perch" (56). Lacking access
to the public's enlightened communication, womanly antics, for
Wollstonecraft, are nothing but charms, meant to lure and seduce
for private gain.

Wollstonecraft formulates the split between the dominating subject and the object on which it acts as a conflict between women's
bodily instrumentalism and male civil society. For Wollstonecraft,
instrumentalism was an effect of tyranny, like slavery, and its manifestation, in women, was their frivolity and sensuousness, their
artificiality and submission, all to be attributed to "the sovereignty of beauty" (55) that they learn. "Novels, music, poetry,
and gallantry, all tend to make women the creatures of sensation,
and their character is thus formed in the mould of folly during
the time they are acquiring accomplishments, the only improvement they are excited, by their station in society, to acquire. This
overstretched sensibility naturally relaxes the other powers of the
mind, and prevents intellect from attaining that sovereignty which
it ought to attain" (61). Unlike for Habermas, who believes that
the learning process of the private sphere will re-emerge as the
redemption of the public, for Wollstonecraft, the resolution to
women's oppression as they are locked up in the private sphere's
self-indulgence can happen only with the erasure of the "agreeable" of the feminine body that limits their access to a more universalized project of political discourse.

LEARNING, INTERSUBJECTIVITY, AND THE PUBLIC

For Habermas, the relation between aesthetics and the public sphere has to do with the way each one functions in accordance with the principle of linguistics, particularly when involved in performative exchanges. That is, "[w]hen participants in communication utter or understand experiential sentences or normative sentences, they have to be able to relate to something in a subjective world or in their common social world in a way similar to that in which they relate to something in the objective world with their constative speech acts" (1987: 27). The speech act means that the subject has already incorporated other subjectivities. The linguistification of universalization, which presupposes an understanding or a cultural sharing with the person on the other end of the speech act, is based on my perception of how to make my utterance appropriatable within somebody else's own context and experience. Kant projects this linguistification through the universalization of taste. He says these "generally valid (public) judgments" mix with opposing "merely private judgments" to make "aesthetic (not merely practical judgments)": "[T]he taste of reflection, which, as experience teaches, is often enough rejected in its claim to the universal validity of its judgment (about the beautiful), can nevertheless find it possible (as it also actually does) to represent judgments that could demand such assent universally, and does in fact expect it of everyone for its judgments" (*Critique*, 99).

This does not need to be, as it frequently seems, a statement on the punitive limits of the human that suppresses difference and imposes sameness, often imperialistically. For Kant goes on to explain that someone who disagrees should not be rebuked, but can be educated to acquire taste; in fact, the beautiful for Kant establishes the universal educatability of human moral consciousness.[42] Nor does it have to be true that everyone succeeds in judging beauty where everyone else at least should notice it too, for the judger might have been mistaken.[43] Rather, Kant imagines the social relations that arise from recognition of the aesthetic as socialization, or learning: My recognition of beauty without a concept of beauty means that I can imagine a subjectivity in another that can communicate to form an agreement that makes sense with my own. Though Kant tries to situate the subject temporally before judgment, the subject of judgment cannot really come into existence until the other's judgment is interiorized as/with my own. Habermas reconstitutes this aesthetic through the idea of a linguistically constituted lifeworld: Without requiring the primacy of the subject, the lifeworld, like the aesthetic, allows for a recognition of a shared understanding that becomes situationally visible.

Habermas uses this idea of learning as an *other*, communicational form of reason that the Enlightenment developed alongside its view of reason as the domination of the empirical world in the concept. The lifeworld, for example, as a cultural stock of knowledge, also stores the interpretive knowledge of past generations. This store of knowledge gets introjected, a process which Habermas calls "feedback" and links to the birth of a communal conscience. "Freud also introduced learning mechanisms of internalization [...] in the sense of 'internalizing' relations to social objects" (1987: 9). Habermas weaves the lifeworld through the Freudian narrative of the formation of conscience through mourning, where the maturing mind incorporates its (literally or figuratively) dead parent in order not only to disavow the separation or prohibition, but also to develop into a moral being. In Habermas, however, the parental figure does not get appropriated as a scolding voice to rid the child's consciousness of the confusion that comes with the id breaking through its barriers. Instead, the child identifies the introjected "third person" as an objectified, even transcendent social context of acceptability for validity claims, and, as such, always involved in argumentation.[44] "Freud [...] realized that these patterns of behavior become detached from the context-bound intentions and speech acts of individual persons, and take on the external shape of social norms insofar as the sanctions connected with them are internalized through taking the attitude of the other, that is to say, to the degree that they are taken into the personality and thereby rendered independent of the sanctioning power of concrete reference persons" (1987: 34). In such descriptions of developmental conscience, Habermas centralizes the maternal role within the linguistification process of moral thinking as the "an uninvolved *third person*" (1987: 35) that becomes the transformative principle of the public sphere.

Habermas's interpretation of the beautiful in Kant as a learning process offers an array of qualities to the public sphere, particularly in its identifications with the communicational aspects of the private sphere and women's work. For one, "[T]he person making the judgment," writes Kant, "feels himself completely free" (*Critique*, 96), and this is because the judgment of beauty operates free of concepts and prior representations, outside of both prohibitions and determining directives. The judgment of beauty is an effect of the free play between the intuition and the understanding where the intuition never comes to rest within the conceptual map of the understanding's cognitive categories. It produces a feeling of pleasure in the subject since it gives access to the harmony between the imagination and the understanding expressed in play, without rules or prior determination. As a bridge between cognitive and practical thought that never belongs to either, the beautiful works not so much as a determining judgment, where the general concept must find the empirical object through which its form is represented, but more often as a reflecting judgment—which Kant calls "the faculty of judging" (*Critique*, 15)—where the empirical object must find a concept through which it can be represented, producing the conditions for the formation of the concept. As Jan Mieszkowski interprets it, "[T]he imagination is distinguished not by its ability to create fantastic visions of alternative realities, but by the way in which it prevents thinking from being reduced to a set of forms or propositions" (5). The lack of determining concept is what makes the beautiful unrepresentable. For Kant, however, the judgment of beauty is where learning occurs, where something unthought can start to be thought, challenging the established conceptual understanding. It has also been read within Marxist and critical thought, as Robert Kaufman points out, as "a boot-up disk for conceptual thought as such [...] and [...] the engine for new, experimental— because previously nonexistent (and therefore, free of status quo determined)—concepts [...] With its quasi-social and quasi-conceptual character, aesthetic experiment [...] also provides a prerequisite of critical thought when [...] it offers formal means for allowing new [...] aspects of contemporary society to come into view" (694). The aesthetic is therefore a break into a new origin, a founding moment that neither repeats nor is repeatable.[45]

Addendum

Neoliberalism ushers in a new phase of the public sphere. In it, rationality enters into the service of a nearly complete instrumentalizing of the private sphere. This is particularly evident in privatized work regimes like sweatshops, where domesticity and maternal labor have been reassigned as targets of capitalization, as I analyzed in the previous chapter. In this, women's work *is* the self-regulating mechanism that is the market. This can explain to a certain degree why the global impoverishment of working people—the growing polarization between rich and poor on a world scale—and the diminishment of wages have been concurrent with rising rates of female employment.

However, while intensifying systems' colonization of lifeworlds, private forms of labor—affective labor, service labor, home work, microcredit, and the like—underlie forms of capital expansion that no longer fall into traditional legal workforce regulatory structures where Habermas's public sphere seems to lie.[46]

Habermas's more recent work has tried to approach such questions. His work on globalization has portrayed this new era of capital as destructive to lifeworld processes in ethical forms of life as it destroys archaic village cultures in an accelerated growth of urbanization and technological specialization. He celebrates this as the possible realization of "an association of free and equal citizens" to be held together by means of law that "forms the emancipatory horizon of expectation within which the resistance to what appears as an unreasonable reality becomes visible" (2001: 58). In other words, the new collectivities and modes of interaction crush and replace traditional means of social belonging, creating expanded spheres of action for modern intersubjective communication and learning processes across borders. Habermas places much faith in the new interactive communicational technologies like the Internet that "have the effect of expanding and intensifying networks" (2001: 66). Habermas notes that these new outflows of capacities "for democratic self-steering" (2001: 67) are met with rising trends in unemployment. However, private life has not disappeared under crushing systems and postnationalism. Instead, in the global production that accompanies the formation of Habermas's global civil society, private sphere production has become reentrenched.

Habermas describes new work regimes not as new forms of social organization, but rather as expanding connectivity on the backs of the new electronics of private aesthetic production: "as we busy ourselves with our radios and cell phones, our calculators, video gear, or laptops" (2001: 42). The absorption of the communication structures of the now-disappearing (according to Habermas) private sphere takes shape completely within advances in media, as though media would be the place of systems' resistance. Such global communication networks, according to Habermas, rise to the possibilities of new arrangements for ever more inclusive democratic agreements to be made as to what the laws should be, what modes of political coordination we should adopt, and how we should govern ourselves globally.[47] Such commercial networking "loosens ascriptive ties to family, locality, social background, and tradition, and initiates a formal transformation of social integration" (2001: 82–83). They repair the regressive aspects of the lifeworld that would slow up the speed of modernization: "The spatial and temporal horizons of the lifeworld," he concludes, "no matter how broadly they extend, always form a whole that is both intuitively present but always withdrawn to an unproblematic background; a whole which is closed in the sense that it contains every possible interaction from the perspective of lifeworld participants" (2001: 82). Habermas's account here requires thinking of the media as escaping from colonization by the money and administrative power that currently control it.

As the pivot through which the archaism of the private sphere would structurally form the redemption of a public, communicative technological future, women and their work play a central role. However, Habermas's vision of modern democracy relies ultimately on the assumption of a deep and insurmountable division between women's work and the public sphere. This plays out—in Habermas's fantastical descriptions of globalization—in his assumption of the obsolescence of women's work. In Habermas's schema, the private sphere of production is lost to history. Once communications leaves the lifeworld, once modernity steps away from tradition, the private sphere loses its application, its use, its structural necessity, and its connection to a broader democratic dialogue, and democracy as a force of modernity gets carried forward on a combination of aesthetic rationality and technology. There can therefore be no accounting, within Habermas's communicational theory, for the entrenchment of the private sphere of production as a mode of advancing global circuits outside of the circuits once managed in relation to national space and national law, nor about why women are still conceptualized, even assumed, as aligned to the private sphere. Yet, even as the private sphere has become a ground of economic relations that are no longer contingent to the nation-state, even when the transfer of public functions to women's work in the private sphere has served to marginalize those public functions from regulatory discretion or public input, women's work and the private sphere have still come to seem as the conceptual zone where the public sphere evolves globally.

Habermas cannot offer an explanation of why gender persists, of why the opposition between the public and private spheres of production still creates value in work even when it does not make social sense as a lifeworld principle, or of why this opposition not only persists but is regenerated as the symbolic and ideological form of modern global corporate expansion. Habermas's references to Kant's aesthetic theory allow for the public to show itself as only recognizable, feasible, and fulfillable in relation to women and their work. The public sphere's roots in the Kantian aesthetic imply that the body can nei-ther be completely privatized or instrumentalized as the "before" to intersubjectivity, nor can the laws that come into place through mod-ern forms of intersubjective agreement make sense without reference to the pleasures and displeasures of the body. Women and their work are not, then, the block or the limit to modernity or its public, but rather, inevitably, their ultimate story.

3

Beirut Fragments: The Crumbling Public Sphere, Language Privatization, and the "Re-Privatization" of Women's Work

In this chapter, I argue that Jean Said Makdisi's 1990 Lebanese civil war memoir, *Beirut Fragments*, chronicles the privatization of the democratic public sphere through the "re-privatization" of women's work. By "re-privatization" I mean an organization of labor where workers in a postindustrial workforce find themselves in places that resemble or repeat industrialism's domestic sphere, but are subject to more direct forms of exploitation; that is, where obstacles of public regulation and oversight can be bypassed or overcome. Makdisi's book presents a public sphere with its linguistification or background lifeworld communicational understanding unraveling. In Habermas's public sphere, the private sphere disappears into the past so that its quasi-transcending socialization processes are absorbed into its processes of modernization; in the remnants of Makdisi's public sphere, the private sphere is at a historical standstill, its communicational structure no longer forward leaning. *Beirut Fragments* can thus be seen to be criticizing a version of feminism—and in particular I address Toril Moi's quarrels with feminist poststructuralism—that posits agency in contingent, situational, private language use. I argue that such a privatization removes the pedagogical content necessary for the public sphere to perform its critiques (Moi can identify the pedagogical in language use only within a logic of domination). By taking the alienation of women's privatization and the privatization of socialization processes to an extreme, Makdisi's memoir envisions a very dystopian moment of the public sphere's demise as it splinters from the sociality of its pedagogical functions.[1]

The Lebanese civil war raged for fourteen years,[2] and can be said to have destroyed the public institutions through which the state acted. "Here and there," Makdisi describes the crossroads lying between West Beirut and East Beirut, "a tattered flag or a pockmarked national emblem hangs lopsided from a balcony where diplomats once hosted leisurely receptions and chatted and smoked over drinks" (75).[3] Not only the diplomatic quarters, but also the national art museum and other buildings that held the symbols that once cohered a national community have given way to military checkpoints, garbage heaps, and ruins. "The museum building itself now serves only a military function, while dark rumors circulate as to the fate and whereabouts of the treasures that once lay within" (74). "[R]eferences to the museum," she explains, "no longer bear the slightest connotation of culture" (54). With the crumbling of the institutionalized public sphere, Makdisi is forced increasingly to take shelter in her home. Her access to the university where she works gets cut off by the war, and her work turns away from the public pedagogical toward private familial responsibility.

Beirut Fragments is a document that witnesses witnessing. It therefore invites expectations that it will adopt techniques of realism. *Beirut Fragments*, however, fails in adhering to realist form. I argue here that Makdisi's failure in following through on such generic conventions parallels a failure of the communicative conventions of the public sphere in a time of war. With the slipping up of recognizable features of genre, what Makdisi witnesses is a privatization of public-sphere functions implicated in the "re-privatization" of women's work. Makdisi's memoir is a fragmented autobiographical tale where public institutions fragment and finally break down, and where these public institutions' former democratic functions and conventions of citizenship—including witnessing and self-narration—are increasingly "re-privatized" as women's work.

The re-privatization of women's work plays out as a privatization of language. That is, it plays out as a block in the sociational and pedagogical functions of language as well as in the formation of agreed-upon meaning-making contexts that transcend private identities. Makdisi lists words in her glossary whose meanings have been reassigned in the course of the war and have become vague references to a situation without references: the words "*masdar mawthuk bihi*," for example, used to mean "a source in which confidence can be placed" when referring to newscasters, and has come to mean "rumor, painted full of tongues" (60–61). "*Al hawadith*," the definition of which is "the events," now figures a grand gesture toward sequences of the war's history, "a faintly contemptuous understatement," which exposes "the poverty of language in conveying experience" (65). Whereas this vocabulary was supposed to represent the sharing of experience by Beirutis, the words' references, moods, ironies, and intensities end up making them "indistinguishable" (50) between citizens. Private language is all that is left.

With language use fragmenting a sense of common purpose in governance, *Beirut Fragments* stages the effects of public-sphere devastation on the cultural front. Gone with the public is a shared mutual context in which words have mutually understood roles and meanings, or the possibility of projecting meaning by assuming someone else's subject position and finding intersections with my own. *Beirut Fragments* sees this as a challenge for realism and a fracturing of the literary conventions, including memoir and confession, that produce shared identities and community symbols of belonging. Corresponding to the "re-privatization" of women's work, the breakdown of publicness underlies a privatization of language use; that is, a breakdown in the ability of language to respond to its situation, to socialize others, or to change its context and situation through use. Whereas—as I discuss below—some strains of feminist theory advocate that the privatization of language is what makes possible demands on a public saturated in relations of authority, universalism, and domination, *Beirut Fragments* treats language privatization as the inescapable demise of a public communication and citizen agency surrendered to privatization through technology-driven violence.

Just as the buildings that housed national power and national culture as structuring forms of political communication and identification are destroyed,[4] the memoir itself falls short on recognizable genre features of realism and memoir such as coherent thematizations, attention to detail, stable identities (most characters have no names), deep psychology, emotional intensity, interior descriptions (most interiors are exposed to the outside), social analysis, and legible temporalities (she tells about her childhood in Cairo in the middle of the book, the fourth part). Makdisi shows that the crumbling of systematic references to the public sphere parallels a disintegration of the communicative function of literary convention. As a narrative that resists placement in any recognizable concept of genre— that actually fails genre—Makdisi's memoir can be read as a reflective account of literary conventions as supplying the rules of the game necessary for a language of the public: The memoir makes visible such a reflection on literary conventions by discarding them along with the conventions, institutions, and rules of the public. This culture of communication at risk finds its most strident formulation in three repeated motifs that disrupt the generic codes for stabilizing meaning: (1) the abandonment of a language that would create a bridge of mutual understanding on which a public sphere depends; (2) the transformation of the pedagogical language of the public sphere into a public sphere of domination, governed by privatized language use; and (3) the "re-privatization" of women's work, the current institutional form of the industrial division of labor.

Part of the way that *Beirut Fragments* narrates the fragmentation of the public is in descriptions of the blocking of roads and open spaces between sites of interaction as they come to pose countless possibly fatal threats. Such wartime obstacles to movement in public space drive civilians to hunker down in the concealment of their homes. The sense of outside danger and devastation that forces social life into private enclaves characterizes much Lebanese civil war fiction, expressed as the constant tension between the war on the outside and inside spaces of refuge and separation from it where trauma and alienation unfold. One thinks, for example, of Elias Khoury's *Gate of the Sun* (first published in Arabic in 1998), where the Palestinian freedom-fighter, run into exile in 1948, leaves his family behind in what is now Israel, where he is lured back by the memory of desire and home life, while the Lebanese border is where the struggle for future nationhood gains material, representative, and political form, and, after the Shatila massacre, gets hazed over in helplessness and despair. Also, one might recall the main character in Hanan al-Shaykh's *The Story of Zahra* (1986), who repeatedly dodges from her domestic seclusion through the war zone to reach her lover who is an enemy sniper, stationed on a nearby rooftop. In Rashid al-Daif's 2001 novel, *Passage to Dusk*, the main character is hit by gunfire near the museum and loses his arm. As explosions continue to echo from the frontline, he returns home to find a pregnant, recently widowed refugee and her son living in his apartment, and the three continue to live there by secluding themselves from each other in the bedrooms, locking each other deeper inside, while in a hallucinatory haze groups of knowns and unknowns knock on their apartment door, some of whom are violence-prone, threatening with guns. Even more starkly, Hoda Barakat in *The Tiller of Waters* (1998) depicts the outside war zone as a desert filled with rocks, remains of dead children stuffed into funeral urns, and rabid dogs on the prowl, forcing the protagonist to hide away with his fantasies and memories in his textile-draped cellar under an abandoned market stall. As public or common space, the outside becomes dystopically unusable.

This spatial movement between outside and inside as narrative technique is, of course, standard for much war fiction (if not for fiction in general). Samira Aghacy sees spatiality in Lebanese war fiction as diagramming connections between psychological problems and political events, where characters search interior spaces "to achieve a stable, coherent and noncontradictory identity" (83) in a merciless environment, or where "[h]ousework becomes a medium of self-expression" (87) that transcends the chaos and urban upheavals. I argue that such Lebanese civil war stories are using spatial dynamics in order to create a vision of society without a state or public sector. "The state," remarks Makdisi, "is as powerless as the individual" (41). Much like the prophecies of neoliberal economics, such chronicles are raw thought-experiments in social and political engineering that simulate the outcomes of radically slashing the public sector.

Critics of Lebanese war fiction note that such fiction explores "a condition of a state that is no longer a state, a state that has little or no sovereignty, a state that is bereft of the means to uphold or impose the rule of law in its territory or at its borders through the mechanisms of force" (Hassan, 1622). In agreement with Makdisi, I do not want to minimize that the fault for the brutalities of this war lies with the Israeli military,[5] its U.S. counterparts, and their expansionist policies, as well as with the religious sectarianism instituted in Lebanon as a defense of minority rule and the multiple histories of colonialism that litter Lebanon's coming-to-nationhood. Yet, besides serving as the backdrop for a criticism of geopolitical power plays, religious sectarianism, or the struggle for land and sovereignty, war devastation here doubles as a superlative metaphor for an economic system that has succeeded in overriding the traditional institutions where citizens in a democracy stake their claims, make demands, deliberate, and decide. The undermining of public institutions has four effects that countervail democratic governance: (1) communicative structures of generalized social integration breakdown; (2) in the absence of symbols of commonality, shared values, and core purposes, individual actors become privatized, thinking is reduced to instrumentalism, and gender conventions come to be defensively guarded as the only remaining protector of culture and the social order; (3) with the takeover of the public sphere by technological means of instrumental rationality, the communicational public sphere is reduced to impositions of authority and command; and (4) the public's capacities to represent and to mediate the intersecting interests, communicational bonds, and mutual understanding between populations and citizens are shredded.

ALIENATION IN THE LIFEWORLD

Makdisi's memoir picks up on a transformation in the relationship between political action and the public sphere that I believe is a feature of the neoliberal age. Liberalism's narrative of increasing inclusion and expanding rights has given way to a divisive narrative of decreasing government involvement and expanding privatization of capital and labor. This decrease in the power and even in an idealized representational value of government has led to a decrease in citizens' abilities to change the course of collective life, to create safety and security in the face of crisis and disaster, or to turn private anxieties into programs of social action. As Zygmunt Bauman puts it, "In a fast globalizing world, where a large part of power, and the most seminal part, is taken out of politics, these [political institutions] cannot do much to offer security or certainty [. . .] Assuming for a moment that the extraordinary happened and private/public space was filled with citizens wishing to debate their values and discuss the laws which are there to guide them—where is the agency powerful enough to carry through their resolutions?"[6] This diminishment of power in the public sphere is at least partially made possible through the "re-privatization" of women's work.

Makdisi shows that liberalism's narrative is being challenged by the "re-privatization" of women in the neoliberal age. The public sphere is not represented by its ability to expand what it can represent—to call forth more concrete identities into its abstract categories of rights and recognitions, because of the inherent universalizability of language use—but rather as its ability to divorce itself from its representations: its representative populations, values, and effectualness. When the bombs come, Makdisi gathers her family together, retrieves her kids from the yard, and descends to the shelter in the garage, where she hunkers down under crashing debris, defenseless, on her own. The war itself forces her inside, where she attends to the needs of her children, finding them a place to urinate and other motherly tasks of seeing after simple biological function. The exploding technologies trap them inside as the outside lots, streets, and neighboring residences crumble and fall.

The situation that Makdisi describes as the Lebanese civil war exposes a deep alienation that occurs in war as a result of a decline in politics that war inflicts. I am reading this, however, as a broader metaphor of alienation, and particularly for the type of alienation made prevalent under neoliberalism, where needs previously administered by state bureaucracies now fall onto individual responsibility and private initiatives. As David Harvey states, "Neoliberalism is in the first instance a theory of political economic practices that proposes that human well-being can best be advanced by liberating individual entrepreneurial freedoms and skills within an institutional framework characterized by strong private property rights, free markets, and free trade. The role of the state is to create and preserve an institutional framework appropriate to such practices."[7] Makdisi faces a loss of symbolism, social integration, or public agreement through which she can identify with other citizens. She denounces the PLO and the Lebanese government "for ignoring me, for not saying a word, for their silence," and society "for leaving me out" so that "I felt myself to be only a useless, discarded, redundant object" (165) like the dust she is constantly sweeping away. The waning power of the state and the public sector that happens with the deregulation of capital causes a disassociation with the institutional structure through which citizens in democracies have traditionally made claims to recognition or made demands to influence policy, vision, and agendas.

Though wars such as this are certainly extreme examples of political culture and civil society getting wiped out, Makdisi's own account gestures toward a more general concern of an ensuing global disorientation and loss of meaning. This disorientation is due to a destruction of a once-realizable communicational bonding across boundaries of identity. In the memoir, this communicational ideal takes the form of the budding enlightened cosmopolitanism in a once-thriving Beirut, now lost: "an almost boundless tolerance and freedom of thought," she writes. "Its cafés had been meeting places for dissidents, intellectuals, and refugees. It was here that they could speak and listen, read and discuss each other's books, often published in Beirut even if banned in their own countries" (79).[8] The loss of this ideal leads to seclusion: During the course of the war, it becomes more and more difficult for Makdisi to get to her workplace at the university or to perform her duties as a professor, as courses are continually interrupted by explosions or student absences, or the wartime atmosphere creates distractions and changes commitments. "Books remain unopened," she describes the setting at the university, after the first bombing,

> but having been carefully stated by the administration at the last crisis, "Carry on" is the order of the day, so carry on we do. Descartes gets a quick going-over, his thought irrelevant and distant, the whole exercise adding to our sense of futility [...] I try desperately to concentrate my thoughts on rationality in seventeenth-century France as Beirut intrudes with yet another series of explosions. (40)

Descartes is the optimal philosopher of privatization, situating private and contemplative life as completely divorced from any ability to affect the world and thereby creating a sense of unreality of the world. As the philosopher who distrusted external impressions as illusions or tricks of the devil and withdrew secular, human reason and certainty into the deep interior of the isolated subject, Descartes himself brings to the fore the communicational breakdown in the institutional ruins and the loss of reason's relevance. The class's shortcomings in producing a conversation about Descartes is the utmost in just punishments for a philosopher who imagines thought bounded by the metaphysics of the private self and without any translatability to an outside other. The decline in the functioning institution that houses the use of a universalizing transnational public reason surfaces as a story about a woman whose movement and workspace are gradually reduced, where language has become detached from its public function of instituting human commonality in human reason.

Makdisi acknowledges that the failing of public institutions is tied to a legitimacy crisis that is linguistically structured. That is, the Habermasian participatory public sphere that provides the basis for social integration and intersubjective recognition between citizens has lost its points of reference, in this case due to war. In addition, Makdisi emphatically states that the continuation of a communicational public sphere that becomes visible through teaching is tied to the continued presence of women's communication, even under siege: "Women grew in the war [...] Our work in the universities became more important," she declares, "as it became more difficult and complicated. As all this happened, a new woman grew up in me, and my skin molted. The question remained, however, how to write" (21). Though *Beirut Fragments* appears as a now conventionalized chronicle of hybridity, where the West meets and mingles with its others and the author takes on the identity of the in-between, on another level it records a structural transformation of the public sphere as assimilated into the character of a woman who teaches through witnessing and writing.

Makdisi imagines that the narrative of the Lebanese civil war is a narrative about the end of language and the breakdown of the public sphere,[9] particularly marked, as she says, by the closing of publishing houses, the demolition of art houses, and university interruptions—that is, by the end of pedagogy. *Beirut Fragments* is not so much a tragic tale about a system of referentiality that has seen its metaphysical roots chronically lose their hold and become unhinged, as in poststucturalism. Rather, Makdisi interprets the war as the destruction of everyday communications that would foreground a correspondence between subjects made possible by a shared substratum inherent in the use of language. Internalized in consciousness through the process of socialization, this shared linguistic substratum would, through teaching, anchor mutual understanding and coordinated action with others.

PRIVATIZATION OF LANGUAGE

The neoliberal context of Makdisi's narrative makes evident that neoliberal political configurations, though borrowing from the symbolic coding of the industrial age's private/public split, are based in a distancing from the utopian communicational ideals that liberalism projected onto the separation of labor spheres. In distinction from liberalism, neoliberalism gives rise to the replacement of ideal public sphere or state universalizing consensus by isolated private-sphere functions, often represented through women's work. Though often liberalism—including Habermas's version of it—sees the private sphere of women's work and socialization as the necessary precursor that merges into a communicational, consensual modernity to come (as I traced it in the last chapter), Makdisi interprets women's "re-privatization" as a replacement of modernity and an end to its political formations, abstract inclusiveness, philosophical ideals, concept of abstract citizenship, and promise of progress. Makdisi shows this "re-privatization" occurring at the level of language, as a separation.

Makdisi's memoir narrates the unraveling of modernity's public sphere as an unraveling of a consensus imminent in language—the kind of consensus, that is, that Habermas pairs to the public sphere. Her insertion into a contemporary feminist theoretical tradition reveals women's work as gradually distancing and detaching itself from the public sphere, and the public sphere defined through conformism, consensus, and a pedagogy of domination as the basis of communication. Feminism has been wary of such constructions of the public sphere through consensus. Such critiques want to amend the universalisms of the public sphere by alternatively constructing a public sphere that would privilege or exclusively recognize the nonconforming differences inside, or privacies. Many feminists—I focus in the next section on Seyla Benhabib—are suspicious of the public sphere because it requires a conformity and agreement that can only really be achieved, they claim, with an external and dominating imposition, a leveling or devaluing of difference, or a forced hegemonic identification. In the following section, I discuss how feminism—in this instance, as developed by Toril Moi—has celebrated, in the name of contingency and difference, the privatization of language as liberating the body. In this, she marginalizes the public function of the symbolic or dismisses it as structured through a desire for unification or a tendency toward domination that I understand as allied to publicness. Moi's idea, however, depends on a Wittgensteinian concept of consensus in language, where, contrary to her conclusions, private language breaks through hegemonic domination with a difference, interacting inside public regulatory relations: For Wittgenstein, private language is private insofar as it reproduces the public only by challenging it. Private language is not a break from the public, a replacement of the symbolic, a singularity, or a radical contingency as much as it represents the conditions of possibility for a public connectivity. As acquired socially, private language is a testing of identity through an enunciation of difference. As I go on to show, Makdisi's memoir, in its neoliberal orientation—in contrast to Habermas, Benhabib or Moi—exhibits the end of the liberal narrative.

Private language challenges a consensus idea of language use that might tend toward a language of domination. Yet, the privatization of language might also carry a sense of undermining consensus altogether as its logic corresponds to the privatization of the economy under neoliberalism in the following ways. On the one hand, as language and human association are privatized, the possibility of understanding others' sensations and connecting with them in my own understanding diminishes. Wittgenstein's famous example of this is in the expression "I feel pain," where it is not possible to assume that another's feeling of pain is based on a picture of pain that corresponds with my own.[10] "The essential thing about private experience is really not that each person possesses his own exemplar," he clarifies, "but that nobody knows whether other people also have *this* or something else" (§272). Staying in Beirut—continuing day to day, doing common errands—privatizes Makdisi's experience by privatizing her pain. On the other hand, private language is an action without rules or regulations, at least not yet. Through a teaching exchange, "private language" gives rise to rules of understanding that have not yet formed: "Could someone understand the word 'pain', who had *never* felt pain?" he asks. "How do we know?" (§315).

Consensus by the Rules

In the last chapter, I discussed Habermas's vision of the public sphere. For Habermas, the public sphere takes communication out of the certainty of the localized everyday encounter that is governed by tradition, familiarity, and sacred symbols. In its place, the public sphere assembles abstract symbols of cohesion that transcend the immediate context, ritualization, and familial socialization, which, in turn, fade into the background as the "lifeworld." In modernity, systems of money and administrative power "colonize" the lifeworld, distorting communication. Habermas believes, however, that there is a part of the lifeworld that cannot be instrumentalized by systems. This part is what gets left behind in the receding of families and sacred authority, and is linked to the socialization tasks that women perform.

Habermas's theory of the public sphere rests upon his concept of consensus, or the ability to reach an agreement. I argue here that Habermas's concept of consensus depends on Wittgenstein's ideas about private language and its relation to rule following. In elaborating this theory of the public sphere, Habermas misreads Wittgenstein's way of understanding rules in order to clarify his narrative of consensus, but only in the section where he cites Wittgenstein directly. In other sections, Habermas uses the idea of private language in order to present the public sphere as a consensus without domination. In this view, private language can never be disassociated from the formation of the public, as it is in the war that Makdisi describes. In its depictions of radical contingency and symbolic breakdown, Makdisi's account shows the incompatibility of the current economic organization through alienated privacy with the Habermasian narrative of the public sphere as a public forming itself out of the communicational structures of privacy.

Habermas's concept of consensus is developmental. He starts out by analyzing an interaction between two animals that can recognize and respond to each other's gestures, perhaps because of genetic likenesses or instinct. Habermas interprets such instinctive behaviors as carrying symbolic meanings that give rise to others' expectations and symbolic responses. This is the first instance of the lifeworld. In other words, if an animal makes a gesture of warning, the gesture must also fit in with the gesture world of the responding animal if that animal is to respond by fleeing. From there, Habermas needs to build an explanation of how societies follow rules, thus acting within a perhaps unacknowledged set of generalized symbols and expectations that organize collective behavior and so transcend the one-on-one interaction: the generalized other. For this, he invites in Wittgenstein: "With this analysis of the concept of 'following a rule,' Wittgenstein demonstrates that sameness of meaning is based on the ability to follow intersubjectively valid rules together with at least one other subject; both subjects must have a competence for rule-governed behavior as well as for critically judging such behavior" (1987: 18). The concept of rule following, Habermas insists, "is key to our problem because we can explain what we mean by the *sameness* of meaning in connection with the ability to follow a rule" (1987: 17). Rather than presuming the regularity of behavior, his consensus idea forces behavior into conformity through internalization: "[P]articipants learn to internalize a segment of the objective meaning structure to such an extent that the interpretations they connect with the same symbol are in agreement, in the sense that each of them implicitly or explicitly responds to it in the same way" (1987: 14). The relationship between the pedagogical community and the individual being socialized would therefore have to be one of top-down management.

However, as I go on to discuss, Habermas understands Wittgenstein's concept of consensus through rule following as not composed of rules that preexist their usages, but rather as a constant negotiation with "private language" or difference. Without testing private language applications against the rules that define the community, private identities, for Wittgenstein as well as for Habermas, could not form in reference to community-based symbols and practices. Rather, public authority would be completely disassociated from and alien to the private lives it is supposed to govern, as it is for Makdisi. However, Habermas explains that in order for rules to work, one person has to act in response to the symbolic expression of another, and that other has to assess the response as either fulfilling the expectations set by the symbolic expression or not. If not, the second person needs to utter an understanding of the initial presuppositions, and the first person would recognize the response as falling or not falling within the horizon of expectations, and so on until agreement is reached. "[O]ne has grasped the meaning of a rule when one has learned to understand the exhibited formations as examples of something that can be seen *in* them" (1987: 16). In other words, the action of following a rule must be validated by the other as recognition that the rule is an expression of a shared convention: It can be neither individualized nor privatized, nor can it be coerced through the domination of the social. "The sequence can be repeated until one of the participants fulfills the other's expectation of recognition, the two arrive at a consensus grounded on critical positions" (1987: 19). The representation of the other is eventually internalized as the community standard of behavior or parental voice against which individual behavior must be checked, or what Freud might call the internalization of the other, mourning, or the socialized superego. This is what Habermas calls "consensus."

Habermas's consensus idea is related to a construction of genre that Habermas himself later realizes is overly deterministic: Consensus dominates as an agreement on the real. Habermas argues that everyday communication is necessarily realist for consensus; that is, for problem solving, pragmatic exchange, and validity claims. Public-sphere consensus depends on realism, is constituted by realism, and breaks up with the dissipation of realism. Realism includes here the eyewitness or documentary report (1987: 202). In the critique of poststructuralism that he fleshes out in *The Philosophical Discourse of Modernity*, Habermas says that realism assumes a specialized linguistic function and pedagogical practice of "mediating between expert cultures and everyday world" (207), between the teacher and the student, that calls into play a shared context with the other that more self-referential or world-creating forms of expression, like fiction and poetry,[11] can suspend.

Makdisi's descriptions concur with Habermas's view by turning it on its head. Instead of saying that the public sphere is maintained through realism, Makdisi depicts realism as dying with the public sphere. Her eyewitness report/war documentary formulates public-sphere consensus as fundamentally broken and along with it the documentary function of mediating between an event and a broader public that needs to know. As Makdisi's teaching duties get crowded out by the war, as her children are forced to stay home from school, as the university itself turns into "modern ruins, reminding me [...of] the Pyramids or the temples of Baalbek" (223), the text itself takes over the function of teaching (i.e., representing the event to a foreign public through the act of witnessing), but through literary devices and genre conventions that fail. Her form of memoir does not, as Lukács outlines the rules of realism, "determine theoretically the origin and goal of human existence" (21), but rather wanders around in a wasteland, without motivation. Neither does her character reveal a depth that would give insight into "a fragment, a phase, a climax, in the life of the community as a whole" or the "specific social or historical circumstances" (20), but rather the character itself flattens, motivations never appear, and in their place arise only basic biological responses, reflexive shudders, and unmotivated impulses.

Realist consensus has been a target for critics of Habermas and for feminist critics in particular who think of the public sphere as a betrayal of difference in the name of abstract and disembodied equality. Seyla Benhabib has taken Habermas's emphasis on consensus to mean an imposition, a limitation to an otherwise useful theory of democratic interaction: Habermas's theory of consensus, she says, does not take adequate account of the "concrete other." For Makdisi, on the other hand, in the sense of neoliberalism, the privatization of language or particularization disrupts and disengages the consensual public sphere, incapacitating it totally. She does not conclude, with feminism, that public-sphere consensus locks out private differences of identity and experience, and its concept needs to expand in order to embrace them; rather, she understands the private to be locking out publicness in symbolic communications.

This limitation of Habermas's conceptualization of consensus has to do with its reaffirmations of the private/public divide of industrial labor: Habermas sees language and its genres as moving from the life-world to the public sphere in the processes of modernity's formation. Benhabib reads Habermasian consensus, with its realist emphasis, as a kind of decisive homogeneity in thinking, the idea of governing through generalized agreements between all those governed leading to the connected idea that the agreement will assume conformity in its generality, and will be imposed on others who do not necessarily agree, that is, imposed from the outside, either against their will or through some form of persuasion, blackmail, brainwashing, or terrorism. Such a reading of consensus is suspicious of universalism— Benhabib calls consensus a "counterfactual illusion" (8)—inferring that universalism is stuck in abstractions and decontextualizations that ignore or neglect difference, sensuality, context, particularisms, localisms, and concrete bodies.

For Benhabib, the focus on consensus is of particular concern for feminists. This is because, she says, universalist theories have traditionally paid insufficient attention to the distinction between the "generalized other"—or the abstract subject of rights and public discourse—and the "concrete other"—or the embodied individual with sensual needs, particular histories, and relational (situational, contingent) moral orientation, usually associated with women. She argues, for example, "The gender blindness of much modern and contemporary universalist theory, in my opinion, does not compromise moral universalism as such, it only shows the need to judge universalism against its own ideals and force it to make clear its own unjustified assumptions" (51). Universalism's insufficient attention to concrete, particular bodies "has everything to do with the gender division of labor in western societies subsequent to modernity" (13); "[t]he norms of freedom, equality, and reciprocity," she continues, "have stopped at the household door."[12] The oppositional categories put in place by consensual universalisms—for example, of the universal of justice versus the particularisms of ethos, ethical life, or the good life—and which Habermas sometimes adopts, leave "the line between the public and the private pretty much where it has always been, namely between the public spheres of the polity and the economy on the one hand and the familial-domestic realm on the other" (13). Valuing universalist theory that does not base itself on consensus, Benhabib wants to adapt the Habermasian public-sphere theory of utopian discussion toward what she calls "the standpoint of 'interactive universalism'" (227), weakening consensual agreement while understanding differences as sparking an ideal of freedom that does not fall into "hermeneutic monism" (226) or atomized appeals.

However, it is not at all clear that Benhabib's view is offering a "step up" on Habermas's idea of consensus. Habermas's presentation of consensus picks up on a debate over interpreting Wittgenstein's "rules of the game" that could be read in a much more complicated way than Benhabib reads it. Implicitly, the public sphere's connection to the private sphere's work of socialization is the source of Habermas's public sphere's resistance to foundational logic, totalizing gestures, or social alienation, as analyzed in the last chapter. Socialization and pedagogical processes work through rules that cannot determine future behavior because the use of language is not determined by the rules of its use.[13]

Habermas does at first imply that Wittgenstein's view of language compels conformity to rules,[14] whereas, in contrast, as he admits elsewhere, the way Wittgensteinian language theory works is by presupposing behavioral regularity, and the type of regularity that Wittgenstein imagines is closer to Habermas's lifeworld concept than a rigid compulsion to language rules would imply.[15] Habermas's adoption of his consensus idea from Wittgenstein's ordinary language theory would suggest that consensus cannot be absolute, preset, or imposed externally because it is a recurrence of private-sphere practices of socialization and pedagogy.[16] Wittgenstein thinks of language as nonconforming to the rules that its use brings into being. As the rules are learned and repeated as part of a pedagogical process of socialization, language deviates from its rules, or the rules themselves do not dictate particular scripted responses, but rather make responses available, as in chess, or are opened up to response. *Philosophical Investigations* is written as a series of conversations between a teacher figure and a student figure or between a mother and a child. In these conversations, the teacher figure is confirming or denying the student's validity claims with "yes" or "no" assertions, and vice versa.[17]

These "yes" or "no" assertions are parallel to the ones that Habermas maintains are the substance of the public sphere (as discussed in the last chapter), as they demand that I make myself understood within the understanding of the other—that is, in a lifeworld or language world that I share with other subjects[18]—or, as Habermas puts it, that I take on "the attitude of the other" (1987: 32). The private sphere of training, reproduction, imitation, confirming, and education—the socializing work of women in the private sphere—is what renders public consensus other than a form social compliance.[19] This is because only with the application of the rule can the validity of the rule be tested, consented to and affirmed, or opposed and rejected through a pedagogical process.

Wittgenstein's descriptions of rule following explain how ordinary language users identify within a community of language users, not how rules are authoritatively imposed. Following Wittgenstein, Habermas understands that the pedagogical relationships of the private sphere are absorbed into the public sphere as what makes the public sphere into a process of deliberation and dialogue rather than conformity and control from above.[20] In Wittgenstein, the application of the rule is followed by the teacher's affirming or denying that the application fits the rule, and so the rule only becomes a rule after the pedagogical negotiation, with the pedagogue channeling the values, ideals, and regularities to which the human or cultural community sees itself adhering. Wittgenstein's examples of pedagogy do not give the master the final say: Whereas one voice says that "the instructor *imparted* the meaning to the pupil" (§362) where "someone else grasps the sense of my words" (§363), the second voice counters, "If he then does something further with it as well, that is no part of the immediate purpose of language" (§363). Wittgenstein explicitly denies that the pedagogical use of language can be causal or imposed from the outside: When one voice asks for an explanation of how words give rise to actions, the other answers: "I have been trained to react to this sign in a particular way, and now I do so react to it" (§198), but the other voice immediately, and maybe even reprovingly, rebuffs the suggested causality. Habermas adopts Wittgenstein's idea that the educational processes performed by women (training and reproduction) in the private sphere develop as the public sphere's forms of noninstrumentalized communication in modernity. Pedagogy is necessary for the public sphere. Yet, pedagogy becomes unworkable in Makdisi's accounts of Lebanese "re-privatized" private life in war, as rules become unreadable, inapplicable, and unusable.

Rules are not followed through repetition. In Wittgenstein's pedagogical sociology, the "rule" that "guides" behavior only becomes a rule after someone applies it and someone else agrees that this application fits the rule. "Hence," Habermas interprets Wittgenstein to mean, "it is not possible to obey a rule 'privately'" (1987: 18). This is not to say that there is no such thing as private life, difference, or autonomy. Wittgenstein reads through examples that, on close inspection, tear apart conceptions of meaning and knowledge based on reference, logic, or "pictures"—words that point to things. He then replaces such conceptions with an analysis of words according to the principle *"this is how words are used"* (§180). Wittgenstein explores how rules function and what relation functioning rules have to the experience of using words. For Wittgenstein, the importance of rules in ordinary language use insinuates that meaning is never pointing to an internal depth, consciousness, causation, logical structure, or interiorized picture of a prior concept or experience. Instead, word use makes meaning through others' approbation and further use, and Wittgenstein models this confirmation process on socialization or teaching: "I influence him by expressions of agreement, rejection, expectation, encouragement. I let him go his way, or hold him back; and so on" (§208). The process of meaning making is a pedagogical process of making public—that is, subjected to judgment, reuse, the interpretation of rules by others, and a collective unbound and constantly reconstituted agreement on what would count as the rules' applications.

In the *Philosophical Investigations*, it is often difficult to discern where one voice ends and another begins, or who is doing the talking, or if the student voice (or the teacher voice) gets replaced by other student voices (or teacher voices) or remains permanent throughout, and how many characters are triggered in the give and take of assertions and counterassertions. At times, it seems the interlocking voice is a private inner voice, and that Wittgenstein is talking to himself, but the inner voice might also at the same time seem external, answering to an outside challenge.[21] At other times, it seems as though many voices crowd into the text, sometimes taking different annotations: Certain lines appear in quotation marks, others come after double dashes and seem as breaks, some come after double dashes but seem as continuities, some after paragraph breaks and some not. "When I ask this," Wittgenstein notes after one of his questions, "a hundred reasons present themselves, each drowning the voice of the others" (§478). The teaching context does not follow the formation of a Platonic dialogue, where one voice is tempting the other to reveal a truth that is already known, but still forces the recognition that words are used and acquire meaning within a social framework that presupposes and takes into account inequality.[22] In such an account of meaning making, rules can always go wrong in a variety of ways, applications can deviate from them, custom cannot determine, and consensus can therefore never be stabilized or guaranteed, is always by definition in the process of formation.

Though Wittgenstein's language use is not determined by preset categories, it does depend on the possibility of interference by both particularized and generalized others. On the one hand, using language has to do with mastering a set of community-enforced rules that repeat through a number of sanctioned actions;[23] on the other, the identity of the rule can only be decided through its private individual application, meaning that the rule only becomes a public or collective rule when an action that gets performed claims it as a rule. For Wittgenstein, the possibility of rules working as rules has to do with a presumption of regularity of our behavior, or, as he himself put it, "The sign-post is an order—if, under normal circumstances, it fulfills its purpose" (§87). Though Wittgenstein does not admit previously established agreements, contracts, or institutions, as language use needs to be more basic than that, Makdisi's analysis of basic private language use does demonstrate the failure of language use "re-privatized" outside of public institutional permeation or the presumption of regularity.[24] For Makdisi, on the other hand, language use is not checked and internalized against an outside framework of symbolic cohesion, agreed-upon realist conventions, pedagogical negotiations, or rules of communal identification: "[W]e are playing a game," she says, "with an unseen opponent who sets the rules and capriciously changes them, and who can therefore never be defeated. We haven't tried not playing at all" (41). Here in Lebanon, she says, there are only privatized rules to obey.

THE PHENOMENOLOGICAL TURN

Beirut Fragments provides an extreme example of social crisis catapulted, at least in part, by the failure of the consensus-making function of language and its institutional sedimentation: the complete privatization of public life. Makdisi's narrative of the privatization of language through the "re-privatization" of women's work follows a trajectory within feminist theory that traces the gradual marginalization, displacement, and disappearance of the public sphere in relation to a politics of women's freedom. On the one side, as presented above,

Seyla Benhabib challenges the universalism of the public sphere in the name of feminism. Like Wittgenstein, she advocates that the universalism of the public sphere can adapt to a recognition of concrete differences in private life and experience. In contrast, Toril Moi has not only questioned feminism's attachment to the public sphere, its realisms, and its universalizing, but also has imagined the privatization of language use altogether, outside of regularity or consensus. One technique Moi uses to address women's liberty is to envision it outside of pedagogical consensus where signification implies determination and only that. Theories of signification, she implies, must suppose that signification determines behavior completely or not at all so that even nonvoluntary behaviors are governed in some sense through the administration or imposition of social identities. Experience can only be "free" when it is divorced from such determination. Any worry that social identities might determine social ideas as natural forms assumes that this determination tells the whole story and leaves no room for autonomous acts or repositionings, Such a model, Moi says, is inadequate for describing the ways subjectivity works. Moi insists that the bodily attribute of "femininity"— that poststructuralism considers as always, in a certain sense, influencing the relationship between women and the social world—is also an attribute that a woman might avoid, depending on her projects: "There are innumerable different ways of living with one's specific bodily potential as a woman" (1999: 66), she elaborates. This suggests that there are some projects that women do when their bodies fall outside of determinations by a fixed sense of gender (her examples, are, curiously: "a ballet dancer, a model, a nurse, or a nun" (1999: 66)). The idea seems to be that gender determinations, if they determine anything at all, must work like a cookie-cutter, a tight mold, a command to conform within superlatively narrow boundaries, and not, as in Wittgenstein, as a sense that is tested against convention and against which convention is tested. Going beyond Benhabib's compromise with representationalism, Moi's critique of poststructuralism can be understood as a theory of radical contingency.

Following Wittgenstein, Toril Moi believes that the body is not, cannot ever be and does not really have a relation to a picture that determines future behavior based on stored rules and past performances, like a Saussurian signifier. Rather, "[e]ach woman will make something out of what the world makes out of her [... T]he relationship between one's body and one's subjectivity is neither necessary nor arbitrary, but contingent" (1999: 82). The "world" she is talking about here is not necessarily always the world of the social or its symbolisms, but rather a combination of social and natural surroundings that extend through the body. In this, she is channeling Wittgenstein and Charles Taylor's reading of him. According to Taylor, the idea that the internalization of a rule (like gender) determines its future application depends on understanding language through a logic of representation, demanding that everything be explained through preset, causational mental pictures or foundational inner consciousness. Such a conceptualization of rule functioning presupposes that the subject is monological, private, and isolated before a world of things, and that the subject is composed of "inner space" where representations reside, like a machine (49). What is missing from this sense of the subject of representation, says Taylor, are the body and the other, and their relation—or, our lifeworld. "The background understanding," Taylor resumes,

> which underlies our ability to grasp directions and follow rules, is to a large degree embodied. This helps to explain the combination of features it exhibits: that it is a form of *understanding* (original emphasis), a making sense of things and actions, but at the same time is entirely unarticulated, and, thirdly, can be the basis of a fresh articulation [...] At the same time, it allows us to show the connections of this understanding with social practice. My embodied understanding doesn't exist only in me as an individual agent; it also exists in me as the *co-agent of common actions.* (my emphasis; 53)

Toril Moi adapts this interpretation of ordinary language in order to address her concerns over the direction feminist theory has taken with its poststructuralist turn. Poststructuralism, for Moi, favors an interpretation of representation as mostly caught up in domination or instrumental logic, that is, as an imposition that language use can only escape through privatization. However, unlike Taylor, Moi believes that the only challenge to poststructuralism's representationalism is to avoid social consensus altogether, in any form, even in the form of a social understanding or background cohesion. In contrast to poststructuralism's representationalism, Moi describes the possibility of liberation through a spontaneous experience of the (gendered) body, a voluntary enactment of undetermined gender-meaning. The tale of language Moi wants to tell is where we wake up every morning and use words without needing to pay attention to the possibility that others might already be using them.

As in Makdisi, the pedagogical as an acknowledging of social integration and mutual understanding, in fact, slips out—the fatality of a politics that has already failed. Moi rejects the pedagogical because the pedagogical seems to impose reality from outside, like idealist realism, by stabilizing meaning within ideological systems. Moi's critique of realism veils a critique of the pedagogical public as only possible in an impositional form, as representational, rather than in the Wittgenstinian model of testing and negotiated approbation. Moi's attack on realism, therefore, is not against all realisms, but mostly against a realism of consensual reference, the kind that Makdisi describes as the missing commonality of all Beirutis. Moi's recent work on realism, *Henrik Ibsen and the Birth of Modernism,* does admit that "it is impossible to banish all forms of reference from language" (2006: 24), "[d]ifferent realisms must be theorized differently" (2006: 67), and "our task as literary critics is to account for their specificity, not to try to demonize them all as naïve 'representationalism'" (2006: 31). Moi's target, rather, is a specific, idealist discourse that espouses "freedom" as "the world of consciousness, imagination and the will, the world in which we make moral and aesthetic choices" (2006: 72), that says ideas of truth and beauty as revealed in poetry can serve as "'*the teacher of humanity*'" (2006: 72). Moi's preference for modernism is not, then, a refusal of all realism, but rather a refusal of the type of realism which defines art as pedagogical, as the practice of improvement through teaching; that is, her preference is for an aesthetics that is "severed from ethics."[25]

Moi's interventions in feminist theory likewise rebuff an internalization of any idealist or realist symbolism that transcends immediate use. In *What Is a Woman?*, Moi is suspicious of what she calls the post-Saussurian thinking she finds in poststructuralism because it describes language, she says, through spatialized pictures that determine representation.[26] Moi's direct target is the sex/gender distinction.[27] The sex/gender distinction, she notes, has become an obsession within feminist thinking since the seventies in a defensive reaction to theories of biological determinism that turn sex into the real of gender. Moi disapproves of such poststructuralist thinking where any allegation that the body exists leads to the conclusion that social values are being naturalized and determined in assertions of biological fact, or rules.[28] Alternatively, Moi thinks that there can be a real of the body that can be known through private experience outside of the agreed-upon rules and symbols through which we collectively and mutually identify.[29] She thinks the sex/gender distinction is unnecessary for describing the way a woman "makes a political and practical difference in conflicts of everyday life" (1999: 7) and just lends itself to a shallow representationalism, a hyped-up defensiveness against biological essentialism that makes it "easy to forget that generalizations about gender may be just as oppressive as generalizations about sex" (1999: 7). The category of "femininity" and its methods of signification are not always and everywhere the problem for women or for feminism for they do not, she says, ultimately restrict or impress upon the variety of expressions women use to confront their daily needs, even when those daily needs include confronting or changing sexist practices or traditions. Many of the body's uses might not be inside the picture, have any relation to it, or be guided by its rules: the relation between the body and its picture as "femininity" might be arbitrary or capricious in a given context, but not pedagogical. For Moi, there is nothing inherent in the concrete body as fact that would determine its future uses. Moi's conclusions, then, about what feminist theory needs to move forward, or to reconceive its premises to confront sexism more smartly, are based in a reading of poststructuralism that assumes all determinisms to be set in the body; she thus does not investigate other of poststructuralism's determinisms that are more socially and politically placed, or methods to challenge them.

In place of the dominant poststructuralist idea of language as a picture that points to determinate things and future applications, Moi proposes, then, that feminism consider the body as a situation.[30] The body, for Moi, cannot be bounded or regulated as it moves between its different callings and uses. "[A] situation," she writes, "is a structural relationship between our projects (our freedom) and the world (which includes our bodies). If I want to climb a crag, my situation is my project as it exists in the encounter with the brute facticity of the crag [...] If your project is to climb, and my project is to enjoy the mountain views, then the very same crag would present itself to you as being easy or difficult to scale, and to me as 'imposing' or 'unremarkable'" (1999: 65). The experience of coming upon the crag, of having a project in relation to the crag, reveals the world of relationships of which the gendered body is a part.[31] The social use of symbols is replaced by a sublime natural landscape that individual bodies float through to experience variously, as though nobody were responsible, and its magnificence is both self-generating and self-referential. As a result, the gender of the body and the world that we are might be understood differently in relation to each different project. "In this way, each woman's experience of her body is bound up with her projects in the world. There are innumerable different ways of living with one's specific bodily potential as a woman. I may devote myself to mountain climbing, become a ballet dancer, a model, a nurse, or a nun. I may have lots of sexual relations or none at all, have five children or none, or I may discover that such choices are not mine to make" (1999: 66).[32] According to Moi, I reinvent what it means to have a sexed body every time I use it. My sexed body is real every time I use it.[33] It is not made real by my internalized sense of what it means to use my body as a woman's body, nor does my use of it affect the way another woman internalizes and projects her bodily potential as a woman. Through its experience, the real body is for the most part isolated from its collective or representational symbolism[34] and its social context, understandable on its own merits, reinstituted through every specific use, revealing a new world every time, without pedagogical potential or idealism.

Moi's rejection of the sexed body as a place that determines social norms allows her to see the subject as "an agent who actually makes choices" (1999: 56). However, though her source here is still Wittgenstein, there is no correction from a generalized or particularized other, no exchange over what those conventions are based in dialogue over how they are applied, and no acknowledgment that such uses are defined in social contexts of inequality. The Wittgensteinian recourse to a language use structured through teaching has vanished. Realism or documentary, Moi goes on, can provide information but cannot "unveil the world," only considering "language a means to an end, an end that is always outside language" (2009: 191). Moi grants that this kind of writing can teach by conveying information, but that is all it can do. She rejects teaching as a realist idealism with an ethical project of human understanding and improvement. Literature, on the other hand, as opposed to realism or documentary, brings the world and other subjects into concert with the expression of a private experience of the world. Referencing only a singularity—for instance, my body encountering the crag for the first time and never again—language can have no prior use, other use, effectiveness, alternative interpretation, or future destination—can have no sense of its public as an ideal. In this, like war, it privatizes experience.

"CRISIS, WITH GLOSSARY OF TERMS USED IN TIMES OF CRISIS"[35]

Beirut Fragments is a tale of the privatization of language, experience, and politics through the privatization of women's work. Makdisi depicts the loss of realism, of teaching, and of a language of consensus as explicitly connected to the ruins of the public sphere nationally, as in its parliamentary form, and internationally in feminism. However, she also suggests a world that the war reveals: a more fundamental commonality, beyond impositional consensus, representationalism, and realism. Makdisi's memoir shows what happens when attempts to gain common understanding by giving reasons that are communally identifiable fail, and have no choice but to fail. Such a failure can be attributed to a failure of public institutions as symbolic references that can organize social order or a failure of language to connect its users through a sense of mutual understanding. For Makdisi, communicative language has been reduced to desperately repeating the private experience that she represents through the women's work of witnessing. "I have no answer," she admits, "except to say that I have seen what I have seen" (149).

The Lebanese war novel is, as critics have noted, particularly well suited for linguistic experimentation precisely because social chaos has splintered referential certainty. Observes Ken Seigneurie, "The war's rapid ideological transformations, shifting alliances and rampant opportunism shattered the notion of a knowable, objective reality and with it faith in realist depictions" (2003: 22). Unlike the novels that such criticism addresses, Makdisi is writing a memoir. Caught in the paradoxes between the realism that is demanded in the eyewitnessing and memorialization of history on the one hand, and, on the other, the radical upheaval of meaning that war entails, Makdisi's techniques of memoir involve a constant coming up against the limits of realism.

In the face of war, Makdisi wants to reverse the senselessness by reconstituting the nation through symbols, but with varying success. At first, Makdisi understands symbols as the experience of the everyday that becomes the language through which people recognize themselves as part of a collectivity that shares such experiences. Makdisi distinguishes her telling of the events from the genre of diary, for, she says, diaries recount personal experience. She prefers a type of recounting that catalogues social episodes around a certain theme like prevalent car thefts precisely because, she says, there was "little government authority left" and the "police [were] increasingly powerless" (27). Even more than in official documentations that were often wrong, such experiences, she remarks, seem trivial, but are situations through which the afflicted can recognize "the realities of Beirut life" (28) as a set of experiential everyday involvements that connected them.

The absence of legitimating institutions parallels the inability of such narrative symbols to constitute the experience that binds a collectivity, what Habermas calls its "linguistification."[36] Makdisi soon realizes that writing on war cannot be reduced to anecdotes because war extracts referents. "It is like looking through a kaleidoscope," she remarks. "Shake it, and a design appears; shake it again, and an altogether different one replaces it" (30). The search for a common language becomes a game for the search for consensus: "The favorite parlor game for a while was finding an appropriate name for the pink militia, every new entry making the rounds to hilarious applause. Thus, 'The Pink Panthers,' 'The Pink Brigades,' and 'The Pink Army' were entered, but judgment was finally given by consensus to 'Die Rosenkavaliere'" (29). There follows a glossary of colloquialisms that are particular to Beirutis, coming to "represent a body of experience, memories, and hopes for the future" (49) that express the living together of wartime. Nevertheless, Makdisi states, this vocabulary, like the experience itself, is unstable: "like an organic being, the vocabulary is in a constant state of growth and change" (49), playing between the literal and the figurative, the ironic and the improbable, defined differently in different contexts, interrupted and transformed as one faction or another gains charge of the political terrain. "[T]he street that symbolized one group's triumph yesterday," she intones, "is the symbol of its rival's triumph today. The town that was once symbolic of this people's sorrow, has become their enemy's burial ground" (31). This continues until the reality becomes "unspeakable," and she loses the ability to find "a metaphor or image capable of expressing some of the pain of Beirut" (31).

The loss of common linguistic reference underlies Makdisi's explicit rejection of feminism as much as it brings attention to the dusty remains of what was once a state. As an instance of imperialism, feminism, for her, cannot be a symbol that allows the formation of an ethical community: Feminism can only refer to a contained situation in the West and, having no referent outside that context and no possibility of stretching beyond the indelible border of the word's meaning structure in its own indelible time frame, cannot be communicated across cultures through common bonding, examples, or translation. Feminism is "private" in its belonging to the West. The religious dimension of the war, she notes, makes "the question of women" particular in such a way that it does not necessarily connect with the concerns of a Western feminist tradition. She tells of a time when she attended a university lecture given by an American woman academic who was "immured" by her own background. "She quoted from all the best writers," Makdisi concedes.

Simone de Beauvoir, Germaine Greer, Kate Millet. She said all the right, if by then a little hackneyed, things in just the right order. Why then did I squirm in my seat as she spoke? I think it was that she had produced not an argument based on the real experience of women here but an ideology ready for immediate consumption [...] In the West the question of women was waiting to be picked, like a ripe fruit off a tree [...] Here, on the other hand, the question of women lies at the bottom of things and cannot be touched without upsetting the whole order [...]. Can the question of women be separated from religious arguments? Can it be separated from social or cultural ones? Is there not a connection between class oppression and the oppression of women? Are Western and Eastern values not at cause here? Are all these issues not the ones over which a war is being fought? And are women not often the symbols of the issues? (143–144)

"Real experience" becomes here an absolute border between cultures, across which signifying structures cannot expand.

However, the questions that Makdisi generates are not necessarily unexplainable in the terms of Western feminism, nor is there an absence of correspondence between the agendas she claims as situational and contextual on the one hand, and, on the other, those inherent in the intellectual toolbox of feminism from other places, even from the West, and other times. As Lila Abu-Lughod has demonstrated, such defenses of cultural uniqueness or relativism work to reify culture, and this tendency to set "culture" off in scare quotes and drape it in the cover of righteous localisms is particularly prevalent, she points out, in treatments of "the question of women" and "cultures at risk." The idea behind such rhetoric, which Abu-Lughod attributes to imperialist conventions, is to employ the moral symbolism of saving defenseless women that are victimized by their own cultural practices and immediate communities and so need saving, rather than focusing on generalized geopolitical constructions like war and imperialism that particularly affect, dispossess, impoverish, and endanger women. Such cultural reifying discourse enables culture to be made into an absolute difference, she says, that lacks an understanding of repetition in the historical record of conflict and declares some cultures to be beyond comprehension or outside of common human value, understanding, or the possibility of political association in common cause. "One of the things we have to be most careful about," Abu-Lughod warns,

in thinking about Third World feminisms, and feminism in different parts of the Muslim world, is how not to fall into polarizations that place feminism on the side of the West [...I]t is also strategically dangerous to accept this cultural opposition between Islam and the West, between fundamentalism and feminism, because those many people within Muslim countries who are trying to find alternatives to present injustices, those who might want to refuse the divide and take from different histories and cultures, who do not accept that being feminist means being Western, will be under pressure to choose, just as we are: Are you with us or against us? (788)

Abu-Lughod is particularly concerned about the veil being used as an excuse for drawing communicational barriers between enclosed cultures. Though Makdisi is Christian, the idea of women's differences forming the basis of resistance to imperialism repeats a similar sense, where women's seclusion in Islam stands in for cultural resistance and the assertion of difference. As Miriam Cooke observes, the privatization of Muslim women was a standard trope of cultural difference that Europeans confronted in the nineteenth century: "Europeans in the Muslim Arab world found themselves obliged to respect the line that separated the private from the public [...] The Europeans interacted with or, better, controlled the Muslim men outside their homes. Women's autobiographies and fiction as well as court records describe a place of privacy where the colonizer could not go" (111). Such images have succeeded in pitting feminism against an authentic Islamic religiosity. They have made Muslim women and their life stories seem outside of history, modernity, and intercultural interaction because their outsidedness and re-privatization have been made to seem necessary for the culture to continue. "In this paradigm," Afsaneh Najmbad, for example, explains, "imperialist domination of Islamicate societies was seen to have been achieved not through military or economic supremacy, [...] but through the undermining of religion and culture, mediated through women" (30). Najmbad goes on to show that feminism in contemporary Iran—rather than representing a foreign and imperialist obsession with otherness that has no local application—has been applied to help build a civil society through journals, public intellectual discourse, and even participation in interpreting religious doctrine in public argument.[37] Such feminist political involvements, "by positioning women's needs as grounds for interpretation and women as public commentators of canonical and legal texts [...] promise that the political democratization currently unfolding in Iran would no longer be a 'manly' preoccupation" (31). Rather than privatization, feminist engagement here is what makes civil society and public culture possible as discussion and debate that recognize background commonalities and allow for agreement.

For Makdisi, on the other hand, the "question of women" is being used to stand in for a narrowly circumscribed communicational action bound by sacralized private belief. Certainly, such communities have cause to project themselves strategically into static, even archaic, ethnic practices and particularistic, noncommunicable expressions that organize difference for the purposes of defense and survival against imperialism or other forms of power. However, the border placement of "the question of women" in such cases means that the role of women—in economic and political as well as social relations—is limited by its necessarily standing symbolically against communicational practices that would transcend bounded local contexts, situational thematizations, and technological advancement. If women need to stand in for the besieged culture, their identities would have to be conceived as resolutely in opposition to modernity, as the last recourse of an untouchable "core" needing protection, outside of the influence of modernity's economies and political institutionalizations.

The breakdown in language that Makdisi witnesses therefore obstructs a cosmopolitan connection that feminism might offer, but also partializes the political commons. Against the literary experimentation that characterizes much of the new writing on the Lebanese civil war, Makdisi's choice to write a memoir has, too, a further, contextual function that reaches beyond a commentary on the failings of realist representational practices in Western historical genres. In addition, Makdisi uses her critique of referentiality to upset the political form of Lebanese confessionalism by exposing the inadequacies of the literary form of confession.[38] Like language, confession in Lebanon has been emptied of content and divorced from its role in maintaining social adhesion in the parliamentary compromise: "Believers and nonbelievers alike," Makdisi disgustedly expresses her scorn for the staid system of distribution of political office according to confessional denominations, "struggle though we may, we are being corralled into the separate yards of our fellow coreligionists by the historic events of the moment. Belief and political vision have less to do with how one is seen, and then is forced to see oneself than with external identification—the brand." (137). The private sensation of belief has become detached from the public action of believing. For Makdisi, the branding of identity through confession results from the "colonization" of spiritual values and cultural qualities by political, military, and demographic strategies. The Foucaultian confession that binds us to the institutions that produce individual subjects through discourse here takes on the form of the brand that breaks apart governing institutions by breaking down the linguistic exchanges between them. The religious feuding broke apart identifications beyond the immediacy of an archaic context and, contingently, incapacitated any imagined possibility of intervening in the construction of coexistence, as the subjective conditions and representational connections were unbound from the surrounding reality. "[I]n the morass of religious feuding [...]," Makdisi concludes despairingly, "the assurance that it is in one's power to change the world seems an enormously important weapon that has been lost" (130). If this is true, then why would "confession" be the literary form of choice for Makdisi?

In fact, the question that the confession constantly forces to the center—that is, why Makdisi, as a university professor married to another university professor, as well as a U.S. citizen with roots in Cairo, decides to stay in Beirut with her three then-quite-young children—this question alludes to the confession, and remains private, never answered: "[Those who have left] remind us that we may be making a fatal—literally fatal—mistake in choosing to stay," she admits. Then she drops the question: "But soon the unpleasant feeling receded, leaving only melancholy" (87). This movement of raising and then dropping the real question repeats multiple times. Within a memoir without memory, using realist techniques to stabilize an inherently unstabilizable but inescapable reality, Makdisi produces a confessional that refuses confession against a background of failed confessionalism. Having foregrounded the collapse of literary form, the lack of representation, and the failures of realism, all constituting public obsolescence, Makdisi resorts to the privacy of watching.

PRIVATIZATION OF WAR AND THE PRESERVATION OF GENDER

Private spaces appear then as the only remaining trace of social cohesion, and therefore as the defensive upholder of gender rules, particularly in ascribing work. The now-distorted communicative functions that have been truncated in their institutional forms are handed over to private appropriation. "I wrote as a witness to the common experiences of a common people," she offers, but nevertheless, "I wrote secretly" (20). With the state made inoperative and its structures fallen to rubble, Makdisi's *Beirut Fragments* envisions the only remaining form of public discourse in a politics of testifying that replaces public representation with the everyday practices of private life and women's work. Unlike in Habermas's liberalism, private life does not deliver the imminence of communication in modern life, moving from its archaic origins to an emancipatory alternative of modern systems' appropriation, but rather is defensive, self-referential, drawn back upon itself, unable to associate beyond its immediate context because of the violence on the outside. Makdisi's depictions of war-torn Beirut provide a parallel case study for the social relations that neoliberal ideologies also envision, where the public sector and its languages can no longer function intersubjectively or communicatively because they have been overtaken and dominated by private power.

Makdisi's descriptions share with neoliberalism a sense of the private sphere as empty political space. The private sphere's behaviors are relegated for the most part through the relegation of women's work; these behaviors are determined by the rhythm of war events into patterns of order and repetition, what Makdisi calls "the drudgery of daily chores" (175). The war sets the rules. The only response is to follow the rules in everyday gestures that reproduce a sense of normalcy: "simply being there, looking after my family" (172). Not only does the private sphere seem to resist time, in terms of being spatially removed and alienated from the main sites where history is playing out, but also it is subject to crises not of its own making. Those in it are barricaded inside, against their will, by the violence outside, and yet do not feel a part of the violence or the decisions that make the violence. Yet, the circular pattern of meaningless tasks, the endless but inconsequential internal war against dirt, was also, she says, "the most meaningful political act of my life" (172). This "meaningful political act" "redefined our community": the continuity of patterns of normalcy—of making beds and boiling the water for pasta in isolated private spheres.

As in neoliberalism, the Lebanese public sector is replaced with women's work as a synecdoche for the privatization of public life. "[T]he war," she explains, "imposes more and more responsibilities on me and other women. The crises of the war were often ones which fell into the traditional realm of women. We had to provide domestic supplies, deal with wrecked homes, create alternative shelters, cope with death" (21). Makdisi's response is neither to challenge nor to affirm these impositions, just to follow their rules. In the aftermath of a bomb attack, Makdisi time and again "[d]ecide[s] to clean the house [...] Start[s] dusting" (22) in a futile attempt to restore order and normalization. "I also remember every now and then going into a frenzy of housecleaning, but this had less to do with normal housewifely motives than with a kind of manic desire to clean up the whole world, the whole cruel world, the world of killing and of babies dying from drinking salty water and of horizons sooty with fire and pain" (175). "I start feverishly cleaning my house," she goes on, "unable to bring any meaningful order to my life, I work desperately at creating order in my immediate surroundings. This is the only part of my universe over which I exercise any control, and so I wield my broom and my cloths, never pausing in my idiotic labor until I collapse" (42). "Even in an apocalypse," she notes, "you have to wash children's clothes; to think of ways to flush the toilet; to eat and drink and smoke" (175). She runs home, worries about her kids, attends dinner parties, cleans, and cleans again.

Makdisi's unending mechanical tasks keep her locked in; the debris constantly needs removal. Makdisi's seclusion in the home is organized around work routines. Doing housework, like witnessing and confessing, reimagines the social plane through distanced, removed, confined, closed spaces governed by circular temporality and machine-like recurrence. For Makdisi, in the face of a loss of symbolism, social integration, or public agreement, the writing of the witness—like housekeeping—is an endless and noncommunicable repetition of empty form. A bomb falls, she rushes home, examines the damage, clears it away, and then this happens again. She needs to tell, even if she tells nothing. Makdisi's maintaining of the home is integral to her role of witnessing, as she usually stands on the balcony or behind a window to watch the outside war from a removed position on the inside, her work alienated from the history that shatters through the walls around her.

For Makdisi, the war had become an extension of housekeeping. The war, like housekeeping, privatizes the language of experience. For instance, Makdisi's description of Beirut's cosmopolitan culture before the outbreak of war is interrupted when "crowds from the suburban slums and refugee camps, as well as rural areas, moved to the city" (79). Commercial and café culture is transformed into "piles of garbage [that] dot the street" (80) as the elegant boutiques and stylish offices of downtown are taken over by masses of the unwashed and unkempt that need to be cleared away. The piles of garbage stand in for "a tragic human flotsam that no institution now functioning has the capacity to handle" (82). "Cigarette boxes, newspapers, sandwich wrappers, plastic bags patiently swept up by the street cleaners every morning—or at least those mornings when there are no battles— magically and instantly reappear" (81) in the place of the refugee. Now, "No sooner is one huge mound of refuse scooped up and piled onto the truck than another sprouts up in its place" (81). The warring city, like the housewife, is caught in a circular routine of clearing away the dust. Contrasting itself to its public, city governance has been privatized as women's work. The war has turned the technologies of city power into a great housekeeping machine.

Makdisi parallels her housekeeping with her other main project of witnessing. Both are steeped in routine, both are silent, both require detachment, both set agendas through the care of others, both are oriented toward the other, but neither have an interlocutor who responds; both have a space for the other with nobody there. Housekeeping organizes cultural difference, creating a spatial hierarchy between, on the one hand, the housekeeper/witness/organizer of details watching from the balcony, alone, a spectator, an outsider, mastering the modern technologies of cleanliness and order, and, on the other hand, the noncommunicating objects under her observations who, interspersed with the dirt and discarded, are engaged in expressions of pretechnological raw and primitive passion. Doing housework, like witnessing and confessing, reimagines the social plane through privatized, distanced, removed, confined, closed, quasi-sanitized spaces. "From the balcony of my flat" (35) she watches the city, where "I saw a red glow in the distance" (107), or "from the edge of a field" (153), or "from the hills" (184), or from the inside of her home through a gaping hole in the wall made by the latest bomb explosion (25), "being on the outside fringe of things" (169), "trapped in the ignominy of being a mere spectator to my people's murder" (167). "I stood on my balcony and watched the crowds of young men," she describes one New Year's Eve right before the war:

> They were doing no mischief, merely blowing whistles and horns, beating on the tin trash baskets [...] and banging on the hoods of parked cars, laughing loudly and calling to each other—in general making a terrific noise [...] I felt a deep alarm that night, sensing that their celebration, though apparently good humored, was not entirely so; that the line between a laughing crowd and an angry mob was a fine one, and that it took the merest spark to transform one into the other. (133)

From her position of nonparticipant observer, Makdisi is terrified by the language that she can neither translate nor identify, the language of bodies. The tasks and chores of cleansing on the inside keep her experience immured in private life, away from these eruptive dangers of the war on the outside and the threatening non-symbolizable waste needing removal. This confession does not infer a category of "the human" based in "care" and commonality, but a post-humanity that has taken on an existential difference as terror, hazard, nonsense or rot. The intrusion of those others' private lives into her own frightens her as different and untranslatable in terms of her own, and she then resorts to the safe refuge behind the walls of her own isolated house care.

It is notable, however, that Makdisi does not—even in her desperation—give up all senses of the public. Rather the public becomes a marginal form, secluded in private practices, as ideal or potential, a ghost of a concept. The shadowy figures on the borders of the text give her privatized experience in the war its significance. Makdisi's daily meanderings lead her past an abandoned patisserie, which, one day in 1985, became the refuge of a group of Palestinian women who made their home there while waiting for their husbands, Palestinian resistance fighters, to return. While she never speaks with them, Makdisi observes them—distanced as her role of witness always figures her—in their chores of cooking and caring for children, washing clothes and utensils. Though unknowable, they mirror her and she learns from them. Like her, they produce "an endless stream of chatter and banter" (195). They stand in the place of the mutual understanding that declines with the loss of language as well as of the self-revelation that her confession demands and does not deliver. Makdisi experiences her encounter with these Palestinian women as a pedagogical moment, where she lets everyday life challenge, alter, and even rearticulate her conventionalized responses and given meanings. Standing outside of any rule structure, Makdisi is unsure if the Palestinian women are the same as her or different, if they apply to her preconceptions and learned experience or if they burst forth as never before applied, as the outcome of the rules gone astray. Her identification with them sometimes amounts to something like pity and other times exposes her humility in the face of their self-sufficiency, "reality," and "substantialness" (195), but never has to do with her identicalness. Rather, it has to do with something that exists on the frame of Makdisi's private world and makes the borders of that world blurry, doubtful, and endangered. She recognizes this in her admission that "they were what the war was all about" (195). Though realizing that sense in this context makes no sense, she affirms their unrepeatable private utterances as what makes sense of her own.

CONCLUSION

Beirut Fragments presents a picture of neoliberal privatization by illustrating the extreme effects of the destruction of the public sphere in wartime. The waste of commerce and consumption comes into focus as undefinable, quasi-threatening outsiders, inarticulable like the New Year's Eve revelers and so turned to garbage. In the absence of public institutions and the public sphere, "the human," as universalizing, has been lost to something Makdisi cannot understand, a concrete difference that can be represented only as garbage. Makdisi is barred from entry in the public sphere, defensively secluded at home. Her separation from the public sphere is narrated as a femaleness that reclaims her by restoring her to private life. It is the last remaining defense of culture against the systemic escalation of the modern technological violence that has taken over public space. In place of the signifying structures and generic conventions of public communication are left the indeterminable idle chatter of a housewife caught in cycles of repetition, a reality without anchor, enforced intimacy, and a walled-in confession empty of a content to confess, unable to articulate a response to its situation. However, in parallel with Habermas, *Beirut Fragments* also gives a definite sense that even with the systems of money and bureaucratic power pushing hard for the most extreme impositions of privatization, the public is imminent in language.

Again, I do not want to minimize the seeming absoluteness of a neoliberal system about which Margaret Thatcher once claimed that "there is no alternative," the saturation of market ideologies and institutions into every aspect of the private and the everyday, or the seamlessness with which the invested interests have taken hold of the production of ideology to the point where people who talk about civil society seem like crazy hippies on drugs, or worse. What this reading of *Beirut Fragments* proposes is the necessity of the following: (1) Thinking about the institutionalized public sphere or consensus in other terms besides through the model of a punitive, impositional pedagogy. A nonauthoritarian pedagogy of the public sphere includes understanding the meaning of words as subject to use, with meanings developed only through use, undecided except through use, application, and deliberative affirmation. The use of such words has a greater context of reference, shared meaning, mutual understanding, and mobility, a greater potential, than the sedimented moment of appearance.[39] Such words constantly come up against the conventions they might or might not represent, measuring themselves against these conventions even as these conventions are corrected against them. (2) Taking seriously Habermas's formulation of the private as what grants citizens the idea of self-legislation in liberalism that "requires that those subject to law as its addressees can at the same time understand themselves as authors of law" (1996: 120).[40]

Makdisi's memoir indicates that the takeover of consciousness toward the acceptance of privatization ideologies can never be total or complete, that a public sense is even articulated in its most severe statements of compliance, alienation, and rejection. In *Beirut Fragments*, the indeterminable, uninterpretable waste heaps of humanity that

block urban circulation merge into the spaces of the falling munici-
pality, the buildings that once housed government bureaucracies. The
person without a state appears in the exact places left behind by the
now functionless state. The witness without a state might recognize
herself and a possibility of consensus in the subjectivity of the stateless
others, even if this recognition is the glimpse of a memory that has
not yet formed and has since been wiped away. The text becomes a set
of unordered, nonsequential, and un-unified glimpses of thought and
experience, with genres collapsing, characters unnamed and uniden-
tifiable, and time sequences and events stopping and starting without announcements or orienting brackets. In place of the consensus
codes that make sense of literature, Makdisi recognizes an appearance
of a possibility of a public. This public, in Theodor Adorno's terms
(which will be further addressed in the following chapter), "remains
the antithesis of that which is the case," because "it is not real in
the same sense as social reality" (1977: 159). Makdisi's lockdown in
her own private world makes impossible a representation of a state
that would point through agreement or through force to her and all
Palestinians. Yet, their shared lifeworld reveals an idea of a type of
public sphere—as human association—that moves us from the ruins
of a language of reality that is, in order to suggest a reality that has
yet to be thought.

Addendum: Family Resemblances?

As Edward Said's sister, it is not surprising that Jean Said Makdisi
premises her witnessing on exile. As Said famously remarks in *Culture
and Imperialism*, exile allows the historian to transcend the restraints
of identity and experience: "Regard experiences then *as if* they were
about to disappear: what is it about them that anchors or roots them
in reality? What would you save of them, what would you give up,
what would you recover? To answer such questions you must have
the independence and detachment of someone whose homeland is
'sweet,' but whose actual condition makes it impossible to recapture
that sweetness" (1993: 336). Unlike Makdisi, who understands family work as a replacement for the work of the public, Said can only
imagine the private family as a prohibition on his publicness, a prohibition to be overcome. His sense of himself as an exiled author and a
public intellectual is not fashioned in response to a shared lifeworld,
but rather through his narrative of a gradual acquisition of autonomy
and independence that gets likened to his exile, his alienation, and,
finally, to his creative originality.

Said's take on exile in his autobiography *Out of Place* barely accounts for the family he leaves behind with its customs, ritualized relations, rules, and intimate ties: "[I]n the deepest sense 'home' was something I was excluded from" (1999: 42), he begins, and then concludes: "the only hope for me as a man was in fact to be cut off from my family [...] Better to wander out of place, not to own a house, and not ever to feel too much at home anywhere" (1999: 294). At times, Said expresses a regret over this, as though his gender privilege creates an insurmountable barrier between his worldly ambitions and the closeness, belonging, and predictability of a more femininized existence in the lifeworld, the family, and the nation: "I envied my sisters at Cairo's English School." He gives a rare sideward and patronizingly nostalgic mention to them: "the comfort of being together and at home, the solidity, as I imagined it, of well-furnished certainty, all of which were going to be denied me except during brief returns in the summer" (1999: 245).

Said's reflections on his own coming-to-exile focus predominantly on his relations with and eventual rebellion against his strict parents, rules, and paternalistic controls. As a child, political exile for him turns on the irreconcilability between how his parents-in-exile imposed an identity on him and the way his body insisted, privately, on feeling. The loss of Palestine is coded as an alienation that he first experiences with his parents' prohibitions on private sexual feeling, masturbation, and erotic reading, leading to the splitting of his consciousness between the morality of parental love and the language of his own desiring body. "Sex was banned everywhere, including books, although there my inquisitiveness and the large number of volumes in our library made a complete prohibition impossible to enforce [...] So in my above-ground life I was steered carefully away from anything that might excite sexual interest, without really talking about it at all. It was my own powerful need to know and experience that broke through my parents' restrictions, until an open confrontation took place whose memory, forty-six years later, still makes me shudder" (1999: 69). This type of scene repeats throughout the pre-America sections of the book, foreshadowing, through sexual alienation, the political exile of the later years. Early childhood tensions with his parents coalesce in the development of the character "Edward"—always in quotes—alienated from the first-person narrator "I" and representing the "incoherent" or "disorganized" part of Said's self (1999: 74) that was closer to his bodily experience: "the complicated but mostly inarticulate inner life I cherished and lived through the emotions and sensations I derived from music, books, and memories intertwined with fantasies" (1999: 202). Alienation from his parents and family results in his educational adventures in the States. In later years, his desire for women as replacements for maternal love seemed "infinitely unattainable" (1999: 282), like "that aspect of America that I could never gain admission to" (1999: 282). In typical Habermasian fashion, Said's private, familial life gets abandoned, to be merged into the public intellectual ambitions of his cosmopolitan adulthood, with his mother exerting a particularly important influence. The idea of cosmopolitanism that underlies his character development, the possibility of learning through travel, literature, education, and imagination, leaving family and homeland behind as limitations to subjective expansiveness—these points furnish the raw material on which Said constructs the development of the literary public intellectual and teacher that he was to become.

4

Adorno Faces Feminism: Interiority, or Modern Power and the Liquidation of Private Life

Theodor Adorno is not the theorist who first comes to mind as offering analytical principles for developing a theory of the public sphere. Perhaps this is mostly because Habermas built his own theory of the public sphere as noninstrumentalizable in opposition to a Horkheimer and Adorno whom he characterized as steeped in instrumental reason,[1] or because Adorno's philosophy predominantly worries over the disappearance of the individual. The problem could also be that Adorno is understood to be the theorist who would update Marxism for a post–World War II perspective, and Marxist theory itself—as it relegates the state to the dustbin of history—is famously insufficient for thinking about the political, or that Adorno was alleged by his biographers (including some of his own students) to have been opposed to the student movement of the sixties,[2] or that Adorno was hesitant—even discouraging or pessimistic—about advocating praxis.[3] In addition, Theodor Adorno's work has not attracted a slew of feminist interest. The reasons for this are multiple as well, and I touch on them below, but they mostly concern the trajectory of subjectivity that Adorno attributes to the bourgeois age as it dovetails with the patriarchal domination of nature.

Despite the unconventionality of thinking about Adorno in relation to these topics, this chapter makes a claim that Adorno does provide fundamental touchstones for a contemporary feminist theory of the public sphere, and that Adorno's thinking on the relationship between the public and the private is closer to Habermas's, as presented in chapter 2, than Habermas would admit. In this reading, I argue that Adorno's formulation of the private plays four roles that I believe would advance feminist thinking:

(1) The private stands for the autonomy of the individual subject in history, yet it also demonstrates the impossibility of autonomy. In other words, what makes the private autonomous is its embeddedness in social history, but then it is still autonomous.

(2) As well, Adorno's controversial reliance on autonomy as an organizing principle in his theory of critique leads him to identify the private/public division as mediating the division between mental and material labor—between subjectivity and objectivity, or, as he says, "of healing the breach between 'outside' and 'inside' that had opened up with the disintegration of the medieval world order" (*Introduction to Sociology*, 93). The idea that the public and private are constantly moving toward total integration with one another that they can never finally achieve—this idea that the division must always tend toward obsolescence but can never finally be overcome—structures both problems in philosophy (the turn toward positivism, for example, where subjective classifications are understood as absorbed in their objective materials) and society.

(3) Adorno's tracing of the private/public split, then, can be said to give a framework for understanding how the perceived need for the symbolics of the industrial division of labor persists even after the industrial division of labor has been made archaic or irrational. The private's opposition or "outsidedness" to the homogenizing forces of social production continues across historical trends, regardless of its particular content. Unlike in poststructuralist theory, where the private/public opposition is flattened out and surpassed, and unlike the perspectives on feminist empowerment and self-reliance in a global age as analyzed in chapter 1 (where the private replaces the public), Adorno's positioning of the private as "outside" insures that it will always have to posit itself in relation to a public (a relation that, in challenging the public, may reinstate it). "You should realize," Adorno informs his students in his *Introduction to Sociology* lectures, "not only that society can be perceived, almost physiognomically, in individual phenomena, but that, far more important, all explanations of individual phenomena lead on much more quickly than is supposed to something resembling the social structure" (49).[4] In other words, the public, even in its alienated form, even when immanent and not yet realized, is necessary to all of Adorno's thought.

(4) The symbolics of the sexual division of industrial labor (the private/public split) is connected to the philosophical development of a position of critique. This connection is becoming newly relevant as the dominant philosophical and political designation of the "private" has moved from signifying an interior space that carries with it some sense of autonomy from the state and the economy. Now, "private" increasingly denotes a decentering of productive and governing processes and a shoring up of governing power behind a private consolidation, control, and ownership of economic and public systems.

Feminism's interest in Adorno therefore ought to reside in the way Adorno's critique of capitalism occurs just when the signs of corporatist consolidation and its schemes of privatization are beginning to appear, affecting the ways that women are absorbed into the workforce. This gives the problem of the public sphere a particular saliency and urgency. Adorno conceives the disappearance of the private sphere—its integration into productive systems—as the pivotal historical moment that allows the public to come into view, when it is most endangered. (Adorno's description, in fact, approximates a current phenomenon, where this private sphere that is integrated in production displaces the private sphere of industrial capitalism that was autonomous from production, but is still modeled on it. I am thinking here of phenomena like piecework, outsourcing, and microcredit.) At the same time, he shows how privatization works by making the public seem nonexistent or historically obsolete at the very point where it is most responsible for the individual's survival. He does this by revealing that consumption is increasingly entangled in production; that is, that production is increasingly privatized as it takes the form of extended consumption. The atomization of working individuals in consumption requires that the sociological context of their emergence be forgotten, she came to be individualized. As the private sphere of consumption is folded into production as its principle symbolic site, the individual loses her sense of her connection to the totality of the production process. This movement of the relations of consumption into relations of production evolves, for Adorno, out of the idea of the concept in idealist philosophy: Like consumption, the concept abstracts particulars into comparable, exchangeable entities. In this, Adorno's works give a sense that global corporate privatization of production has roots in the philosophical legacy of Enlightenment.

My argument in this chapter is that, contra Adorno, poststructuralism's skepticism about interiority really is a rejection of the public
sphere. For most poststructuralism, the interiority of the private subject gives a false sense of something essentially human at the heart of
human behavior as well as a false sense of sovereign individual control
over thought and action; the solution was to deny its autonomy or
its "outsidedness" to social or linguistic forces. Therefore, the trajectory of my argument in this chapter (as well as in the next) makes it
seem as though I am pitting critical theory against poststructuralist
theory and deciding in favor of critical theory. However, I want to
set out from the start that poststructuralism's contributions to literary and cultural theory are really too numerous to chart here, and its
influence on my own thinking is fundamental. In particular, poststructuralism offered a critique of language and the subject that is
too trenchant to ignore, while raising inevitable questions about culture and power, politics, and resistance. Rather, my contention is that
poststructuralism as a project seems to have stopped pushing forward,
and that some of the reason for this can be accounted for in the way
the poststructuralist theorists took up the possibility of critique in a
world saturated in relations of language, particularly in the constructions of identity and difference performed by language. Further, poststructuralism had the perspicacity of seeing the separation of power
from the state that was about to ensue with the multinationalization
of capital, but as a result poststructuralist theory preemptively abandoned the state and the public sector as a target of theorization. This
abandonment, however, did not make the state—or its private/public
split—wither away.

Facing the increasing consolidation of global capital, the ascen-
dance of deregulatory regimes of corporate governance, and the
eclipsing of democratic state institutions by nondemocratized corporate and financial bodies in the late seventies and on, one of poststructuralism's chief questions was, then, in a secular world, how to
account for human action or human agency in other ways besides
what the philosophical or political canon offered; for example, will,
self-determination, or consciousness. All of these thought structures
had the tendency of presupposing the subject as prior to its constitution in sociality and language. Adorno's insistence that the private has
to exist in relation to a public contrasts with a poststructuralist fiat
that assumes for there to be a private, it would have to exist as an end
in itself, a coherent whole, an exclusionary concept, an origin, a self-
sufficient totality, or an imagined safeguard of an impossible truth; in
poststructuralism for the most part, the private has been so invaded

by commercial currents and institutionalizing webs of knowledge that it can only be understood as an effect, a falsification that extends the broad maneuverings of power. For Adorno, in contrast, the private and the public cannot ultimately be conflated because of a dialectic that assumes an antagonistic society; that is, a society that cannot be reduced to the added-on combination of all that it includes, a society embattled against the formation of its future, and a society constituted through enacted class interests that cannot coincide. What is more, Adorno de-essentializes the categories of the self, the individual, and the private by taking out any content that is not historical, and by showing that the self, the individual, and the private are mediated categories. In denying the framing of the subject in terms of a private life that preexists the social, poststructuralism also barred the necessary movement interiority incites toward what Adorno calls "political education"[5] or human improvement, or the "rebellion of experience against empiricism" (*Introduction to Sociology*, 51); that is, the public experience of a society-to-be.

I start out by discussing how Adorno invokes the private sphere through his emphasis on reconstructing the individual, stressing the importance of the individual as the place where the congealed, static relationships of the exchange society open up to dynamic processes; the individual is where history, philosophy, sociology, psychology, and political economy interact by overcoming their methodological instrumentalization within the division of disciplinary labor. I then look at Judith Butler's reading of Adorno to investigate what is at stake for feminism in her desire to read him as abandoning the private/public split that points, for him, toward the possibility of a transformed society.

THE LIQUIDATION OF THE INDIVIDUAL AND THE CONCEPT OF THE PUBLIC

Adorno is predominantly concerned with the private individual. This is because the particular individual grants the possibility of experience and memories of experience beyond the generalized categories of reified intelligibility and repeatable forms projected through the concept.[6] Adorno makes a distinction between, on the one hand, the current phase of the public sphere—where the dominance of communications and media saturation has led to a reification of consciousness, an endless repetition, a totalizing but alienated consensus, a transformation of the public into a commodity[7]—and, on the other, the historical idea of the public sphere, based on independent subjective reason and the liberal concept of opinion. To know what is meant by the public, Adorno specifies, "[o]ne needs to know [...] the processes to which this category of public opinion is subject and which—if anything has—have played an active part in the change in the function and inner composition of the public" (*Introduction to Sociology*, 147).[8] The reified consciousness of the present can only be eliminated by the memory of the individual that was inside it but different than it, even opposed to it.[9] Without this, the present configuration of society seems both timeless and natural,[10] with the nondifferentiable individual absorbed in the objective economic structures: The individual melts into ideology, and the public becomes the congealed substance that solidifies over its historical constitution. The individual, its temporalization, comprises the "outside" to such congealing, the place where history is "stored up" (*Introduction to Sociology*, 146). Through the individual subject, Adorno thus injects history as the public sphere. The private individual is necessary to this history and its memory,[11] even as this history gives rise to this individual as its antagonist: "Even the subject's resistance to the pre-existing categories facing him is mediated by the categories in which he is enmeshed" (*History and Freedom*, 23). Also, the memory of this history of the individual organizes the social.[12] With the demise of the individual, the public sphere is also in danger of dissolution.

Like the private sphere itself, as I demonstrate below, and like history, the individual, though, has no metaphysical guarantee. In the face of the totalizing tendencies of homogenizing media technologies, of a New Deal that made workers identify their interests in the interests of the capitalist bureaucratic state, of Stalinism, and of a fascism whose cultural foundations were not only apparent in Italy and Germany but also in the United States, Adorno understood the individual as disappearing,[13] or, as he more eloquently says, the world has become a totality that "tolerates no 'outside' anymore from which it might be broken" (*Negative*, 274). Reading the working subject as completely caught up in the totally administered society, Adorno's revision of Marxist theory occurs, to a degree, through the replacement of proletariat oppositional consciousness with philosophical consciousness—the historical development of critique—as the principle site of opposition, along with a rejection of revolution itself as a final reconciliation between consciousness and the world. As Susan Buck-Morss has so well documented, Adorno "was fully aware of the inadequacies of the workers' empirical consciousness [...] He insisted on the freedom of the intellectual from Party control, indeed from all direct concern as to the effect of his work upon the public, while at the same time maintaining that valid intellectual activity was revolutionary in itself" (30–31). Since he understood capitalism as having integrated or bought out the working classes, so that the working classes no longer interpreted their interests as antagonistic to ruling-class ownership of the means of production, Adorno surrendered the revolutionary nature of the proletariat in favor of a philosophy of social change that would realize itself through philosophy's own critique of itself in the resurgence of the individual.

The demise of the individual corresponds to what Adorno interprets as the trajectory of Enlightenment reason. Following his idea of focusing on "the elements of cognition that had previously been sought in objects [...and] were now transferred to the subject" (Adorno, *Kant's Critique*, 1), Kant's mapping of the interiority of the subject through concepts was meant to determine general categories to which the representations of particulars from the empirical world could be attached; knowledge and the world did not need to be reconciled because the objects of the empirical world corresponded exactly, without remainder, to the categories of intelligibility that the thinking subject had prepared for them a priori. The inside of the subject itself would form the objective basis for knowing the world. This constituted bourgeois reason's retreat into what Adorno called "identity thinking," where the object-world could be reflected adequately, even discovered, in the subject's unity of categorical representations, independent of experience, without access to the world. Kant was, however, unable to establish concepts corresponding to all objects: "What the objects communicate in," notes Adorno, "instead of each being the atom it becomes in the logic of classification—is the trace of the objects' definition in themselves [...] To comprehend a thing itself, not just to fit and register it in its system of reference, is nothing but to perceive the individual moment in its immanent connection with others" (*Negative*, 25). As all the empirical world was not ultimately accessible to the categories of consciousness as he outlined them, Kant came up finally against a limit to absolute knowledge in the forms of God, freedom, and immortality that were unrecognizable within the categories of the human subject: "[W]e always come up against some outer limit," concludes Adorno. "We might even say that in a sense the vital nerve of Kant's philosophy as a whole lies in the conflict between these two aspects, the impulse towards system, unity and reason, and on the other hand, consciousness of the heterogeneous, the block, the limit" (*Kant's Critique*, 18). The impossibility of autonomy, of a separation from Kant's schemata, gave rise, in turn, to its necessity. This nonreconcilability of objects with subjects, for Adorno, brings up the possibility of self-reflexivity, autonomy, privacy, or critique in Kant.

Hegel, on the other hand, according to Adorno, premised the eventual coming together of the object in the concept. "Hegel left the subject's primacy over the object unchallenged [...] The spirit wins its fight against a nonexistent foe" (*Negative*, 38–39). That is, the particular was subsumed by the universal (which Hegel came to identify with the Subject of History, and eventually with the state), and the temporary space of autonomy was closed down. This also means that the individual, empirical human subject becomes identical to the ideal subject that is (social) History, and History stops moving forward. The inability of the particular to break from the world (the demise of the individual) is the same, for Adorno, as a positive affirmation of "what is" or reality, and "what is" is intolerable. Yet, in his critique of Hegel, Adorno also believes that there is ultimately no possibility of reconciliation despite Hegel's best efforts: Although the negative or the nonidentical has been criticized for having no content of its own,[14] Adorno suggests that the moment where Hegel projects the ultimate reconciliation—"the primacy of the whole over its finite parts" (*Hegel*, 4)—into the identity of the state is when social antagonism becomes visible as the nonidentity of identity, as the experience of the "outside." "In proper Hegelian terms one might say," Adorno interjects, "[...] that it is precisely the absolute subject in Hegel that does justice to an objectivity indissoluble in subjectivity" (*Hegel*, 6). Hegel returns to Kant.

For Adorno, the irreconcilability of objective knowledge and the knowing subject is a problem that develops with the rise of modernity as described by Max Weber. As J.M. Bernstein explains it, the separation of the public world of reason from the objective materials that are supposed to compose it is an effect of what Weber calls "disenchantment" and leads to the individual's surrender to passivity—the idea that the individual's action can have no real concourse within societal rationalization, calculability, standardization, and the like. "Externalism is the view that there can be justificatory reasons for a moral norm that are independent from reasons why any particular agent should act on that moral norm" (2001: 11). Bernstein calls this "affective skepticism" (2001: 6), and says that this bar, limit, or block—where the outside's coherence can have nothing to do with the individual's own understanding of how or why goal-directed action can be achieved—underlies the weakening of human agency within secularism. Outside of instrumentalism, "[W]e have nothing approaching a normative account explaining *how a wholly secular*

form of life can be rationally compelling and intrinsically motivating"
(2001: 18). Adorno believes, says Bernstein, that the disjoining of
inner and outer reason deforms both, leading to what Adorno calls
"damaged life," and this is particularly in evidence in a retreat of
ethical practices into private life.[15] For Adorno, to resolve modernity's disruptions requires an expansion of reason: Instead of what
Bernstein calls the "simple concept," which is independent from its
content, Adorno reads the concept as complex, where the concept
itself would mediate between its logical structure of generalizability
or comparability, on the one hand, and, on the other, its "material
axis," or the "ingredients that do cognitive work" (2001: 33). The
material axis gives a fleeting indication of a "nondiscursive" (2001:
34) aspect to conceptual thought, an "outside" to external reason
that can be internally motivating because action and the intelligible
world overlap. In other words, the mediations of the concept would
be exposed along with its alienating rationality through which the
public and the private got split up in the first place. The problem with
the loss of the private individual is thus a loss of effective and moral
action, the acceptance of an intelligible world that has no need to take
account of the individual wills that composed it.

Adorno's interpretation of the individual in philosophy corresponds to a parallel figuration of the individual in political economy.
A product of the division of labor with its increasing differentiation
between specialized regimes, the individual here grows out of the
individualizing of interests in the search for profit; the individual is
the expression of an antagonistic society. Adorno develops his perspective on social production as in conjunction with his appraisal of
the under-acknowledged intersections between the fields of sociology and psychology. For Adorno, the private individual embodies
the social at the very point where it conflicts with the social: "[T]
he individual, which is generally regarded as antithetical to society [...] is a social category in the fullest sense" (*Introduction to
Sociology*, 112). Adorno believes that—like the divide between the
external logical concept and its material axis—the divide between
sociology and psychology "gave rise to untruths" ("Sociology and
Psychology," 74), where the ego, in its weakness, is made identical
to the primary instincts, and, in relation to this monadic subject, the
social is made opaque, the individual thrust back into helpless isolation over which it has no recourse to prevail. This separation hides the
antagonism between the individual and the social order,[16] explaining
alienation.[17] An extreme manifestation of this tendency is in psychoanalysis, which "was first conceived in the context of private life, of

family conflicts, economically speaking in the sphere of consumption; this is its proper domain, because the specifically psychological play of forces is restricted to the private sphere and has little impact on the public sector of material production" ("Sociology and Psychology," 76). Faulting Freud for stamping the unconscious with a natural and unmediated timelessness, Adorno reformulates the species aspect of the unconscious as the psyche's social moment. He then shows that the unconscious is the product of a distortion of reality and therefore is constantly set against the objective untruths that the social order projects through rationalization.[18] "The irrationality of the rational system emerges in the psychology of its trapped subjects" ("Sociology and Psychology," 72). In this view, the private sphere is made to seem private as part of the distortion of social relations that makes the public realm invisible or inaccessible, reducing it to an alienable "outside." However, this sense of the private sphere reveals it as a congealing of objective relations of production.

The individual's private psyche is thus integrated, at its deepest core, with objectifying public forces. This reverses Marx's base-superstructure relationship by breaking down the divide between them.[19] The private life enhanced by consumerism does not come after, respond to, or reflect something greater than itself because it is impossible to consider the individual apart from the antagonistic system of production that it models: "The rigidly dualistic basic structure of Kant's model for criticizing reason duplicates the structure of a production process where the merchandise drops out of the machines as his phenomena drop out of the cognitive mechanism" (*Negative*, 387).

Adorno's privileging of the private individual has been objectionable to critics as a sign that Adorno gave up on political action, social movements, and utopian change. Also, Adorno's emphasis on the individual seems to feed into today's rampant consumerism that is based on an idealization of individual choice as forming the model of participatory citizenship, where the individual can be nothing but market share.[20] "A critique is only available from a second order, namely the critical thinker," says Nigel Gibson, "or more correctly any authentic critique is made impossible [in Adorno's thinking]. The circle cannot be broken; all praxis [...] cannot by definition be the subject's objectivity but only the pseudo-action of a subject position" (284).[21] According to Gibson, Adorno misreads his philosophical sources—for example, he substitutes "work" for Marx's term "labor,"[22] a rhetorical move that shuts down Marx's activity of self-realization in "work" by seeing it perennially captured into capitalist exploitation, and therefore closes down one of Marx's main avenues for overcoming alienation in the revolutionary project.[23] The subject, then, is, for Adorno, constantly re-alienated, its alienation figuring the "outside" or the negative.[24]

Like feminism as I discussed it in chapter 1, and like philosophy and art for Adorno, the individual is archaic. It finds its fullest expression in the age of Odysseus. The culture industry (or consumer society) has abstracted it into an identity that can be exchanged with any other and integrated it, at the same time degrading it. Even, he says, the division of labor is no longer individuating the identity of producers: "[W]ork processes become more and more alike, to the point that the supposedly qualitative differentiation through the division of labor is finally abolished" (*Introduction to Sociology*, 42). The absorption of the individual is accompanied by the dissolution of the private sphere that supports it along with the type of production, like small-scale agriculture, that went along with it (*Introduction to Sociology*, 133): "[T]he entire private domain is being engulfed by a mysterious activity that bears all the features of commercial life without there being actually any business to transact" (*Minima Moralia*, 23). Within the rationalization of advanced capitalism, the family is irrational and is therefore being broken, with parental authority losing its "impotence" (*Minima Moralia*, 22), and the new generation understands their elders as too powerless to rebel against, to expose their lies, or to insult their version of reality. Marriage is "an abstract parody in a time that has removed the basis of its human justification" (*Minima Moralia*, 30), which "unfailingly means the degradation of interested parties" (*Minima Moralia*, 31). With the needs for self-preservation sucked up into technological systems, the family no longer satisfies the means-ends rationality that is needed for self-preservation: "[T]he number of divorces and that of incomplete families kept increasing" (*Negative*, 302). With the loss of the family, says Adorno, the individual is also being lost, along with the individual's sense of deviation from the society of equivalence: "With the family passes away [...] the resistance which, though repressing the individual, also strengthened, perhaps even produced him. The end of the family paralyzes the forces of opposition" (*Minima Moralia*, 23).[25] The private sphere's disappearance, like the individual's, makes it more emphatically relevant: It makes publicly visible the irrationality that the rationalizing system has become. What Adorno might offer us now is this: Just as industrialism's private sphere was vanishing inside the public world that constructed it as antagonistic to it, today's public is shaping out as similarly nonidentical to the claims to privatize.

Feminism Takes Off Its Shirt

Feminist theory has seen Adorno as an ally but has been reluctant to embrace his thought fully.[26] This has been the case even inside Adorno's own classroom: Lisa Yun Lee, for example, probed into an incident in 1969 when Adorno's counterculture students bared their breasts in class to protest his alleged aversion to radical activism: "A commotion broke out in the seminar room and three leather jacket–clad feminists from the SDS (German Socialist Students) barged up to the podium, surrounded Adorno, and bared their breasts to him, lavishing him with rose and tulip petals and erotic caresses" (114).[27] Hesitance and ambivalence continue currently to rein over feminism's reception of Adorno even as some feminists have sought common cause. Renée Heberle, for example, appreciates that feminist theory shares with Adorno the idea of "immanent critique" (4), the focus on "lived experience" (6), the preference for "constellations" over "determinist thinking" (7), an "open-ended" approach (3), and an interest in "the body and [...] somatic suffering" (3). As well, Andrew Hewitt reads Adorno as privileging the feminine as "an *escape* from the all-inclusive system of power" (73) at the same time as he denies women "the honor of individualization" (76): As the negative, women represent both alienation and instrumentalization even as they suggest the possibility of resistance to totalization and expose that the systemization of capitalism and patriarchy à la Weber is imperfect. On the other hand, Sabine Wilke and Heidi Schlipphacke understand Adorno as infusing the subject and its rationality with masculine domination and also projecting a feminized version of nature as their outside: The problem of posing an idealized treatment of femininity as the exemption to the totality of power is that "the totalization of patriarchal discourse [inhabits] not only its own sites but also the language of its own critique" (297).

Despite such skepticism, I venture a return to Adorno that does not simply see Adorno as a cohort to a poststructuralist analytic, with the negative representing the unrepresentable of power, the limit of reason, or the end of subjectivity.[28] Poststructuralism principally espouses an agency of affirmation, where transformation would be immanent within existing discursive or symbolic forms. The concept becomes an agent for its own transformation rather than being affected by an antagonistic object, an alternative axis or agency on its outside. Foucault's homosexual, for example, is the resistance of the concept against itself. Whereas Adorno's negative opens toward an axis that differentiates itself from the concept, poststructuralist difference is no

difference at all but an effect of difference, a subversion that the concept does to itself rather than an object that stands independent of the
concept, even if the concept once bore it. Often within poststructuralism, transformation is figured as an escalation of the concept, a pres-
suring of the concept to become itself but even more so till it becomes
other, even if the concept itself is an insidious, oppressive, or reifying
expression of power.[29] Resistance in poststructuralism is a crisis within
the concept rather than an object that shows the limits of the concept
by being something else.

In its most extreme forms, poststructuralism's flattening of everything into discourse makes it difficult to conceive of an agency of
opposition or a subject of politics that can have an effect against what
is most intolerable. Feminist poststructuralism, for example, focuses
on overcoming the dominance of the sex/gender divide by integrating
sex into gender and demonstrating that each is equally constructed.
The sex/gender divide presupposed that "sex" or the body would be
a material object "outside" of the cultural construction of gender, in
fact, as contrary to it. Yet, poststructuralists deemed "sex" unworth-
while as a differential category that insists on the naturalization of the
body; that is, that the body essentially has its meanings determined
as an extension of the overall invisible workings of linguistic classification and social norms. As Toril Moi summarizes, "[I]f sex is as
'discursive' as gender, it becomes difficult to see how this fits in with
the widespread belief that sex or the body is concrete and material,
whereas social gender norms (discourses) are abstract and immaterial"
(1999: 46).[30] (On the other hand, Moi, as I discuss in the last chapter,
wants to minimize the relevance of the concept to subjectivity and
understanding, to make meaning contingent, constructed according
to the context of individual projects.)

Adorno, on the other hand, would understand an "outside" to
discursivity in the private sphere outside of the generalizability of the
general concept: The private sphere of industrial production is created by the social organization of industrial labor in order to become
independent of it, even conflicting with it. Adorno indicates that the
overall category—be it gender—is always involved in the appearance
of the private, individual form, even if invisibly so, and both are transformed by the encounter. Poststructuralist appropriations of Adorno
tend to assimilate him to a denial of interiority (as does for example
Judith Butler, analyzed below) in order to foreground his rework-
ing of the concept, denying in turn the "material axis" of the body.
Butler uses Adorno to support her thesis that "there is no 'I' that
can fully stand apart from the social conditions of its emergence"

(*Giving an Account*, 6). This reading, I believe, goes against the grain of Adorno's dialectic, in particular by overlooking that dialectic's entwinement in a history of separate spheres. Here, "the private" does indicate a standing apart, the necessary ideal of particularized autonomy on which social history rests.

My own critique, therefore, proposes some redemption of Adorno's thought as a way out of some of poststructuralism's impasses, and particularly its impasse in thinking the public. That is, poststructuralism tended to push theory away from a deep psychology of the subject, or consciousness—where the subject's inner formations are the origin and the essence of being and knowledge or where rationality, representationality, and language stand opposed to the facts and objects of wordly empiricism or where motivational structures reduce action to cause-and-effect linearities. Adorno, in contrast, restores interiority to the subject. Instead of resurrecting an old Freudian cartography of consciousness or an emotional core of self-knowledge and causative sensibility or a regressive living-out of conflict within the closed circle of the autonomous family, Adorno's interiority is premised on what Fredric Jameson regards as an "analysis in terms of the economic system or mode of production" (9), that is, on the division of labor. Adorno's formulation of interiority often follows the standard narratives of psychoanalysis in likening it to domestic and familial life. As domestic and familial life, like the individual, are, however, in the process of disappearing under the reigning forces of capitalism, interiority, as Jessica Benjamin demonstrates, takes shape as the "isolation and powerlessness" of the individual under capitalism. This isolation and powerlessness form into the "critical and emancipatory reason" that makes the individual, even in its disappearance, excessive to capitalism. History inhabits interiority, takes it over, even as interiority, the outside of history, limits history and resists it. The interplay between interiority and history that is based on the division of labor in Adorno parallels the interplay between Kant and Hegel, where Hegel's subject of history rewrites Kant's interiority of the subject play by play in order to dismantle it.

This is not to say that those feminists who refuse Adorno are somehow misguided. In assuming for the most part the maleness of both subject and history, Adorno blames women for the alienation that accompanies the disassociation between the social and individuals under capitalism, and then he turns around and blames them again for the conformity of individuals to the social forms that repress them; that is, for the disappearance of the individual. For example, in "The Culture Industry," Horkheimer and Adorno give women the role of promising the fulfillment that never comes in a cruel, erotic tease. "There is no erotic situation," they note, "which, while insinuating and exciting, does not fail to indicate unmistakably that things can never go that far" (140). Eroticism seems to lure us in as an escape but then defers the pleasure, often with a punishment. Though often at odds with Freudian-type narratives,[31] in this instance Horkheimer and Adorno give the culture industry the same castrating role as women, just as later the hysterical woman, personifying the film industry, "tries to ruin the happiness of her opposite number" (152), and the housewife promotes mass culture by identifying with the drama of the "idiotic women's serial" (152), which ends tragically. All the promise of happiness offered in encounters with women thereby turn into flirtations with death for a moment of happiness until the order of suffering is restored, confirming the way things are.

Likewise in "Odysseus or Myth and Enlightenment," women stand in for the regressive myth, magic, sensuality, and nature that need to be resisted, controlled, and dominated in order for the bourgeois subject to come into being. "Circe tempts Odysseus' men to give themselves up to instinct: therefore the animal form of the tempted men has always been connected with a reversion to basic impulse, and Circe has been made the prototype of the courtesan" (69). Against the provocations of women and his eruptive anger at "the faithless women who had reverted to prostitution" (79), Odysseus "rebukes his heart" and is forced to tame his body that "is reacting against his will" (47n). In order to survive the call of instinct of the Sirens' song and master it, the individual man—Odysseus, the hero of reason—needs to punish himself by tying himself to the mast, while his crew members submit to their ordeal by renouncing their senses and desires and becoming slaves to the rhythms of work. As Wilke and Schlipphacke conclude, "The female subject serves mainly an instrumentalized function on the male's way to self-actualization. Beyond that, the female subjects in this text are all associated with forbidden, though socially and politically impotent, forms of sensuality and are thus reconstructed out of stereotypical patterns of female images in patriarchal culture" (299). In effect, Horkheimer and Adorno are criticizing the systematization of sex relations under capitalism, that "speak of women as the Eternal Feminine that draws us onward," while treating them "in reality as minors" and holding "them in permanent subjection" (*History*, 47). Yet, they repeat the gesture.

INTERIORITY AND THE PRIVATE SPHERE

Despite such limitations, I would like to look beyond a reading of how women are imprisoned in oppressive and disparaged images, associations, or positions within Horkheimer and Adorno's descriptions of a capitalist world system or of how women create the demand for conformity toward what they theorize as the concept. I would also not want to follow Adorno in posing women as the purely negative form that empties out conceptual thinking and exposes its limits without necessarily having a positive content. Rather, I want to propose that Adorno's continued reliance on the division of labor is what makes possible a mediated model of interiority that is neither wholly a blank slate for inscriptions of social or textual values nor a protected difference, a pure identity. Adorno sees the private sphere as what breaks apart the repetition of the concept and, in so doing, brings out the sociality that the unified concept as repetition represses. Opposite Odysseus, Odysseus' faithful, now-bourgeois wife, Penelope, waits for him to come home from work. In the meantime, she weaves. Reflecting the bourgeois subject, Penelope, like him, is "cunning" (*Aesthetic Theory*, 186). Penelope's work is about unifying the multiplicity of experience by abstracting from its sensuous particularity, gaining conceptual "mastery" over it by imposing a form on its empirical objects, and Adorno calls this "violence" (*Aesthetic Theory*, 186), just as he does with Odysseus' gaining mastery of the rowers by desensitizing them. Unlike Odysseus, however, Penelope feels guilty: "multiplicity must, like the ephemeral and alluring images of nature in antiquity's myths, fear unity" (*Aesthetic Theory*, 186). Penelope realizes that the production of the commodity inflicts unity on the object in the same way that it inflicts unity within herself. She therefore unravels her work at night. Though Adorno calls this "art," the process reveals that the unity of the ultimate form is "nonidentical" to itself, and one could equally call this the unbinding of sociality and recognition of concrete difference in the public sphere: "In every instance the renunciation of unity as a principle of form itself remains unity sui generis, however mediocre the quality. Yet this unity is not binding, and an element of this absence of bindingness is probably binding in all artworks. As soon as unity becomes stable, it is already lost" (*Aesthetic Theory*, 187). As industrial capitalism creates a purposeful singularity out of the private individual interests that compose it, the private sphere repeats the whole by showing its incompatibility with the whole. In this primary scene of sweatshop labor, the private sphere reveals the illusory and chaotic quality of the material—nature, the impulses of the body, the nonconceptual, the nonidentical—that is incompatible with the repetition of the concept in unity of the commodity form. The private sphere thus brings into view the false synthesis of the whole, the disparity of the parts in reference to the whole.

As Carrie L. Hull formulates it, Adorno's model of interiority "provides many of the tools of poststructuralism while maintaining the grounding I think is necessary to engage in an analysis of various aspects of the division of labour" (32). Hull's essay compares Adorno's and Butler's interpretations of materiality, and concludes that though neither thinker reduces objects to thought, ideality, or language, Adorno premises an outside to the subject that thought cannot completely capture. I add that for the object to be a "something more," it needs also to exist as a limit to the system of production and exchange through which the social totality gets formed, and as antagonistic to it.

The private sphere reveals an internal multiplicity to the concept that, irrational according to the current unity in the sphere of production, becomes its external limit. This is in part because the private sphere's archaism makes it constantly at odds with the modern organization of the means of production. As Horkheimer intones in a chapter on the family, written with Adorno, "[In modern bourgeois civilization, t]he family remained essentially a feudal institution based on the principle of 'blood' and thus was thoroughly irrational, whereas an industrialist society (though itself including irrational elements in its very essence) proclaims rationality, the exclusive rule of the principle of calculability and of free exchange following nothing but supply and demand" (382).[32] In his book on Kierkegaard, Adorno treats bourgeois *intérieurs* similarly to how the family is treated in this chapter. The *intérieur* extends outside space through a window mirror into the inside, but the objects inside are alienated, having become mere decoration—abstract representations of use-value to-be-exchanged, and sometimes "abandoned inwardness" (46) as the semblance of a nature that is past. "Space does not enter the *intérieur*; it is only its boundary [...] Just as external history is 'reflected' in internal history, in the *intérieur* space is semblance" (43). As reflection, the "interior" is alienated; yet, the inner space also discloses the unraveling of the unity of nature's reflection in the concept, that which cannot be absorbed.

This structuring of the family and private space as an "outside" that is "inside" to the rationalized world of modernity and exchange is closely tied to Adorno's structuring of the individual. For Adorno, the individual is coextensive with the social sphere of material production and the system of bureaucratization that grounds modern rationality, just as the bureaucratic system crushes the individual through homogenization and abstraction. That is, the individual repeats the social, but this repetition means that the individual must be differentiated, act independently according to the demands of reason, and outlive its self-sacrifice to the whole. As Adorno explains in *Negative Dialectics*, "Now as before, the social process of production preserves in the basic barter process the *principium individuationis*, private disposition, and thus all the evil instincts of man imprisoned in his ego. The individual survives himself. But in his residue which history has condemned lies nothing but what will not sacrifice itself to false identity. The function of the individual is that of the functionless—of the spirit that does not agree with the universal and is therefore powerless to represent it" (343). The individual appears as an internalization of the atomization that the unity of productive forces imposes on the social totality of an exchange society. The individual is formed as the depository of independent economic reason and calculation that is necessarily autonomous from the sum of objective social relations but still absorbed in them. That is, the individual, like the family and the *intérieur*, reflects the social totality through its alienation from it. Though the object's outsidedness is never absolute, I contest with Hull that Adorno, unlike Butler,[33] does provide a sense of something over the border of knowledge that can be known, a guilty survival, a "beyond" to the forces of reification and assimilation into concepts, and that this "sense of something" depends for its formation on the disappearing memory of a bourgeois private sphere.

Modern Power and the Liquidation of the Private

With Toril Moi, I want to emphasize that my engagement with Butler's theoretical work does not imply any sort of disparagement of her political commitments.[34] Her involvement with feminism; gay, lesbian, transgendered, and transsexual activism; her support for disabled people; as well as her active and continual speaking out against U.S. imperialist wars, torture, Zionist aggression, curtailments to academic freedom, and the production of dehumanized bodies on the border of social norms and intelligibility—all of this proves Butler to be an inspiration as well as an aspiration to generations of scholars and students, including myself.

Embracing the poststructuralist embrace of affirmative philosophies, Butler, however, wants to oppose the politics of domination by a logic of repetition. Butler's subject is formed by performing aspects of the symbolic, constituting itself by assuming them, repeating them with a difference. This limits her thinking on the connection between social agency and empirical or practical action. The social only exists as a linguistic demand. Change might happen when the forming subject is misrecognized within the symbolic structure. Though Butler certainly believes in collective social action and speaks frequently in its favor, her critics have noted that her theoretical paradigms deny any intersubjective component to political change. That is, Butler's readers have had trouble discerning in her political vision any possibility of a normative ideal to be developed and differentiated from the subject and the language world that embeds it. Amanda Anderson, for example, contests that Butler has "distinctly mapped [...] her intrapsychic model [...] onto her collective model" (39), because she fails "to elaborate any basis for its normative commitments," implying that "intrapsychic maneuvers translate directly into political realities" (38). For Amy Allen, Butler's account of the subject's formation through subordination, subjection, punishment, and self-beratement means that she does not flesh out any mechanism for judging between "subversive reiterations or reenactments of the law from those that reinforce and uphold it" (78). In other words, Butler's subject is so attached to the punishing power that forms it or calls it into being, Allen continues, that her positing of a possibility of being "elsewhere or otherwise" (78) seems disenabled.[35]

One might tentatively say that poststructuralism's interest in language, and its thinking on the social as a relation of language, is one place where it adopts and adapts idealist philosophy's focus on the concept, though the analogy is necessarily incomplete. Where the concept was a category of understanding that made the external empirical world intelligible to the subject that was independent of it (in some form or another), poststructuralist theories of signification necessarily imply that the subject is already caught up inside of empiricism, already relational, an effect, indiscernible from the object it contemplates. By reading Butler through Adorno, my point here is to question whether the dominance and inescapability of language as concept in poststructuralism gives inadequate resources to address the recycling of the private sphere of industrial production inside today's most prevalent forms of exploitation, of female labor in particular (as explored in chapter 1). I am suggesting that the problem of the "concept" has overlapped with the private sphere's problem of independence and autonomy in liberalism. The absence of the private as an oppositional concept in poststructuralism might indicate

an absence of any but the most insinuative concept of the nonconceptual, the "outside," or the differential future, even to the limited
extent of Adorno's principle of nonidentity.

Since neoliberal ideologies marginalize the development of the
public, exclude it, reject it, or project it as irrational, the prevailing
indications of its survival might be located in the symbolic persistence of the private sphere. However, poststructuralism's distrust of
the private/public split might reduce the theoretical tools available
for confronting the ways that the current division of labor is put-
ting the symbolics of the private sphere to use as the replacement
of the public rather than as the "outside." Rather than a rejection
of the private/public divide, what need to be worked out are the
different ways that the private sphere is called into being; that is,
whether as (1) the disappearing private sphere of the industrial division of labor; (2) the persistent private sphere of neoliberal modes of
exploitation and ownership, from outsourcing to microfinance, that
bank on the appropriation and commodification of traits and work
regimes traditionally recognized as "feminine"; (3) the understanding of the human individual as having an inner core of the self that
precedes entry into the social, like a soul, a personality, desire, sex,
or freedom, particularly manifest in formulations of human rights
and civil rights; and 4) the place of critique, consciousness, autonomy, and reflection. This last category of the private is needed to
challenge market philosophies and the privatization of everything
through preserving ideals of social and political improvement and
public participation that are not necessarily just an extension of private power, and Adorno distinguishes this mode of the private as the
private sphere's survival through disappearing—its outsidedness.[36]
I believe that Butler's analysis of Adorno as being in conformity
with Foucauldian disciplinary formations exhibits that the theoretical exclusion of the private sphere "forecloses"—to use Butler's
terminology—the necessity of thinking in affirmative terms about
an emergent public agency or intersubjectivity. Poststructuralism
via Butler relinquishes the category of the private, I argue, with the
result of privatizing everything.

SEX AND SOVEREIGNTY

Michel Foucault had, in fact, worked out a reason that the private/
public split needed to be surpassed. Foucault's project consisted in
describing modern power as a network of intersecting institutionalized discourses emerging within very specific social disciplinary sites

of identity production; for example, the police, the army, the prison, the health clinic, the asylum, and the school. He needed, then, to distinguish this way of thinking about *modern* power from a *premodern* idea of power based on the sovereignty of kings. Kings, he said, displayed their power in disconnected periodic spectacles, like public torture and executions, meant to work both as deterrents and as performances of might and control. Such displays operated in discrete moments. Modern power, on the other hand, is everywhere: continuous, seamless, invisible, and without gaps. However, according to Foucault, modern understanding of power, including among its critics, still assumes the older version of sovereignty. This means that the thinking of power is limited to forms of power like the state's exercise of repression, as though modern forms of power simply stood in the place once occupied by kings.[37] Critics of modern power do not take into account, for example, that modern power mixes a discourse of the limits of governing authority with a discourse on the law as setting the conditions for market growth.

Foucault's revision of power, then, requires him to abandon the private/public split that institutes the outside/inside split in nonmodern power regimes. He does this by changing the two synchronous functions through which his teacher, Louis Althusser, characterized the modern state. Foucault divided the two Althusserian functions of the state into two distinct but overlapping time periods. Those state apparatuses that Althusser identified as working through force, coercion, and suppression (Repressive State Apparatuses, or RSA) were relegated, by Foucault, to a time when power was located in rights and the body of the sovereign king. Those that work through the distribution of ideologies and competencies (Ideological State Apparatuses, or ISA) represent, for Foucault, modern power, based on discipline rather than sovereignty, based in techniques of domination and permanent surveillance rather than the discontinuous application of codes and punishments. Althusser maintained that Marxism had no theory of modern state power that could take into account how working-class consciousness and identifications reproduced themselves to continue producing in support of the interests of the ruling class, without overthrowing the state that propped them up. To Althusser, Marxism's shortcoming can be discerned in its descriptions of state power only as repressive state power, or coercion. Althusser wants to add to this description other mechanisms, or apparatuses, that would cast "light on all direct or indirect forms of exploitation, [...] on the subtle everyday domination beneath which can be glimpsed [...] what Lenin, following Marx, called the dictatorship of the bourgeoisie"

(133). For this purpose, Althusser sees the distinction between public and private spheres as unnecessary. "[T]he state," notes Althusser, at the beginning of his discussion of Ideological State Apparatuses (ISA),[38] "which is the State *of* the ruling class, is neither public nor private; on the contrary, it is the precondition for any distinction between public and private. The same thing can be said from the starting point of our State Ideological Apparatuses. It is unimportant whether the institutions in which they are realized are 'public' or 'private'. What matters is how they function" (137–138). Addressing the issue of what Antonio Gramsci called the "manufacturing of consent," Althusser—like Adorno—basically acknowledges that cultural work draws subjects into identification with the state of capitalist interests, despite that their interests are contrary to it. This identification against one's interest is inherent similarly whether power takes on the form of socialist centralization, public welfare state policies, or private ownership. Althusser, however, does not completely abandon the private/public divide and does not insist that private institutions and public institutions are identical to each other in all instances, but rather announces that the private/public divide does not explain how capitalism reproduces itself: Private institutions (e.g., the media or the church), like public institutions (e.g. the school), are all just as likely to call the subject into existence in relation to the state and its social classes.

Foucault formulates Althusser's distinction between Ideological State Apparatuses and Repressive State Apparatuses as a principle of historical periodization. Instead of through repressive mechanisms like decisions, edicts, violence, and spectacles of punishment as in the premodern power of kings, modern power works as a system that controls populations by knowing, without gaps, the norms and the laws through which populations get constituted. The interiority of Foucault's prisoner is exactly an extension of the prison house in which he resides, just as the "private bourgeois bedroom" is an instrument that expands the external reach of surveillance. Public sovereignty no longer marks the limits of state identity, its borders, decisions, periodic rituals, and singular acts, but instead is spread out among the multiple networks through which power is exercised. There is no inside or outside of power, just power everywhere and always. "This state of government, which essentially bears on the population and calls upon and employs economic knowledge as an instrument, would correspond to a society controlled by apparatuses of security" (2007: 110). Unlike in Adorno, knowledge in Foucault is fully identical with what can be known; the subject and the object are completely reconciled. There is no variation between the big structures of history and the little subjects that inhabit them. Adorno would disparagingly call this positivism.

Butler does not see a disparity between Adorno's theories of power that work through the suggestions of autonomy and Foucault's that explicitly deny it by extending discourse even through what is oppositional or resistant to it. Butler's project appropriates Foucault's breakdown of modern power in order to encourage feminism to abandon the sex/gender dichotomy, which she says has been its principle organizing structure since the sixties, as well as one of its principle blind spots. "Sex," for Butler, exists as a category expressing an inner truth as a private, prediscursive, stable, coherent identity, located in the body, whereas "gender" stands for a force that imposes itself from the outside, preformed, retractable, culturally sustainable, and grounded by the law. Butler argues that the inner/outer distinction naturalizes gender identity by creating a sense that something—some fixed "hidden depth" (1990: 134)—precedes the internalization of the law of gender. Rather, she contends, the category "sex" provides just a fiction of a distinction between "inner" and "outer" that stabilizes a coherent subject with a fixed and intelligible boundary. "In other words," she clarifies,

> acts, gestures, and desire produce an effect of an internal core or substance, but produce this *on the surface* of the body, through the play of signifying absences that suggest, but never reveal, the organizing principle of identity as a cause [...] This also suggests that if that reality is fabricated as an interior essence, that very interiority is an effect and function of a decidedly public and social discourse, the public regulation of fantasy through the surface politics of the body, the gender border control that differentiates inner from outer, and so institutes the "integrity" of the subject. In other words, acts and gestures, articulated and enacted desires create the illusion of an interior and organizing gender core, an illusion discursively maintained for the purposes of regulation of sexuality within the obligatory frame of reproductive heterosexuality. (1990: 136)

Language, here, with its dispersed institutions and myriad of unconnected practices, substitutes for the state, its institutions of governing and production, as where the principle of power's reproduction gets enacted. Butler imports Althusser's thesis on the state and its affiliations to the private ruling classes to talk about gender identity: As Althusser asks how workers end up complying with regimes of work, becoming workers, regulated by a state representing the interests of an opposing class, Butler asks how girls and boys learn to be girls and boys, even when such an identification attaches them to an organizational or categorical social organization within which they cannot recognize themselves or recognize the multiplicity of their desires, and which subordinates them. Where Althusser raises the question of what could constitute the internal consciousness of the worker before it is called by the ideological apparatus to assume the identity of worker, Butler asserts that the very idea of an identity before the call of public knowledge is false, arbitrary, and, in fact, a belated proposition, a backward projection.

Though Butler seems to be discarding the "private" and the "public" in a similar gesture to Althusser's, the way she is describing the "public" is as a screen of display, a social space for individual acts and gestures. Though the private seems to be reduced into the public as just another instance or effect of language, the public has been redefined as a series of what we think of as interior moments, or of reconstructions of what we have thought of as psychic depth. There is no materialization of the subject prior to its constitution by and absorption in the apparatus of the social;[39] there is no separation, partial, apparent, conceptual, periodic, or temporary. The individual is indistinguishable from the linguistic formations that constitute it and that it constitutes, in turn, through its repetitions.

THE INTRASUBJECTIVE MAPPING OF THE INTERSUBJECTIVE PUBLIC USE OF REASON

Althusser's dismissal of the private/public divide makes evident that state-run institutions and administered bureaucracies (the school, the police, etc.) on the one hand and, on the other, non-state-run institutions, businesses, and households (the church, the family) work together to call into play the subjects—with a lowercase "s"—that learn to recognize themselves within capitalism's historical Subject positions, or classes, that reach their final historical moment in the modern state. The problem is in how to identify what it is that is called into existence by the hailing process if that subject does not yet exist: "*the category of the subject is only constitutive of all ideology insofar as all ideology has the function (which defines it) of 'constituting' concrete individuals as subjects*" (emphasis Althusser's; 160). For this, Althusser likens the separation between subjects with a lowercase "s" and historical Subjects to the Lacanian imago, where the prelinguistic child feels physically alienated from his image in the mirror even when he knows the image is referencing him: "all ideology represents in its necessarily imaginary distortion not the existing relations of production (and the other relations that derive from them), but above all the (imaginary) relationship of individuals to the relations of production and the relations that derive from them" (155). As with Lacan's mirror stage, the subject that gets constituted by the call of the state in Althusser is made to cut off some of the sensuous, affective, incoherent, or private experience not reducible to her idealized relationships with the realization and enactment of ideology.

Whereas Adorno translates the Marxist idea of proletariat consciousness into a post-industrial form of autonomy in the private consciousness offered through philosophy and aesthetics, and Althusser raises the question of an autonomous consciousness outside or before the call of the state, Butler poses interiority only as a linguistic effect. Translated into gender terms, the private/public divide is not, for Butler as it was for Althusser, so dominantly a problem of the division of labor, its separate interests that get dissolved, the structures or organization of ownership, areas of control, or a mark distinguishing government's exercise of power from civil society's. Her rejection of it is not because she wants to make a point about how the state and the private institutions that exist alongside it have interwoven interests when it comes to reproducing a labor force whose interests are different, but rather that autonomy is co-extensive with the power that constitutes it: "The politics to which we refer is not the politics *of* the state or the politics *of* the public realm but the particular political power of delimitation that constantly divides private from public on questionable grounds" (2009: 782).

In her *Critical Inquiry* article on Kant and Enlightenment, the private/public divide is a "delimiting power" (2009: 783), with questionable legitimacy. Like "man" and "woman," the "public" is an arbitrary designation whose identity is formed through an exclusion that constitutes it in language. In Kant's "What is Enlightenment?" Butler notes, the authorizing power of the state designates a "domain where the exercise of state supervision takes place free of critical intervention" (2009: 778), a domain set aside for the practice of philosophy. This works by drawing a border between this space of free critique and another "unfree and private domain" (2009: 778). In actuality, whatever "outside" the public has is an effect of constituting, naming, or differentiating: "any opposition to the norm is already contained within the norm" (2004: 51). Since the public's very identity and existence depend on the establishment of the division, any determinations or inquiries coming out of the public cannot question what exclusions brought it into being, what allowed the determinations or inquiries to take place. Yet, the "unfree and private domain" sets the terms of that limitation from within. The public, in its free exercise of reason, necessarily limits itself against the unfree, but does so only under the regulatory structure that calls it into being as such. The "public" is a discursive closure like any other, a creator of legitimating exclusions.

Butler's reading of Kant's version of the public here parallels an earlier reading of Habermas's public, where Butler questions the reference to the "we" in the public sphere's establishing interrogative: "[W]hat are we to do?" Butler understands Habermas to be presupposing, in this "we," a normative structure outside of the public sphere's evaluating practices, and that the normative structure would designate a content of critique, a set of rules, judgments, or legitimating rationales that Butler identifies as would-be enabling foundations.[40] Amy Allen calls Butler's project in such declarations to be "a form of social suicide" (83), where any intersubjective relation can only be considered as a form of subordination, and no social attachment, mutual recognition, or situation of dependency can arise except for pathological, submissive ones.

Butler's project—and this particularly concerns her in reading Foucault—consists in showing how regimes of normalization, particularly in relation to gender, operate outside of central and sovereign controls, police action, law, punishment, and the like. She emphasizes that the nineteenth-century "emergence of the norm as a means of social regulation [...] is not identical with the operations of the law" (2004: 48–49). "[P]ower is not reducible to state power" (2004: 116). For Butler, the rejection of the private/public distinction is not any longer focused on working through or marginalizing the differences between the state and civil society in their conjoined preparation of workers for production. Instead, her rejection of the private/public splits appears as a rejection of the difference between an outward sign or performance—a public norm—and an internal meaning, a truth of the self, a deep structure of the linguistic sign that it might not integrate and claim.

Butler's idea that the public is but an effect of language—an identity formed through exclusion that cannot question the exclusion that brought it into being—repeats an analysis that Butler makes in other places about subjectivity. In *The Psychic Life of Power*, Butler sets her analysis of Foucault against a Freudian narrative in which the psyche is excessive to consciousness; the Freudian psyche cannot be reduced to the norm that demands its conformity. Within the narrative of psychoanalysis, power is therefore incomplete in its subordinating function, guaranteeing resistance: "[T]he psyche is precisely what exceeds the imprisoning effects of the discursive demand to inhabit a coherent identity, to become a coherent subject" (1997: 86). In Foucault, on the other hand, she says, the body is a prisoner of the soul. This means that power's inscriptions on the body, its call, gives the surface a fictive sense of a preexistent interiority, or soul.[41] In turn, gender is a manifestation of power playing on the body. This play of power produces a fantasy of depth or interiorization that gives gendered identities a false sense of private meaning and coherence.

Just as individual interiority is not opposed to the social of language (as it is in Adorno), Butler cannot describe any sort of oppositional consciousness or effort in other than indefinite terms. Butler does see in *The History of Sexuality, Volume I* the possibility of where "psychic resistance thwarts the law in its effects" (1997: 98), producing "unanticipated effects of symbolic interpellations" that she calls "subversions" (1997: 99). The field of sexuality, of the imaginary, is where Butler locates what Althusser calls "misrecognition"—the imago, or small "s"—or the blurriness where the name that the apparatus uses to call out does not capture the entirety of the subject being called, producing an excess. Neither a revolution nor a rebellion, this excess, says Butler, is an "instability and unpredictability" (1997: 96), a "non-place of subversion" (1997: 99), a reformulation, a transmutation of the law, an atopicality, a "condition for the subject's de-constitution" (1997: 99). Elsewhere she calls this "the possibility of savoring the status of unthinkability" (2004: 106), "sites of uncertain ontology" (2004: 108), or "middle regions, hybrid regions of legitimacy and illegitimacy that have no clear names" (2004: 108). Though certainly Butler is identifying "something," and the "something" is mutable, she does not specify distinctly what could have a positive value. As Carrie Hull points out, in Butler, "There is no absolute other of discourse because we can only conceive of that outside in relation to discourse [...] Thus, Butler has basically asserted that there is no distinct reality outside of discursive, social practice, yet we may one day know that reality" (27). Butler's reluctance to name or describe an outside in affirmative language has to do with her skepticism of the static, meaning that any call by name would, as it does in Althusser, exclude parts of what constitutes it and fix meaning as partial. Hull goes on to contend that Butler's inability to formulate a distinct and positive outside limits her ability to address a variety of social issues, including "domestic and/or other types of either socially abject, low-paying, or dangerous labour" (32). I would add that this indistinctness or unnameability of any exteriority, limits, or outsidedness—even a diminishing one—is, simultaneously, where Butler abandons thinking the public.

GIVING AN ACCOUNT

Butler's insights into language and subjectivity build out of a rejection of the individual. For Butler, the individual, like the private and like subjectivity, is a division, instituted by language and its exclusions and maintained by normativity. One would expect her, then, to express insurmountable differences with Adorno's work, particularly with his reliance on the individual as an interiority that bespeaks the social, as a possibility of difference within history, and as what breaks from the unities and repetitions of reason under state capitalism and scientific positivism. Amy Allen notes that Butler's 2004 book, *Giving an Account of Oneself*, is one of the sole instances where she tries to theorize a sociality not completely driven by relationships of subordination, and where she almost opens her thinking up to "the recognition of our commonality [that] provides the basis for political community and collective resistance" (93). Contingently, this is the book where she also does her most extensive reading of Adorno. However, Butler's formulation of social relationships is based on reflection—an extension of the individual through likeness—rather than on antagonism. As she says in a slightly earlier article where these ideas are percolating, "Judgments operate for both thinkers [Adorno and Foucault] as ways to subsume a particular under an already constituted category" (213). Though this may be true for Foucault, it is explicitly contrary to an Adorno who believes the integration of empirical particulars into intelligible concepts exposes the inadequacies of concepts for understanding. This blending of Adorno into Foucaultianisms leads Butler to a skewed appropriation of Adorno, as though his thinking could be assimilated to the Lacan-Althusser-Foucault trajectory, with its (nearly) seamless continuity between the individual and its social call or concept, the individual not being anything before the concept gives it a name.

Butler does realize substantial differences between Adorno and Foucault, but at the same time, wants to show a set of parallels. These parallels have to do with the relationship between the individual and the social. She does, for example, note differences in their readings of Kant—for Adorno, Kant represents the individual of abstract reason, while for Foucault, he represents the appearance of the conditions of knowing and acting, of the constitution of selves. Foucault sacrifices the individual to the discursive regime, where the subject becomes subject only "through an ecstatic movement, one that moves me outside of myself into a sphere in which I am dispossessed of myself" (2005: 115). Butler also recognizes that Adorno is a dialectical thinker, where the individual is bifurcated from the world,[42] and Foucault is not, meaning that the subject of critique for Foucault is immanent within historically oriented regimes of intelligibility, and there is no possibility of either autonomy or transcendence.

For Butler, such differences do not, however, nullify the thinkers' compatibility in their allegiance to Hegelian thought: "[Foucault] turns to confession to show how the subject must relinquish itself in and through the manifestation of the self it makes. In this sense, the manifestation of the self dissolves its inwardness and reconstitutes it in its externality. This dialectical inversion is worthy of Adorno and no doubt bears Hegelian resonances" (2005: 113). In other words, where Foucault and Adorno converge for Butler is at the moment when the private individual disappears into the social, "giving oneself over to a publicized mode of appearance" (2005: 114), when the interior of the subject is called out by the epistemological regime or the historical norms, and becomes visible. What gets left out when the subject comes into these public forms of rationalization is, for Butler, variously "something" (2005: 120), "a price," "a cost" (2005: 121), or a loss. Again, there is an exclusion that gets constituted—from within discourse, by means of discourse, as part of discourse—as an excess, but cannot be distinguished or identified; the nonconceptual has no positive existence, no movement away from its ideal or ideological constitution.

What Butler seems not to notice in Adorno is that he reads in Hegel the idea that "discontinuity and universal history must be conceived together" (*Negative*, 319); that is, that the totality of the social, the organized processes of production, must always alienate those it absorbs and produces, those that compose its unity. Adorno, for example, shows the possibility in philosophy of "the idea of depth" (*Negative*, 17), where Kant exists as a moment of independent deduction inside of or alongside the repeated reconciliations of Hegel's dialectics of History: "A prime example of the modern age is the Kantian deduction of pure intellectual concepts, which the author, with abysmally apologetic irony, called 'somewhat profoundly arranged.' Profundity, as Hegel did not fail to note, is another element of dialectics" (*Negative*, 17). Butler repeatedly denies Adorno's ideas about the private interior as the limit to the social, its alienation. For example, explaining Adorno's position on "private ethics" or love and its injuries, Butler cites a passage from *Minima Moralia* in which an individual's pain leads to his realization of and enthrallment to the general social norms, that we are "implicated in a mode of relationality that cannot be fully thematized" (2005: 102). Adorno, on the other hand, gives a firm sense that the individual is never fully drawn into this relationality because of his interiority. Where Butler ends her citation with "he who is rebuffed becomes human" (*Minima Moralia*, 164), Adorno goes on to talk about how this individual is at risk of disappearing into the call of this "human," of immediately assuming its identity as his own, but ultimately cannot be reconciled inside of this "human": "[H]e who has lost love knows himself deserted by all" (*Minima Moralia*, 164). Contra Adorno, Butler, through this exclusion, is reading both sides of the dialectic as harmonizing, as cross-identifying; that is, as categorical equivalents that reflect each other like the imago, even with a little bit of distortion.

What Butler has left out in her reading of Adorno is the idea of contradiction. The idea of contradiction is central to Adorno's thinking that Adorno develops from an analysis of the private/public division of labor. Though the contemporary configuration of the market and the economy would seem to support Butler's supposition that the private has disappeared into the public, or that the private is just an extension of the public, it would also give credence to Adorno's postulate that the disappearance of the industrial division of labor and the private sphere is coterminous with its reemergence in various symbolic forms. For Adorno, this division still traces out through the play between Kant's and Hegel's formulations of the subject of reason. "[F]or Adorno," Butler writes, "there is always a bifurcation" (2005: 110). A bifurcation implies two paths leading out separately but at the same time; a bifurcation is different than a contradiction because, in a bifurcation, the two paths might coexist without crossing; they might coexist without canceling each other out. Butler reads Adorno's Kant as he who "represents the culture of abstract reason, which is bifurcated from the consequences of its action" (2005: 111). The world, she interprets, and the individual who thinks it, can coexist. In fact, they must coexist, because the world sets out the conditions of legibility in which the individual enters it, so the individual is an extension of the way the world knows itself, at least for the most part. By existing, the individual repeats the regulatory principles by which the world calls her into being. This is not a fair reading of Adorno, or rather this is a reading of Adorno that denies the dialectic. For Adorno, critique as theorized through the Enlightenment contains within it the contradiction that "things-in-themselves," or the objectivity of the material world, are a projection of subjective human categories, and so identical to what can be thought, and yet, at the same time, "things-in-themselves" have their own "affections": "[T] his human product must not be allowed to mistake itself for objective reality, but must become conscious of itself as something internal to human beings and thus limited" (*Kant's Critique*, 67). Adorno's Kant therefore realizes that the external world is critical because it stops reason from making an absolute of itself. Critique is, then, what Adorno calls a "somersault" (*Kant's Critique*, 67) of reason acting against itself.

In his lectures to his students, commenting on Kant's same essay on Enlightenment that Butler engaged in *Critical Inquiry*, Adorno proposes that Kant's critical insight into the limits to the theoretical coincides, not accidentally, with modern bureaucratization and its division of labor. Adorno cites Kant as saying that the universal implicated in the free public use of reason, like the universal of the Kantian subject, suddenly finds itself against the limit, or block, of what calls it into being (for example, the individual is opposed to or alienated from the bureaucratic system that made it possible). Whereas Butler sees the production of the free public use of reason as a subordinating exclusion that is substantially indifferentiable from what it excludes, Adorno understands Kant's production of the free use of reason as an irreconcilable antagonism instituted by the division of labor:

> This predicative use of "as" [as in "as a writer," "as a scholar," or "as a servant of the state"] signals a restricting of reason in line with the division of labour in which human beings find themselves involved; the restriction imposed on enlightenment here is in fact a matter of the division of labour [...]—the purely theoretical human being is free to be enlightened in a radical sense. The moment he has a particular function, the post of civil servant, for example, all reasoning is at an end. (*Kant's Critique*, 63).

Whereas Butler dismisses the private/public split as a linguist ruse, a function that creates fictive effects of differentiation, Adorno translates the division of labor between public and private spheres as the operative principle behind critique.

Adorno's underlying focus on the private/public split and the state could be said to make his work dated and no longer applicable. This might be particularly true when measured against Judith Butler, who, in abandoning the sex/gender division, also gives up the categories of the public and the private as no longer describing the ways identities are constructed in a so-called "postindustrialized" setting. Butler's setting aside of the private/public split allows her to develop a description of the present that marginalizes the state or the public as the principle site where power is exercised (in line with Foucault). For Butler, with the state no longer foremost in the construction of power, sex/gender identity is a result of the actions of regulatory norms rather than regulatory enforcement mechanisms and production distributions. As Valentine M. Moghadam points out, however, "[W]omen's organizations around the world remain focused on their societies and states. Some lobby for the return of the welfare and developmental state and social rights that prevailed before the onset of neoliberal economics; others for the protection or expansion of reproductive rights; and yet others for equality and empowerment in the family. The state still matters to women" (256). Without the state, and without any alternative to the state in a transnational public body, Butler is left without a framework for an analysis of—among other things—the interpellation of labor through privatization that currently shapes how gendered relations are controlled and managed on a global scale, and left without a framework for an analysis of what kind of construct, theoretical and practical, that could oppose the extensions of such power.

Butler's abandonment of the private/public split also leads to a philosophical abandonment of an "outside" to this present except in the form of its repetition, its extension, and its excess. This could be seen as a historical "given" in that both the private sphere and the individual that inhabited it are products of an industrial age that is receding, and the survival of both is put at further risk by the proliferation of a global consumer society. However, the private sphere has not been buried in modernity's wreckage, but rather has been recycled. As in the industrial age, it still affirms the values of infinite productivity, private accumulation and limits to state authority. In fact, the private individual, in the form of its economic rationality, seems to have taken the role of Kant's transcendent consciousness and the free use of reason, setting itself against the unfree domain of public reason or even the limits of the empirical world. On the other hand, the public stands in the place of the critical individual of Enlightenment reason: The public is disappearing. Butler's theoretical enterprise is a symptom of this disappearing public. While Adorno, a self-avowed Kantian, believes that the reconciliation between the social and the individual that Hegel could be said to predict is stopped by the Kantian block— the incompatibility between the subject and the world, the principle of alienation —Butler, who could be said to be a Hegelian, believes with Kant that the subject extends without stopping because it really is the social. For Butler, a series of individual acts produce the social by affirming its linguistic concepts and pushing them to an extreme, where they turn Other. Adorno would see the disappearing public as evidence of a lingering autonomy, the possibility of thought, and the construction of difference in the "what ought to be." Whereas Butler affirms a fragmented reality that imagines no reins or "block" to private individual production or private consumption but only its repetitions, Adorno understands the individual as limited by the social totality that engenders it; the private individual is, in turn, barred in its tendencies toward making itself absolute by the irreconcilable work of its outside, the marginalized public body.

5

BAGHDAD BURNING: CYBORG MEETS
THE NEGATIVE

This chapter attempts to locate an appearance of the public sphere within a critique of the "re-privatization" of women's work regimes. The marginalization of the public sphere is shown to be coterminous with the marginalization of women's work, so that the remnants of public sphere practices are still discernable within private sphere settings and their representations. In this chapter, I compare Donna Haraway's views on the technological public sphere with Herbert Marcuse's. According to Donna Haraway, new political visions and identity formations for the neoliberal, postnational age assume a surpassing of the private/public split of industrial capitalism, whereas Marcuse believes that the private sphere's continued temporal, spatial, and conceptual "outsidedness" gives it the symbolic force of a radical alternative. Moreover, Haraway bases her analysis of cyborg culture on the idea that markets have taken over where nation-states once were, reducing all social values to values gained through positionings in the market (so that the private is just another market position), whereas Marcuse sees the private sphere as a check, an "outside," to the indefinite expansion of nation-state-backed private interest.

This chapter goes on to show how the idea of the outside, critical detachment or the negative difference that Marcuse works through the national private sphere needs to be identified within a postnational and public analytic that Haraway brings into play. Writing from a country whose public sphere has been transformed into a technological display of total destruction that seems to have no end, Riverbend takes on this project in her now famous two-volume witness to war, *Baghdad Burning: Girl Blog from Iraq*. Unlike Haraway, Riverbend does not believe that future identity-formations will make invisible the private/public divide, but understands the incipient construction of a public sphere outside of the privatizations and appropriations of imperialism depends on a defense of the public realm revealed through domestic practices. In opposition to a technological public culture extending imperialist investments, work privatization, and endless administration, Riverbend envisions an internationalized private sphere constructed through technology as an embryonic pedagogical public culture.

Rather than understanding neoliberalism as an age which no longer sees its identity in the private/public split, as does Haraway, I argue here that the relationship between the public and the private has been structurally reversed: while the private gains decisive power in its avoidance of state control and regulation, the public is pushed off to the outskirts of economic and political activity. I call this "reprivatization," and see it as relating to an emergent formation of gendered labor where women's work is still subordinated but as the intensified site of capitalization. These new forms are not science-fictiony suggestions of new networks of alliance that are no longer identified through affectivities produced in private and familial life, as Haraway predicts. Rather, the private/public divide of industrialism, that seems to be destroyed in the violence of the new economic age, is, actually, functionally turned over: the public is now the "outside" and, in this, symbolically is represented through new identities of women working. Within the symbolic structure of the endangered industrial private sphere can be discerned the marginality of a future public sphere unfolding.

AUTHENTICITY, OR THE LIMITS TO THE PRESENT

The comparison between Haraway and Marcuse indicates that the private sphere, as a relic of nation-state-centered productive practices and development, must be read as an autonomous space of opposition or transcendence to the totally administered society that Haraway believes has disappeared: for Haraway, politics in neoliberalism has to do with arranging and rearranging codes rather than with conflict, contradiction, or struggle. Her idea of is that market relations have completely saturated the social. This comparison also suggests that often the remnants of communicative public functions can be attributed now only to the margins of the post-national technological takeover of the national public sphere, in such margins as the private sphere formerly resided under industrialization (where Habermas located the lifeworld, as analyzed in chapters 2 and 3). This public communicative function is what is being leveled in the leveling of the private/public difference. As an explanation of women's work within a corporatist, neoliberal, biotechnological age, Haraway's cyborg culture describes women's private work as the point of entry of inescapable forces of appropriation and exploitation that transform the very nature of the human to be exploited; there is no longer a line dividing technologies from biologies, or production from reproduction. She understands this new nature of the human (the posthuman) to be full of new political possibilities for social and material transformation.

Marcuse's vision of the relation between technology and labor is limited by the context of the nation-state, while Haraway's internationalism disrupts the private/public binary in such a way as to make invisible the emergence of an oppositional public sphere that Marcuse identified in the forms and temporalities of women's work. Haraway describes women's work as the underlying basis of the cyborg system, totally defining the core of possible relationships between work and system, while Marcuse sees women's work as the "outside" to production. As a result, Haraway's analysis lends itself more fervently to a critique of the present while Marcuse's analysis does not account for the incorporation of women's work as central to the corporate organization of labor globally. Yet, Marcuse traces a complexity of thought that holds the structural place of women's labor as drawing out the possibility of thinking outside of the administered present, whereas in Haraway, no such possibility exists.

For Marcuse, the "pastness" of the private sphere is an expression of modern alienation, in particular the alienation caused by a totally administered society, state-centered production, and their technologies. The lingering private sphere is a ghostlike figure, a time within the present that contradicts the present. As much as the industrial private sphere is embedded as shoring up the economic logic that extends the present indefinitely, it also abstracts itself as the outside of that form. Much as Heideggerian "authenticity" is an immanent distinction within the present's seeming solidity, the private sphere, as a nonabsorption in the world, is similar to Heidegger's "Not-Being-its-self," an exception that "functions as a *positive* possibility of that entity which, in its essential concern, is absorbed in the world" (1962: 220). Though Heidegger's abstract language of "authenticity" does not apply directly to any discernable concrete historical instance, it constitutes an autonomous element of future historical change, immanent within the present, that Marcuse materializes in the structural position of the private sphere.

For Marcuse, the private sphere persists as the symbolic form of contemplation that resists absorption in the present's administration and national production. The private sphere as a national form parallels technology whose meanings are, at first, restricted to its relations within national production. In Marcuse's thinking about technology's social future, the eventual realization of "a new freedom for man" (1964: 3) results from his imagining of technology as, like the private sphere absorbed in a national form and yet essentially irreconcilable with it. Because national capital is internally focused, investing in machines to satisfy internal needs, its reach is always only partial, nationally bounded. In its uses for national production, technology produces new needs that are outside of the needs that the technology itself is designed to fulfill in its nationally and temporally bounded form. Like the private sphere, technology therefore represents the limit in time to the nation-state's systems of productivity: both the private sphere and technology are material constructions of the present that have essences not containable within their present, economically exploitative forms. Technology opens the way to a collective rebellion that reaches into the sense of inner consciousness, instinctual life, sensuous nature, and private necessity that cannot be accounted for in the present moment: a totally different private sphere.

On the other hand, without a nation-state in reference to which (or against which) to fashion public identities, Haraway's vision of the blending of public and private spheres into a technological/market universe leaves no outside. Haraway understands Marcuse's continued embrace of "outsidedness" as an outgrowth of dualistic thinking, where technology is defined through domination, and redemption is imagined as a return to an originary organicism: "One of my premises is that most American socialists and feminists see deepened dualisms of mind and body, animal and machine, idealism and materialism in the social practices, symbolic formulations, and physical artefacts associated with "high technology" and scientific culture. From *One Dimensional Man* (Marcuse, 1964) to *The Death of Nature* (Merchant, 1980), the analytic resources developed by progressives have insisted on the necessary domination of technics and recalled us to an imagined organic body to integrate our resistance" (1992: 154). Though I see how such a conclusion can be reached, I am reading Marcuse a bit differently here: rather than a "return to nature" thesis, I read Marcuse as positing the private sphere as an empty signifier of difference that is always on the move, always an opening, and always oppositional. Its referential allusions to a sphere of women's labor do not stagnate its meanings and ground them down but rather suggest a broadening of this sphere's communicational potentials that its technological use foreshadows.

SHAHERAZAD ON-LINE

As a collection of blog entries republished in book form, *Baghdad Burning* can be read as two books in one. On the immediate level, it is vitally present. Starting in August 2003 and moving through May 2006, Riverbend presents her impressions of the historical events of the war as they unfold around her, as she watches and lives them, sometimes in short snippets and observations, at other times in sarcastic rejoinders to the news and grandstanding on TV. As James Ridgeway explains in his introduction, Riverbend puts a "real" "human face" on a tragedy that most of us are learning about through impersonal statistics and distanced reports: She "has made the war and occupation real," showing that "war is something that is lived every day—every night" as a "way of life" (xi). On another level, *Baghdad Burning* exists as a two-volume collection that tells a story of war, with stable characters, sustained narratives, identifiable settings, and linked chronologies. The war unwinds both as a series of stills, each one framed and distinct, each one disappearing as another comes into view, without connection, and as a moving sequence in which each shot is opened out as it disappears into the surrounding whole.

These two forms are in constant tension. Each dated entry tells of an event or a set of events that are happening at the same moment as or in close temporal proximity to the writing, is being covered on TV, or has entered fervently as an item of discussion among the neighbors or on the Web, perhaps obsessively so. As well, each dated entry tells of a moment in a trajectory of the war that might reveal itself within some historical significance or contribute a note to an unfolding understanding of a geopolitical formation, giving a fresh perspective on a very familiar thematic setting where we all identify our historical moment. Responses may oscillate from total recall—I remember that as how we got from here to there—to a wonder at forgetting—that seemed so significant at the time, why did it fall out of the war's story, will people in the future still recognize this as part of the history? The entries appear as both an eternal present without memory and as a memory without present.

Certainly, the narrative voice in *Baghdad Burning* appears as a modern-day recurrence of Scheherazade of *The Arabian Nights,* who has to keep telling her tale to survive (even the back cover admits this). It also resembles an epistolary romance like Goethe's *The Sorrows of Young Werther,* (1774) where a single letter writer is posed pouring his heart out in response to unprinted incoming correspondence from absent personages. But the best analogy for *Baghdad*

Burning would be a possible merging of *Don Quixote* (1605 and 1615) and *The Diary of Anne Frank* (1950). Though it is just a raw, day-to-day, personal and emotional response that brings to life a "civilian tragedy" as the yet untold, empirical part of a story about the large, powerful forces, energies, and interests through which we generally confront history and war, at the same time it can look back at itself, reflect on its past, revise, and comment in response to the hindsight of its future and the distance of other places. The difference with *The Diary of Anne Frank* is that in *Baghdad Burning*, the war is as much inside the hidden refuge as outside, brought inside through connecting to vast communications' networks that call from the future or from a nonnationalized territory of participating voices: radio, television, telephone, neighborhood gossip, Internet correspondence, other blogs, international websites, and, of course, the new technologies of warfare constantly exploding, endangering, and interrupting day-to-day life processes. The private inside is saturated and defined by its electronic outside.

MARCUSE ON TECHNOLOGY

The temporal rift in the very form of *Baghdad Burning*'s experientialness gives it common ground with Marcuse's analysis of technology as well as with his analysis of the private sphere. Like Riverbend, Marcuse gives a sense that technology's absorption in its present gives rise to a positive possibility that is different or autonomous from the meanings bestowed on it by its immediate use in production. Marcuse understands technology as locking in the present by buying out the possibility of the present's negation. Modern technology grants workers a comfortable standard of living that invites them to identify their interests in the growth of the technological systems, keeping them harnessed to their own exploitation at the expense of their self-determination and freedom. Technology satisfies immediate human needs and so erases the impulse to revolt, but only by creating new needs, mostly based on fear, that require an ever-larger technological base, an expansion of labor, and a permanent mobilization. As in *Baghdad Burning*, where the very dailiness of the war extends the war as infinitely part of the present, each day a new blog entry, the present for Marcuse's technological society becomes an extension of itself, an automated repetition, standardized and routine, an integrated totality where human life is but an extension of the workings of the machine. What results is a reduction of thought, a collapse of ideals into facts and of possibilities into actualities: "Today's fight against this historical alternative," he laments,

> finds a firm mass basis in the underlying population, and finds its ideology in the rigid orientation of thought and behavior to the given universe of facts. Validated by the accomplishments of science and technology, justified by its growing productivity, the status quo defies all transcendence. Faced with the possibility of pacification on the grounds of its technical and intellectual achievements, the mature industrial society closes itself against this alternative. (1964: 17)

Technological management and scientific thinking (or, positivism), for Marcuse, transform governance:[1] As a result of its dominance, the state itself has lost its Hegelian moment of connection, transcendence, and separation from civil society, and has instead given itself over to practices of containment, arms proliferation, and, consequently, the growth of oppressive productivity—a "thoroughly static system of life" (1964: 17).

On the flip side, by expanding labor, by increasing needs—through its cultures of consumption—which it ultimately cannot satisfy, by freeing up free time, technology gives rise to "the historical transcendence towards a new civilization" (1964: 37). That is, technology reveals "the consciousness of the discrepancy between the real and the possible, between the apparent and the authentic truth, and the effort to comprehend and to master this discrepancy" (1964: 229)—technology expresses the universal, the not yet realized potential revealed in the actual present moment and against which the present moment appears as a positive fact, and for which the present moment eventually is replaced. In technology, the universal bursts out of the walled-in frame of the present, demolishing its facticity.

The dual nature of temporality in Marcuse's work is in part an effect of what critics have identified as Marcuse's reaction to his dissatisfaction with where Marxist theory was headed. Orthodox Marxism had lost a sense of effective action within history because it had constructed the historical process as mechanical and objective in conformity with positivistic science rising in dominance at the time. To solve the problem of historical determinism early on, Marcuse turned to Heidegger, and later to Hegel. The critics, however, disagree on how Marcuse's early engagement with Heideggerian phenomenology addresses the problem of history and its immersion in the subject/object split that both positivism and commodification espoused. Douglas Kellner, for example, believes that Marcuse turned to Heidegger's formulation of "authenticity" as a way of understanding Marx's category of alienation without denying the possibility of the individual's interactions with the historical process. But, "[s]ince Heidegger's analysis does not allow for the possibility of revolutionary change that would overcome 'fallenness' with a new social structure, the most he can recommend is individual self-transformation" (1984: 48). Though Heidegger does develop an account of *Dasein* as able to move apart from the "idle chatter" of the "they" of inauthentic existence, his inability to theorize the concrete historical and social conditions or contexts of inauthenticity, or how such social conditions could be anything but inauthentic, leads Kellner to conclude that "Heidegger [...] scorned the public act" (1984: 48). John Abromeit, on the other hand, separates the first part of *Being and Time* from the second part. The first part constructs a "radically individuated" (133) sense of human agency that is based on this individual's ability to build an awareness of itself in relation to past and future and to "realize [his own-most possibilities] in the future" (135). The second part, meanwhile, indicates that this radical individuation can be dynamized "only through a collective effort to change the material world" (135). "Departing from his earlier analysis of authenticity as Being-toward-death, which had focused on the extreme individuation brought about by existing in the full awareness of one's own mortality, Heidegger [...] shows that [authenticity] can be realized only collectively, within a larger context of Being-with others" (136). This exchange between Kellner and Abromeit demonstrates the tension in Marcuse's work between individual action and objective history, as well as between the present moment and its temporalization that contrasts with the affirmative tendencies of positivism. Marcuse's engagement with the private sphere, I argue below, fashions itself into a theory of individual active autonomy that, at the same time, "can be completely realized only collectively" (Abromeit, 136).

By the time of *One-Dimensional Man* in 1964, Marcuse had distanced himself from Heidegger and phenomenology, in part because of Heidegger's affiliation with the Nazis and their political philosophy, and in part, as both Abromeit and Kellner elaborate, because phenomenology's abstractions were too limiting to develop the analysis of concrete material relations of production that Marcuse thought were vital. When Marcuse takes up the topic of technology, he still borrows this doubled temporality of technology from the term "enframing" that Heidegger develops in his 1954 essay "The Question Concerning Technology." For Heidegger, "enframing" means a "way of revealing which holds sway in the essence of technology" (1977: 20), a temporal potential, the "standing-reserve" that challenges but inhabits the standard parts, or physical actualities, like rods and pistons. Heidegger laments that technics, which is the human capacity to release essences in the forms of things through work,[2] has been replaced by technologies, which only perform the ordering of things already there, never actualizing their potentials, and therefore alienating them from the world. "Enframing" captures Heidegger's sense that the scientific ordering of reality that, as in positivism, "pursues and entraps nature as a calculable coherence of forces" (1977: 21) also could bring out the inscrutable energy concealed in nature, the essence in things, their future. "Enframing" as such is something that can only be acknowledged as it is happening and never subsequently, but at the same time, "never too late comes the question as to whether we actually experience ourselves as the ones whose activities everywhere, public and private, are challenged forth by Enframing" (1977: 24). "Enframing" lets ourselves be ourselves in the present, as radically active, while being, as a question, other than what we recognize as ourselves in the present, part of something else, something indiscernible, ghostly, and collective. Revealing technology's "essence" rather than just its present manifestations, this second "enframing" differentiates from "the inevitableness of the unalterable course" (1977: 25) of technology and frees us from technology's "stultified compulsion to push on blindly" (1977: 25). As technology "opens up human existence" (1977: 3), it cannot be totally instrumentalized in the present nor privatized as a contrivance for a particular, subjectively intended end.

RIVERBEND AND THE TECHNOLOGIZATION OF THE PRIVATE SPHERE

In the 1960s, Marcuse worries that technology has already translated universals and essences into concrete realities and facts: The one-dimensional, technological society "tends to reduce, and even absorb opposition (the qualitative difference!) in the realm of politics and higher culture, so it does in the instinctual sphere. The result is the atrophy of the mental organs for grasping the contradictions and the alternatives [...] It reflects the belief that the real is rational, and that the established system, in spite of everything, delivers the goods" (1964: 79). This "inauthenticity" or absence of alternatives, this technological absorption characterizes all walks of modern life and infiltrates private spaces as well. Marcuse is anxious that technology has succeeded in excising from things the possible world of spatial and temporal relations to which they are attached. "[W] ithout universality," he warns, "thought would be a private, non-committal affair" (1964: 138).[3] This worry has already been realized in Riverbend's descriptions of her experiences in the war in Iraq. Such a technologization of the private sphere coincides with Riverbend's return to it as a computer expert, blending the inside into the outside, the housewife into the worker. As Marcuse fatefully predicts, *Baghdad Burning* documents how, as the private sphere is increasingly mediated into the technological system, technology is increasingly privatized under the control of "the masters of the apparatus" (1964: 166).

At the same time as *Baghdad Burning* is an experiential panorama of war, it is also a story of a professional woman who loses her job, and whose life then gets consumed in endless household chores; Riverbend gets "re-privatized." "Re-privatization" is an appropriation, by the ideologies of neoliberalism, of the symbolic structure of women's labor under industrialization. That is, under industrialization, the private sphere figured the "outside" to the public of production, civil society, and the state. The ideologies of neoliberalism capitalize on these symbolic and moral meanings of domestic labor for the purposes of bypassing the authority of the nation-state in regulative and governing processes. In this case, the return of women to the private sphere comes to replace the state as the main social organization in the wake of the national public sector's total destruction by imperialist forces.

This section presents *Baghdad Burning* as privatizing the public by "re-privatizing" women's work; like technology, the private sphere and its rituals serve as an automated tool to affirm the present by restoring its ordering. In a future section, I explore *Baghdad Burning* as "Enframing" the private, revealing its potential as already public and already past. Technologized, the private sphere becomes the science fiction of the present, what affirms the present by repeating it, but what at the same time proves the impossibility of its repetition, the present's fragility.

Much of the scholarship on new media in the Middle East focuses on issues of identity and empowerment in an era of globalization. According to these critics, new media gives voice and expression to the silenced, and this voice and expression disrupt the authority of the power structure. Such criticism does not, however, situate identity construction within the politics of privatization that globalization, along with its technologies, invites. Neither does it investigate the contradictions between the time of the new technologies (the time of the modern) and the time of the preservation of nature and culture that, such critics insinuate, is the mission of new media (the time of the archaic or the primitive created by the modern as endangered). For example, in a 1999 collection reprinted in 2003, Dale F. Eickelman and Jon Anderson celebrate new media as "fragmenting and contesting political and religious authority" (1), and in a 2005 volume, Fereshteh Nouraie-Simone cites Virginia Woolf in claiming new media as "a liberating territory of one's own" where users can "resist a traditionally imposed subordinate identity" (61) that would challenge both the legitimacy and coherence of the Iranian revolutionary regime. The following article also claims that "the Internet has eroded" the authority "of the family and the educational system" (Yamani, 81) and, as a result, has weakened the hold of the Saudi family on civil society. Such analyses make the Internet seem like a deus ex machina that will bring down governments in a single swoop or end patriarchy by speaking boldly and thereby restoring the natural core of identity. The savior seems always in the hardware. They also assume that the people and their media have spontaneous desires that emerge in self-expression, that self-expression itself is the expression of a culture that is asserting itself against death and desecration, and that the state and the public are in opposition to this self-assertion whereas technology is its friend and thus the friend of freedom. None of this gets explained: not how the technologies get distributed nor how the users of such technologies escape their mediation by the culture of the machine's production as they reach toward a "real" representation of their own culture. Rather, these analyses imply—like positivism or scientific thinking—that to describe the reality of the present gives the imperative to affirm it as the real, to celebrate the affirmation of the real as resistance to the distortions to the real that oppressions orchestrate, and to extend the present by describing it as a return to the really real, even if the real is only accessible through technologies.

In this vein, *Baghdad Burning* has been signaled within optimistic declarations of victories of the technological society, where, as Nadine Sinno reads it, Riverbend presents the non-terroristic side of Iraqi society, playing with language, and thereby challenging the media monopoly that glorifies the war by using a medium that proliferates "alternative producers" (131). Riverbend is evoked as contrary to media culture and its authority rather than as an embodiment of it. The blog "challenges the master narrative fabricated and disseminated by U.S. mainstream media through actively deconstructing the war rhetoric, using sarcasm as a means of ridiculing authority figures and the purported 'achievements' resulting from the regime change, recounting stories of the (otherwise) voiceless underdogs, exposing the underlying colonialist motives and repercussions of the invasion, and promoting global activism and transnational dialogue" (132). Riverbend, Sinno suggests, affirms her reality against its abstractions, commercializations, and misrepresentations, and thus resists colonialist oppression and appropriation (in her use of the colonialist media apparatus). Though it is possible to read the text in this by now stereotypical way, with Riverbend as the transparent representative of the pure reality of Iraqi women made voiceless—the victimized subaltern telling us about her various cultural differences and what they mean, her holidays, her religious views, the relations between the sexes in her country—and their struggle against the colonialist state, Riverbend herself blocks this reading, giving few details about her personal life,[4] no deep psychology or emotional conflict (except in her frustration against "the political process"), expressing mild interest in religion and a belief in God without identifying herself through faith, not revealing herself through romance or sexual intrigue, and labeling herself "anonymous" (2005; 21). Rather than calling into play a deep consciousness outside of the administered totality, a character, a self within an interior soul, Riverbend's identifications are mostly electronic, extensions on her circuits.

Unlike other cultural translators of new media in the Middle East as cited above, Riverbend does not interpret the state or the public as her enemy, but rather the occupation. That is, the privatization of identity, or its separation from the state and the public as private culture—is not the answer to oppression but its catalyst. Offering a course in the human cost of war from the humanistic "pen" of the enemy, Riverbend does not present her cultural practices as a redemptive alternative[5] or as a qualitative or temporal difference. Rather, Riverbend constructs herself as a node in a global public policy debate: She discusses with her invisible interlocutors what the new government should look like, who should be involved in deciding, how should populations get represented, what part religion plays, and what should or should not be the role of the United States. She is engaged in a campaign of clearing up misinformation on the part of some of her U.S. correspondents, but also of learning from others. Her dominant tone, even when ranting, is ironic. One of her favorite targets, for example, is Ahmed Chalabi,[6] whom she frequently depicts as a clown or a circus animal: "A circus-themed gala, perhaps, where Bremer can play the ring-master and Chalabi can jump through red, white, and blue hoops to mark this historical day" (2005: 45). Or, when Donald Rumsfeld announces that there is no chaos in Iraq, she responds with "heaping colorful, bilingual insults on Rumsfeld's head (hope the doves crap on him)" (2005: 51), and when, just a day later, Rumsfeld compares Baghdad to Chicago, she retorts, "Wow. This guy is funny [...] What he actually should have said was, 'It's like Chicago, during the 1920s, when Al Capone was running it'" (2005: 52). Spoofing the Oscars, she nominates George W. Bush for "Best Actor" "for his convincing portrayal as the world's first mentally challenged president" (2006: 180) and Condoleezza Rice for her performance in "Viva Iran!" She awards honorable mention to Bush's speech writers for "writing scripts to make George W. Bush sound/look not great, not even good—but passable" and writing "speeches using words with a maximum of two syllables" (2006: 182). In post after post, she continues, with popular culture references and allusions to the depth of the leaders' incompetence, to expose their decisions as tragically ridiculous. Such irony works not as critique—that is, as showing the limits of the applied logic, using reason to make visible argumentative and factual mistakes or alternatives—but rather through pushing a statement to its extreme, affirming its content by extending its sense. Rather than suggesting alternatives or posing an opposing possibility or a new argument, irony melds opposites together through superimposition, over-the-top affirmation, and mocking agreement, or pastiche.

Rather than celebrating the privatization of culture, *Baghdad Burning* stages a process of developing identity through public involvement, pushing against the forces of privatization that want to construct private identities in order to capitalize on them. Riverbend's critique of privatization is nested within her account of what happens to women and their work as a result of the invasion. At the same time as *Baghdad Burning* is an experiential panorama of a war without end, it is also a story of a professional woman who loses her job, and whose life then gets consumed in endless household chores: Riverbend gets "re-privatized." At the age of twenty-four (at the start), Riverbend becomes a host of the private sphere, not permitted to leave without at least two male chaperones, and this restriction she shares, not only because of the lack of public security, kidnappings, assassinations, street explosions, and militias,[7] but also because of a cultural transformation induced by the occupation; modern identities were remade into the primitive, the savage, the backward, the private, and the irrational. "Before the war," she notes in her entry of August 23, 2003, "around 50% of the college students were females, and over 50% of the working force was composed of women. Not so anymore. We are seeing an increase of fundamentalism in Iraq which is terrifying" (2005: 17).[8] Writing in English, addressing herself often to a U.S. audience, part of Riverbend's mission is to disassociate Iraq from Western fantasies of its technological archaism[9] and to debunk parallel mythologies of Middle Eastern exoticism, particularly in the form of a backward-looking indigenous cultural abuse of women. "([...W]e had equal salaries!)," she describes Iraqi women before the occupation. "We made up over 50% of the working force. We were doctors, lawyers, nurses, teachers, professors, deans, architects, programmers, and more. We came and went as we pleased" (2005: 22). Now, however, "My 14-year-old cousin (a straight-A student)," she continues, in a litany of such examples, "is going to have to repeat the year because her parents decided to keep her home since the occupation. Why? Because the Supreme Council of the Islamic Revolution in Iraq overtook an office next to her school and opened up a special 'bureau'" (2005: 17). Riverbend makes clear that the war is not the defeat of sexism and of the exclusion of women (as many of the war's U.S. defenders claimed) but rather the catalyst to new forms of sexism connected to the privatization of women's work.

Before the war, Riverbend worked as a programmer/network administrator for an Iraqi database/software company. After the invasion, when she gets word that the company has continued operations, she insists on returning. Accompanied by two male bodyguards, she braves the streets, cracked under the weight of U.S. tanks, and enters her old office—where the electricity had been cut—with great anticipation, only to discover that "I was one of the only females" (2005: 23). Approaching her department director, she reads on his face an expression that tells her "females weren't welcome right now—especially females who 'couldn't be protected'" (2005: 24), and he sends her home. "I'm one of the lucky ones" (2005: 24), she concludes, as she tells of Henna Aziz, an electrical engineer who was assassinated in front of her family because she refused to stop working when her country needed her expertise. "How are females supposed to be out there helping to build society or even make a decent contribution," she remarks, "when they suddenly seem to be the #1 target?" (2005: 68). Women's seclusion in the private sphere—through religious fundamentalism, violence, or the imposition of outside labor practices and economic demands—crushes the idea of the public that was made possible in women's participation.

Baghdad Burning depicts the private sphere as a site of technological breakdown. The constant failures of technology make Riverbend's house seem like a workshop, as the day-to-day repetitions of family ritual are impeded and then work begins in order to put them back in order. The private sphere has the function of restoring routine and modernity against the crises to the everyday that the war continually inflicts: The water stops coming through the tap, so they fill the water tank on the roof, carrying pails of cold hose water up the stairs; or the electricity gets cut, and they wake up at 2 a.m. to wash the clothes, during the brief return of the current—"reality is a washer, clanging away at 2:30 a.m. because you don't know when there'll be electricity again" (2005: 197). The time comes for the holiday Eid, with its ritualistic housecleaning (2005: 148), or the carpets need to be cleaned and stored for summer (2006: 82), despite the shortages; or "the furniture is all covered with a light film of orangish dirt, the windows are grimy, and the garden, driveway and trees all look like they have recently emerged from a sea of dust. We spend the days after such storms washing, wiping, polishing and beating dust out of the house" (2006: 93). With rituals out of place and habits disrupted, Riverbend describes the privatization of everyday life and the return of the primitive as alienation: "We are no longer safe in our own homes—everything now belongs to someone else. I can't see the future at this point [...] It's like trying to find your way out of a nightmare" (2005: 8).

To restore the (modern) present, Riverbend portrays daily life during war and occupation as a constant attempt to make household technologies functional despite their constant crashing, or to substitute human acts for technological automation, so that human acts take on the automation of the failed technologies. She does not achieve lasting success. Riverbend, with her family, washes clothes when water is only sporadically available through the tap; fills empty bottles with water in preparation for the next water stoppage; vacuums the house when electricity is rationed at two or four hours a day; fuels the generators when the lines at the gasoline station are four, or eight, or eighteen hours long; prepares meals when the refrigerator is down or when groceries cannot be delivered through road blocks or rubble; tries to get some sleep in the stifling summer when the air conditioner stops functioning, the ceiling fan is not working, and it is too dangerous to sleep on the roof; blogs, even when the Internet connection is available only at night; and then does this all again, when the clothes get dirty again, or fuel runs out again. The repetitions of daily routine life in the private sphere also reflect the annualization of rituals—the continuance of the yearly cultural rituals, from Ramadan to Eid and back, with their family visitations, phone calls, and traditional dishes (at one point, Riverbend starts to exchange recipes over her blog (2005: 130–131))—these practices get disrupted by curfews, road detours, gasoline rationing (in a country, Riverbend points out, that is rich with oil), car bombings, and threats of violence. The private sphere is endangered by the deprivations of war, but, more fundamentally, also by the kidnappings, killings, street explosions, and security raids, both U.S. and Iraqi, where family members are removed or disappeared, and all semblance of order or attempts at restoration get suspended in searching for them: a traumatized young woman's mother and three brothers are captured by authorities, interrogated, beaten, and held in custody, and a customary visit to a sick friend's house then turns into a conversation about what interventions need to be made to bring back the family (2005: 234–235). A cousin's husband disappears while driving his parents back home after the feast of Eid, and, with "[g]oing home no longer an option" (2005: 204), the family stops its daily routine to search for him, pay ransom for him, and await for his return. The purpose now is to re-establish the ritualistic order of time by re-establishing the private sphere as foundation, as protected against the outside. "Houses are no longer sacred...We can't sleep...We can't live...If you can't be safe in your own house, where can you be safe?" (2006: 175). The private sphere has come to seem mechanized, functional, its work rhythms and routines like a production line. Human acts have take on the automation of technologies, as well as their failures: the human is but an extension of the technological.

With its essential purpose to provide security for a culture at risk, the technologization of the everyday has the job of stopping time, of keeping the "is" as is. In "re-privatizing" women's work, Riverbend's private use of technology also privatizes the public sphere. The conflating of public and private life in the "re-privatization" of women's work affects, as well, any public engagement. The automation of daily home tasks even affects the outcome of the constitutional referendum in October 2005; it wipes out the public, quite literally. As Riverbend's neighbor tells her: "I don't have time or patience to read it [the draft constitution]. We're not getting water—the electricity has been terrible and Abu F. [her husband] hasn't been able to get gasoline for three days...And you want me to read the constitution?" (2006: 129). She emphasizes this by grabbing the paper out of Riverbend's hands and washing the wall with her copy of the Constitution; the most basic political acts have been privatized as women's work. Sure enough, "there isn't real public involvement" (2006: 130) in discussions of the referendum.

The technologization of the private sphere extends the private sphere indeterminately, blending it into the outside from which it is

meant, in liberalism, to be separated. As the inside is constantly bar-
raged in electrical failings and dry faucets, the outside is similarly
seeped in wreckage, blasting bombs, falling buildings, car explosions,
and infrastructural collapse. Like the private sphere, the technological devastation is met with a staunch effort to repair things by
privatizing them. In fact, repairing things means their privatization.
Riverbend recounts how her cousin, a bridge specialist working for
an Iraqi firm, was asked to calculate the cost of rebuilding the New
Diyala Bridge in Baghdad; although his estimate came to $300,000,
the contract was granted to an American company who made an estimate of $50,000,000 (2005: 35) (Riverbend compares this negatively
to the successful reconstruction efforts of Iraqi engineers after the
1991 Gulf War). "A few rich contractors are going to get richer,"
she laments, "Iraqi workers are going to be given a pittance and the
unemployed Iraqi public can stand on the sidelines and look at the
glamorous buildings being built by foreign companies [...This war]
is [...] about huge corporations that are going to make billions off
of reconstructing what was damaged during this war" (2005: 37).
The re-privatization of women's work, the production of unemployment, is made to seem like part of an effort by the multinationals to
grab jobs, productive forces, territories, and profits. As in the private
sphere, the destruction and reconstruction, the breaking and repairing of technologies, make the war seem caught in an endless cycle,
a repetition of the day-to-day of the occupation in private life. Like
the re-privatization of women and in parallel to it, the privatization
of Iraqi sovereignty, infrastructure, and public space makes the future
continuous with, framed in by, and, in fact, indeterminate from the
present.

HARAWAY AND THE END OF DIALECTICS

Twenty-seven years after Marcuse wrote *One-Dimensional Man*,
his classic study of technology, Donna Haraway, in "The Cyborg
Manifesto," describes a vastly altered technological universe, much
more in line, it seems, with Riverbend's. The world of technology
is no longer organized along nation-state lines or bordered territories. Instead, it fuses along on electronic circuitries and informational
nodes tied to corporate productivities.[10] There are no boundaries to
the reach of technology, spatially, temporally, or materially; technology has penetrated even into biology and consciousness and can
no longer be discerned from them. There is no longer a firm separation between the worker and the machine, or the possibility of

identifying the workers' interests against those of the machine, even essentially so. Time has flattened out, as have concepts flattened into particular empirical demonstrations or isolated information bits, and even essences and ideals that contradict have flattened into existing reality; fiction has collapsed into fact, imagination into experience, construction into organism, public into private, idealism into materialism, man and woman into the postgendered body of the cyborg. Potentialities appear as actual: The "cyborg is a condensed image of both imagination and material reality, the two joined centers structuring any possibility of historical transformation" (1991: 150). Instead of the negative ushering in a qualitative historical difference because it makes no sense in the present, as in Marcuse, Haraway's present, like Riverbend's, solidifies around blasphemy, or irony; in contrast to the ultimate resolving of contradictions that she identifies with dialectics,[11] irony for Haraway maintains "the tension of holding incompatible things together because both or all are necessary and true" (1991: 148). It would seem that the possibility of technology's essence, or the restoration of its technics, can no longer dislodge the present in its immediacy, no matter how irrational it appears.

Haraway's cyborg theory extends the present infinitely, and it does this—just as *Baghdad Burning* does this—through the extension of women's work or "women's experience" (1991: 149). Women's worlds highlight the structuring dynamics of microelectronics as well as biotechnology, new photographic imaging as well as ecosystems' management, communications technologies alongside practices of agriculture and energy industries. "The actual situation of women is their integration/exploitation into a world system of production/ reproduction and communication called the informatics of domination. The home, workplace, market, public arena, the body itself— all can be dispersed and interfaced in nearly infinite, polymorphous ways" (1991: 163). Instead of the private sphere becoming obsolete and abandoned as a historical form—as it is for Marcuse and Marx as well as becoming the hope of the early second-wave— it is absorbed and integrated in the total structure, where "the factory, home, and market are integrated on a new scale and [...] the places of women are crucial" (1991: 166). There is no longer an outside to work or working time; there are no longer class differences. Indeed, things have always been this way[12] even if arranged differently. The idea that we got here somehow from a place that was different is replaced with the idea that the difference of the historical past is nothing but a fiction that is one of the ideological components required, if rearranged, for the system to function. Irony here means that the site of women's oppression is also, simultaneously but not contradictorily, the site of alternative political affiliations, associations not based in biological or geographical identities, but in other forms of commonality and electronic connection that challenge exploitation even without ending it. Such "high-tech-facilitated social relations," though at times dominating and oppressing, can also lead to "effective progressive politics" (1991: 165). Cyborg systems take current forms of exploitation to an extreme intensity till they push into another form. This is what constitutes change. The political needs identities constituted through work, impoverishment, and technological emergence as what grants it identity and substance; it is an extension of exploitative systems. We have seen this in Derrida: The most dire pain is its own relief.[13]

The end of the private/public distinction continues to underlie descriptions of the present in Haraway's later work, where private and public have merged together into a new and productive corporate/governance combination that is also the site of oppression. In *Modest_Witness*, for example, biotechnological research has made markets that trade in human or animal cell tissue, patenting laboratory animals like OncoMouse™ that are used to target disease. Haraway compares this to slavery and the trademarking of life itself even while she extols it for its innovation, advances in scientific and pharmaceutical knowledge, and for creating fruitful new capacities for interconnectedness, genealogy, and category fusion, including mixing insides with outsides, natural origins with corporate productions, public and private, state and corporation: "From conception to fruition, [...] these millennial offspring required massive public spending, insulated from market forces, and major corporations' innovations in their previous practice. In the strongest possible sense, OncoMouse™ is a technological product whose natural habitat and evolutionary future are fully contained in that world-building space called the laboratory" (1997: 83). In *When Species Meet*, Haraway explores the marketing of pets and pet products as heralding new forms of labor and its exploitation, new forms of obedience that also "work their magic to build subjects for a world not so fiercely divided into outside and inside" (2008: 65). Analyzing a program on Animal Planet called *Cell Dogs*, where prisoners train dogs not only as house pets but also as therapy and assistance workers, she explains that such programs are lessons in discipline and subjection that are also outside of traditional categories and violent tropes of commodity-making. They forge kinlike connections between humans and others, based in intimate identifications, that are not caught up in the dichotomy between use value and exchange value, production and reproduction, or inside and outside.

In setting aside classifications of productivity based in an overlapping of private and public control, between oppression and its opposite, Haraway tries to find a new method of description that belies norming. The idea would be that any kind of judgment in relation to norms or ethical principles would imply an outside, a separation from ideology that would be required for this ideology to be reflected upon. Instead, Haraway's method of retooling fuses theory into descriptions of reality as corporatized, as public-private partnerships—as though describing this reality as what it is substituted for an explanation of why it is or what is the problem—and actually carries within itself its own theorization. She defends this by saying that she herself can only be an extension of the "what is": "Since I can't be outside ideology, I'll take that one, face-to-face and eyes open" (2008: 65). The question for Haraway parallels the one Amy Allen asks in a different context: "If we reject theoretically the source of resistance in a psychic domain that is said to precede or exceed the social, as we must, can we reformulate psychic resistance *in terms of the social* without that reformulation become a domestication or normalization?" (77). In other words, if autonomy and agency are deemed impossible because they are determinate social categories, is there any way of thinking resistance to the social or change from within it?

For Haraway as for Riverbend, there is no alternative to the technologized body; it is everywhere simultaneously, part corporate and part domestic, hopeful in its despairing. The cyborg is the possibility of everything as it already exists, as it can be discovered and then affirmed as what we already have and have had all along; the present has always existed, even if arranged or ordered variously, and even as it will be reordered eventually. In a gesture affirming the "as is," Haraway has abandoned the position of critique along with dialectics, as there is now no outside to the current system, just irony. Even systems' breakdowns are just rearrangements or new designs,[14] assemblies, disassemblies, and reassemblies. Words themselves, now "codings," blend together with their opposites without major disruptions or discomforts, but as synergies and circuit-breakage. Though the cyborg immerses us in the "intensification of insecurity," "cultural impoverishment," and the "failure of subsistence" (1991: 172), it also gives grounds for a "serious potential for challenging the rules of the game" (1991: 173), new "political imaginations" (1991: 174), "complex political-historical layerings" (1991: 174), and "a simultaneity of breakdowns that cracks the matrices of domination and opens geometric possibilities" (1991: 174). Political vagueness opens politics to variability that cannot be ground into binary struggles or determinisms. Cited out of feminist science fiction, such alternatives to "the public" are not concrete or clear since any identification would be "totalizing and imperialist"—descriptive terms from an older time of nation-states and empires but rearranged to mean referential determination. Such categorical precision, realism, and word definition could only represent a desire for a "perfectly true language" (1991: 173), a reconciliation and resolving of contradictions as in Haraway's reading of dialectics.

Haraway's cyborg relates to the world-disclosing function of the Heideggerian workshop. Heideggerian disclosures play the part of revealing the underlying abstract relationships that are more primordial, more basic than the division between subjects and objects or public and private. According to the world-disclosing logic of the Heideggerian workshop, taking up a piece of equipment that is lying around ready for use lets that piece of equipment concern itself with a "totality of involvements" (1962: 118), an understanding in relation to its unity with its surrounding world or global system, not separate from it and without boundaries from it, not inside or outside, not first or last within it.[15] That world then becomes visible: "The cyborg is our ontology; it gives us our politics" (1991: 150), says Haraway. The equipment gives access to the primordial essence which projects/anticipates itself through objects at work, just as the cyborg projects/anticipates "the tradition of racist, male-dominant capitalism; [...] the tradition of nature as resource for the productions of culture; [...] a border war" (1991: 150). Ironically, the cyborg also reveals itself as—simultaneously and without contradiction, primordially—a borderlessness, a "post-gender world" not defined through physical borders (like identities: racial, ethnic, gender, nation) set down by narratives of reproduction or biological origins, but technologically symbiotic, more primordial then the temporal and spatial boundaries of the subjects and objects it comprehends.

MARCUSE'S TECHNOLOGIZED PRIVATE SPHERE

It is tempting to leave it there: Marcuse was shortsighted in developing analytical paradigms through reference to nation-states and their industrialized work arrangements, welfare states, state-centered imperialism, Cold War bipolarism, and nuclear détente, and so in retrospect Haraway's prescience wins. Yet, unlike in Haraway, Riverbend's assimilation into a technological society does not mean that the essence and possibilities of technology have been exhausted in its present facticity. The privatization of production is not the final word.

Riverbend's private use of technology sets in motion a technological option that cannot be confined within the present, its violence, and its repetitions because the essence of technological use cannot be totally privatized, reduced to isolated incidence, or alienated from the discovery of its universal.

Unlike Haraway, who figures that the disappearance of the private sphere has already been completed, Marcuse, like Riverbend, wants to tell his story about modern technology as a story about how the disappearance of the private sphere as an opposition in or alternative to the present is still in process. Marcuse takes the controversial Marxian line that the present use of technology, once it is freed from its restrictions within the irrationality of the capitalist present, "sustains and consummates itself in the new society" (1964: 22). Technology can shed the values and value system that made its production, distribution, and exploitation rational, and carry itself forth as the harbinger of new, revolutionary social relationships. That is, Marcuse believes Marx that technology, even if developed in a profit-based society for profit-based applications, is itself neutral, and once removed from that society, once embedded in different relations of production, the technological apparatus would also alter, unleashing the new possibilities that were already inside of it. Rousing the possibility of a technology that would out-survive its own performative profit principle, Marcuse proclaims that "the completion of the technological reality would be not only the prerequisite, but also the rationale for *transcending* the technological reality" (1964: 231). The technological imagination, when internalized and alienated, fashions a world beyond technology's mechanizations in repressive power and resistant to it. "At the advanced stage of industrial civilization," as Riverbend's situation would exemplify, "scientific rationality, translated into political power, appears to be the decisive factor in the development of historical alternatives" (1964: 230). With their connection within the private sphere, free time, and the post-work society, such historical alternatives are, according to Marcuse, "feminized": "inasmuch as the 'male principle' has been the ruling mental and physical force, a free society would be the 'definite negation' of this principle—it would be a *female* society" (1972: 74–75). Women's link to the private sphere and its productive technologies forms into the public of the future. This happens because society under capitalism is irrational, forcing its potential into alienated private enclaves outside of the direction of production and divorced from social reality, reserving its energies for later use. The revolution would undo or reverse this alienation.

The problem is that this inner alternative of technology may be lost. Along with the proletariat and other manifestations of the negative, as a symptom of the "convergence of opposites" that underlies the one-dimensional society, present technology has been invading and absorbing the private sphere, cracking down on the development of historical alternatives that its private use, according to Marcuse, would release. Total mobilization takes shape as the " [...] invasion of the private household by the togetherness of public opinion; opening of the bedroom to the media of mass communication" (1964: 19). Marcuse worries that technology has "invaded the inner space of privacy and practically eliminated the possibility of that isolation in which the individual, thrown back on himself alone, can think and question and find" (1964: 244). The gradual disappearance of the proletariat matches up—lamentably, for Marcuse—with the gradual disappearance of domesticity, the division of labor, and its corollary private reflection. Like Adorno, Marcuse believed that the welfare state was succeeding in assimilating the proletariat into the interests of the productive forces: "Under the conditions of a rising standard of living," he writes in 1964, "non-conformity with the system itself appears to be socially useless" (1964: 2). Like Adorno and Habermas, too, Marcuse believed that the private sphere, like a working-class opposition, was becoming obsolete with the intensification of production under industrialization.

Marcuse's private sphere is thus "ghosted": always disappearing but continually present. Marcuse's blending of the logic of technology into the private sphere makes the concept of the private sphere something more than its particular appearance in any particular reality; that is, something not just actual but also essential. The positivistic thinking in which technology is embedded expels this ghostly philosophic thinking that recognizes things as concepts; that is, as abstractions that cannot be reduced to any particular empirical appearance. "The philosophic universe," Marcuse further elaborates, "thus continues to contain 'ghosts,' 'fictions,' and 'illusions' which may be more rational than their denial insomuch as they are concepts that recognize the limits and deceptions of the prevailing rationality" (1964: 186).[16]

MARCUSE AND FEMINISM

Marcuse was well aware that his analysis of private contemplation and autonomy as having a relationship with the private sphere—where it develops through socialization—pointed to a revolutionization of

women's lives and social roles. Of all the Frankfurt School thinkers, Herbert Marcuse took the most definitive stand in favor of the
feminist movement. "I believe," he announced in a 1974 lecture at
Stanford University, "the Women's Liberation Movement today is,
perhaps, the most important and potentially the most radical political movement that we have, even if the consciousness of this fact has
not yet penetrated the Movement as a whole" (2006: 147). Earlier
in 1972, he also asserted, "[T]he Women's Liberation Movement
becomes a radical force to the degree to which it transcends the
entire sphere of aggressive needs and performances, the entire social
organization and division of functions" (1972: 75). Such a radical
social transformation as Marcuse envisions would mean "the 'feminization' of the male," that is, "the decisive change in the instinctual
structure" (1972: 75). Unlike Habermas, who thought that the social
relations of the domestic sphere would reemerge within a specialized
communicational function that would check the excesses of purpo-
sive rationality in the systems of money and administrative power,
and unlike Adorno, who thought that the private would take form as
the negativity of the contemplative individual that would be immanent in aesthetics and philosophy, Marcuse saw that, after Hegel,
the values of the private sphere would reformulate sociologically as
the destructive force of immanent qualitative change still linked to
workers' liberation, or rather, the liberation from work: rebellion.
Women symbolized for Marcuse the freedom from work that the
future would usher in. The "feminine characteristics" of the emergent socialism would "activate aggressive energy against domination
and exploitation" (2006: 154), reducing "alienated labor and labor
time" for the "emancipation of the senses" (2006: 154) and becoming the new universal. For Marcuse, the essence of man—his Being
and his potential—is woman.

Marcuse, however, has had a mixed reception by feminist critics.
Some feminists see Marcuse as an ally. As Margaret Cerullo wrote
in the *New German Critique*, "I take Marcuse's serious engagement
with the feminist project both as a testament to his enormous historical openness, his refusal of political resignation, and also as a moving
gesture of respect and solidarity, which may turn out to be the most
important part of his legacy to the male Left in the United States
today" (21). Angela Davis—arguably one of the most inspiring and
admirable feminist philosophers of our time, and also Marcuse's student—lauded him for developing a new political vocabulary for the
1960s that "allowed many of us to understand the extent to which he
took seriously the charge of critical theory to develop interdisciplinary

approaches, anchored in the emancipatory promise of the philosophical tradition within which he worked, that would signal the possibility and need for transformative interventions in the real, social world" (43–44), which included the new social and cultural movements. Stanley Aronowitz agrees that "[Marcuse] came to understand the radical implications of contemporary feminism and also the salience of new social movements" (148). In the realm of queer studies, Kevin Floyd has suggested that Marcuse's revising of reification within the Marxist tradition gave gay and ultimately feminist activism expanded categories for politicizing the body through its various, contradictory objectifications, even nonprocreative ones.[17] Marcuse's conjoining "the erotic, the empirical, and the universal" (1994: 161) has led critic Shierry Weber Nicholsen to read women, in Marcusian philosophy, as, like in Adorno, "the absent other, a link that is mediated by the imagination as the locus in which subjectivity, sensuousness, and possibility co-exist" (1994: 160).

Some psychoanalytic feminist critics, however, have criticized Marcuse (as they have Habermas) for privileging ego psychology over object-relations psychology and intersubjectivity as the framework for his analysis, and therefore formulating emancipatory instinctual life in terms of isolated monads rather than social relationality.[18] Feminists have also faulted Marcuse for subordinating "the issue of gender to that of class," equating "patriarchy with class domination" (Horowitz, 126). Meanwhile, other feminist critics have read Marcuse as essentializing women. As Douglas Kellner points out, Marcuse

> was criticized by women within the feminist movement and others for essentializing gender difference, although he insisted the distinction was a historical product of Western society and not an essential gender difference. Women, he argued, possess a "feminine" nature qualitatively different from men because they have been frequently freed from repression in the workplace, brutality in the military, and competition in the public sphere. Hence, they developed characteristics which for Marcuse are the marks of an emancipated humanity. (2004: 92)

The traits of an emancipated humanity are archaically preconceived as those of women engaged in the work of the private sphere of the industrial age. Though Marcuse essentialized women's traits, he even more fundamentally essentialized the private sphere as the negative. Though historically obsolete like the proletariat, it is sustained even when the proletariat is not, infallible as a resurrected memory, the unrealized essence of an emancipated humanity.

The link in Marcuse's work between women and essence, however, is more complicated that such criticisms make it, because his idea of essence does not fall easily into conventional metaphysics. Remember, Marcuse borrows his treatment of essence from Heidegger's formulation that he borrows from the Greeks, where essence is the meaning that is contained in objects and that is released from objects through human activity, or work. Essence is what remains, ghostlike, after the object's immediate rational use, what exceeds its use, giving the object a meaning that is other, disclosing, different, and future to what its immediacy establishes, and ultimately denies its immediacy, cancels it out. The centrality of femininity in his vision of social revolution is therefore not related, says Marcuse, to motherhood or any kind of biological or matriarchal function, for "the image of the woman as mother is itself repressive; it transforms biological fact into an ethical and cultural value" (1972: 75). Marcuse's reading of woman is abstract, constructed, social rather than physical, and, like Riverbend's, "anonymous." Marcuse sees radicalism in the eroticism that has been sublimated into women's bodies by the social relations of capital and the division of labor. This erotic energy reified in her body has the potential of countering the aggressive needs and performances of the total structure not because of her biology, but because her sexuality has been objectified by the culture industry, giving access to a sensual aesthetic otherness. Women's ties to this sensual aesthetic, the potential of releasing the senses from their repression in work directives, indicates the presence of the new society within the old, currently in the form of its irrationality. Though essentializing the private sphere and women's work within it, Marcuse does not grind the private sphere down into a specific thing, a historical determination. Rather, Marcuse gives women and the private sphere the same structural standing as he gives technology, as a revelation of essence that is not yet materialized. By releasing the senses, technology in the form of the "new science" "gives word and tone and image to that which is silent, distorted, suppressed in the established reality" (1972: 96), outside of the order of work, irrationalized.

Marcuse's merging of women's structural position with that of technology brings into play a central contradiction in Marcuse's work: The technological forces that dominate nature and human nature, partly by objectifying and eroticizing women as the irrational, also construct a new nature that would harmonize within the new society.[19] As C. Fred Alford notes, "The new science is rhetoric designed to soften Marcuse's otherwise terribly harsh [...] goal of the complete subordination of nature to human purposes. The new science is, in a sense, an ideology. It grants the aura of reconciliation with nature to what is actually projected to be humanity's final victory over it" (1985: 64). The symbolic fusing of technology's new science with women and the private sphere explains why feminist critics have objected to the objectification of women in Marcuse's work, as well as appreciated Marcuse's placement of women and the private sphere as the starting point of a rich vocabulary of liberation within the irrational organization of capital and as the structural marker of liberation in a postwork, postscarcity society.

PHILOSOPHY AND THE PRIVATE SPHERE

In much of Marcuse's philosophical work, in his work on aesthetics,[20] as well as in his various treatments of rebellion and liberation, the private sphere is a placeholder for the negative; it symbolically inhabits the place of a history, a temporal sense of qualitative difference in the future, of a present that can be left behind by the revelation of its own essence. Describing the effects of artistic practice within bourgeois society, he states in *The Aesthetic Dimension*: "The 'flight into inwardness' and the insistence on a private sphere may well serve as bulwarks against a society which administers all dimensions of human existence" (1978:38). Reading Freud in *Eros and Civilization*, Marcuse analyzes the historical repression of the private sphere as coterminous with the sublimation of the erotic unconscious into the performance principle, or work. The superego manipulates the "coordination of the private and public existence" (1955: 94), mechanizing the absorption of private consciousness into alienated labor, impersonal associations, and alienated consumption practices.,[21] "The independent family enterprise and, subsequently, the independent personal enterprise cease to be the units of the social system; they are being absorbed into large-scale impersonal groupings and associations" (1955: 96). The pleasure principle would eventually "express rebellion against the subjugation of sexuality" (1955: 49) through a "polymorphous perversity," which would burst out of the order of procreation and all of the institutions that used to keep it in place, diverting eroticism from its sublimation into work.

Marcuse understood the "private" of the industrial age as supplementing a long tradition of philosophical development of freedom and autonomy dating from Lutherism and coming to fruition in the bourgeois political theory of the state; the private sphere embodies the historical trajectory of autonomy and freedom in the philosophical tradition. For Marcuse, the problem of the "private" throughout this tradition was how to make sense of a private freedom against the backdrop of social unfreedom. Each phase of this process had a corresponding phase of private sphere development, from the Calvinists, who set up families under the imperative of absolute obedience to the father with the threat of punishment in the name of God's will, to the Hegelian matrix, where the family served as the "'ethical' root of the state" (1972: 61), preparing individual subjects for identification with institutions, objective morality, and the general community, as well as upholding the communal agreement of abstract legality over property.

Marcuse is basing his ideals about social freedom on early pre-bourgeois ideas about individual freedom, or privacy. Christianity had a concept of humanity as internally free—a *"homo privatus"*—in preparation for a transcendent future, but born into a social community over which it had no authority.[22] Transcendental freedom could coexist with social unfreedom, as separate. On the other hand, Marcuse says that bourgeois thought required the concept of the free individual that Christianity had constructed, along with a "'calculating' character" (1972: 10) that had some power of influence through its actions in the external world as well as a right to property. Kant's job, then, was to theorize a private subjective world in correspondence with an objective empirical world, but without any real effect on it. Borrowing from Christianity its concept of the autonomous individual, Kant had to conceive of a private freedom that would have a public character. Even though, Marcuse points out, in Kant "reason is limited to an inner realm of the mind and is made powerless over 'things-in-themselves'" (2000: 48), his philosophy sets the course by hinting at thinking as "an activity by which the antagonism between subject and object is produced and simultaneously overcome" (2000: 48). Like Christian freedom, this freedom would be free from all empirical determinants and yet would be connected to a general community.[23] The division between internal freedom and external unfreedom materialized, for Marcuse, as the division of labor: "[T]he world," he explains, "is split in half: two relatively self-enclosed spheres are set up and freedom and unfreedom as totalities divided between them in such a way that one sphere is wholly a realm of freedom and the other wholly a realm of unfreedom" (1972: 7–8). As Marcuse traces the history of German idealism, the private consciousness of early Christianity turns into the form of the state in Hegel, the state becoming the self-realization in History that early Christianity attributed to transcendence. Later in Marx, the idea of negativity in proletariat consciousness evolves from pre-bourgeois thinking on separation of conscience: the internalization of consciousness, the ability of social consciousness (like the private sphere) not to be contained by the social relations that engendered it.

THE SPECTER HAUNTING RIVERBEND'S PRIVATE SPHERE

Whereas Haraway has constructed a vision of the world in which the distinction between public and private—between autonomous and social will—plays no part, Marcuse understands the private sphere as a site of historical contention and struggle with the social, similar to autonomy and freedom in idealist philosophies. Haraway abandons the inner, private freedom that idealism poses against social unfreedom for a social vision where the socialized individual is infused with the totality of social relations, without borders between them. On the other hand, adopting Marx's observation that struggle in a capitalist system is rooted in the struggle between technologization and the working day, the private sphere, for Marcuse, represents a reduction in the time of work—at least, of remunerated work— that Marcuse understands as man's historical essence, his autonomy. Within Marcuse's philosophical apparatus, the private sphere assumes a different form in each historical phase.

Consequently, Riverbend's private sphere resembles Marcuse's only in its bare outlines. In fact, in some senses, Riverbend's situation reverses the situation described through Marcuse's private sphere without necessarily countering Marcuse's idea that the private sphere's resistance to conceptualization gives it historical force. Rather than a separation from work, Riverbend's private sphere is a place where work continues, but work of a different sort. In *Baghdad Burning*, nonwork is more exploitative than work, because nonwork (or unemployment) indicates a world owned and controlled by others elsewhere, in their own spheres of private appropriation. In Riverbend's view, her continued work in the private sphere refutes colonialist exploitation through privatization. The private sphere is a site for practices of public sovereignty.

The idea that work linked to technology can be creative and therefore lead to fulfillment and strong identity has been elaborated within strands of German feminism influenced by Marcuse and the Frankfurt School thinkers: Technology in advanced capitalist societies, feminist social critic Frigg Haug ethnographically details, can finally allow for a type of work that resembles what Marcuse means by nonwork. Haug criticizes post-Marxist philosophies: "Behind such post-Marxists positions lurks the question of whether human development and happiness can be made a real possibility, even though the production of material life is still confined within systems of domination. In that event liberation would be restricted to certain aspects of life" (106). Post-Marxism projects that any form of work is a form of exploitation, and only a form of exploitation, leading to the conclusion that liberation can only happen outside of social productivity and therefore can only ever be partial. Haug thinks, in contrast to post-Marxism, that frameworks for nonalienated and nonmarketed labor currently restricted to the private sphere could be blended back into working life.[24] In addition, Haug finds that Marx's sense of a proletariat consciousness developing from work—especially independent, creative work like the kind technology can foreground—means creating the potential for action through work in the world rather than conceiving work as just a mechanism for extending exploitation, dehumanization, or dispossession. The creativity of work could develop into a crucial site of autonomy. The women programmers Haug interviews confess that "[i]n their work the fascination of the computers gives the programmers a kind of self-determination within the general system of determination by others" (124). Work, she says, gives them autonomy over their time, self-direction, a right to control their thought and their time in the workday rather than letting it be controlled by others.

In connection with Haug, Riverbend believes that exploitation in work takes a particular form: undermining the possibilities of becoming independent from the determinations of rationalized, privatizing capital. Therefore, not all work is equally exploitative. As with Haug's informants, Riverbend asserts claims over her own time as self-determination in the cultural and familial routines of the private sphere. The occupation has its own time: "You get to the point during extended air raids where you lose track of the days. You lose track of time. The week stops being Friday, Saturday, Sunday, etc. The days stop being about hours. You begin to measure time with the number of bombs that fell, the number of minutes the terror lasted and the number of times you wake up in the middle of the night to the sound of gunfire and explosions" (2006: 68). Or: "There were days when we lost track of time and began counting not hours and minutes, but explosions. We stopped referring to the date and began saying things like, 'The last time we saw my uncle was'" (2005: 180). Or, a street explosion "had warped me back a whole year and we would have to relive this last year of our life over and over again" (2005: 243). The war claims title to its narratives on certain events; on April 9, 2004, for example, Riverbend remembers that day a year before, when Bush announced the triumphant end of the war, unleashing a torrent of violence, massacres, looting, bomb blasts, and a refugee crisis.

For Riverbend, her work the private sphere—the rituals, routines, and family orders—blocks the appropriation of time by others, its alienation. Dinner or a TV show might be interrupted, for example, by an electricity outage or a threat of a raid; everybody gets up to hide the heritage jewelry, or to check to see that others are accounted for, as the family tries to conclude the narrative moment on its own terms rather than wait for the invading army or national police force to do it. Or the war's disruptions of sleep make the war's world somnambulant and dreamlike. Housework claims back the time that the occupation wants to control in its labeling of events by restoring the time of the everyday: "I have spent the last two days ruminating the political situation and...washing the roof," Riverbend announces. "While the two activities are very different, they do share one thing in common—the roof, and political situation, are both a mess" (2005: 270). Housework can be compared to living under laws that you yourself author, Riverbend proposes. Maintaining the private sphere does more than just affirm the private sphere as a fact that needs securing, as an actuality, a fact, or a hierarchy of value; it also marks an outside, an alternative, contextualized, self-determining, and nondispossessed temporality distinct from the occupation's framing of time, event, and object.

Riverbend's private sphere chores reference not just an immediate group of real-life intimates, but also an invisible audience. This ghostly presence, both inside the house and determinately outside, appears in the frame as Riverbend addresses them—in her exchange of impressions, interpretations, and information—as part of her educational circle, and these are, importantly, not national but excessive to the nation. They also resist the realist tendencies of blog reporting or war witnessing conventions, inserting a kind of gothic glow, as though the war narrative itself would not fit into the categories of the real in war narration. Though the discussion focuses on the political fate of Iraq, it alludes to still bigger conceptual questions, like how to set up a democratic system and how imperialism contradicts those efforts. As formative thought on what might constitute the independent citizen of the future democracy, Riverbend's online informational public offerings form a continuity with her independent household routines: marking holidays from year-to-year; discussing news stories; chronicling the coordination of chores; trying to clean up, sort through, and put in place the disorderly rationality of the political situation;[25]

describing the internal adjustment of household technologies to the new external regimes of scarcity and control.

Riverbend's Internet involvements implicate her private sphere as part of an educational mission, mediating her internal context with absent others to produce knowledge outside of official-speak, referring to the unrealized potential of Iraqi politics. She comments on blogs by U.S. soldiers (2005: 59–61), gives a lesson on private contractors (2005: 78–79), and corrects mistakes in the *New York Times* about the Iraqi tribal structure (2005: 87) or about the veil (2005: 92). Answering some of the criticisms from her U.S. interlocutors, she invites them inside to see outside the standard tropes: "I wish every person who emails me supporting the war, safe behind their computer, secure in their narrow mind and fixed views, could actually come and experience the war live. I wish they could spend just 24 hours in Baghdad today and hear Mark Kimmett[26] [*sic*] talk about the death of 700 'insurgents' like it was a proud day for Americans everywhere" (2005: 254). Sometimes the computer speaks back to her as "anonymous" or the "absent other": "I avoid looking at the computer because it sometimes seems to look back at me rebukingly" (2005: 255). The computer gives a sense of otherwordliness that exceeds the present.

Through the computer screen, these ghostly forms or unreal essences,[27] as outsiders, reveal the internal meaning of the private sphere and its practices as more fundamental, more radical and conceptual, than its actualizations in the present. Riverbend's educational conversations with the absent others have a counterpart within what I would identify as the critical center of the trajectory of her narrative: This is a story told by another, and she reports it as a "haunting" (2005: 210). During a trip to Amiriyah, Riverbend tours a bomb shelter. To this shelter, Riverbend attributes similar structural meaning as a home, its family members gathered in ritual celebration.. The shelter, however, was blasted to pieces by a "precision" bomb during the festival celebration of Eid in 1991, locking 400 women and children inside as fire and boiling water rose and killed them. Riverbend later learns that the woman who leads the tour of the shelter—and who refuses to leave—had lost all of her eight children in the tragedy: She had exited the shelter for an instant during the festival to retrieve food and clothing at her house, and while she was running back, the missile hit.

> She had watched the corpses dragged out for days and days and refused to believe they were all gone for months after. She hadn't left

the shelter since—it had become her home. She pointed to the vague
ghosts of bodies stuck to the concrete on the walls and ground and the
worst one to look at was that of a mother, holding a child to her breast,
like she was trying to protect it or save it. (2005: 211–212)

This private sphere is destroyed. Yet, it still persists in the form of
ghostly, absent others traced onto a screen, witnessing from elsewhere,
in intense engagement. Riverbend's descriptions of her everyday life—
the constant destruction of everyday life in the private sphere, and its
just as constant, extensive, and persistent systems of repair—suggest
that the precision bombing of Amiriyah is repeating itself constantly,
creating ghosts on the wall every day. Like the mother's constant
return to the site of the family gathering, Riverbend's obsessions with
house chores, claiming back time, surviving, and restoring order take
on the function of restoring the ritualized private sphere. This private
sphere provides a communicational setting not totally identified with
the war, not totally appropriable by it, even as it borrows the technologies of the war. As it is destroyed by the technologies of the profit-
seekers and war instigators, these same technologies allow the survival
of a non-instrumentalizable communicational form as a remainder. In
Riverbend's private sphere, the ghosts on the wall are disembodied
and detached contributors to a textual scenario, participating spectators beyond definition or location, who come into existence through
technological use. Against the technologies of imperialism and their
destructive privatizations, the private sphere has revealed its authentic
potential as the public's "Being-with-others." In the face of the privatization of the industry in which she worked and the privatization of
her job, Riverbend herself creates a public alternative in the private
sphere's autonomous time.

The technologization of Riverbend's private sphere at first seems
like an affirmation of the present: The disruptions to the repetition of
everyday practices caused by the war lead to a constant effort to repair
what was broken in order to restore a private order that seems, regres-
sively, to be secluding women and offering up the nation for the profit
of others. This perspective shares with Haraway's a confirmation that
survival demands an affirmation and reconstruction of the facts "as
is," and an imperative to rearrange the facts rather than to change
them. Yet, Riverbend's work in the private sphere also reveals itself
through an autonomous wired world populated with absent others.
In this instance, as an exchange of perceptions, the technologized
private sphere cannot be walled in and turned into a thing for sale.
In other words, the world concept to which it gives rise cannot be

reduced to its concrete factuality: It reveals a future that uses technologies differently, as mechanisms of rational argument, intersubjective recognition, reflection, and autonomous critique rather than as tools of appropriation, dispossession, and destruction. The private sphere that Riverbend envisions offers her the autonomy from the social necessary for social criticism, an autonomy prepared by the social technologies of the present, and released by them, but not confined to them. Like Marcuse's, Riverbend's privatizing private sphere exists as an actual exploited labor form to be differentiated from a private sphere that reveals itself essentially as a ghostlike sovereign, public future.

CONCLUSION

Feminist Theory in Pursuit of the Public addresses how the concept of the private sphere of industrial labor persists within the defense for global regimes of privatization. Though the private sphere is an archaic formation, it continues to evoke the liberal tradition in order to create a sense of separation, for certain practices, away from legal frameworks, oversight, regulation, and public interventions. Even with the distinction between the home and the workplace diminishing, with the unsustainability of the traditional family and a general awareness of the irrationality of the nuclear organization of the family within the current economic organization, the ideology of the private sphere lives on in the re-privatization of women's labor. This takes the form, for example, of microfinance, which grants debt financing to women with home businesses that manufacture commodities or services by employing traditional family and community structures.

The symbolic trajectory of the private has moved from the industrial division of labor to underlie the structure of contemporary fashions of corporate privatization and "re-privatization", as well as a rhetorical attack on all things public: claims of the public sphere's obsolescence, defunding of public education at all levels, the end of welfare, the end of development, the righteous anger arising violently against taxation, deregulation of private business and financial institutions, the transfer of public money to bail out large corporations and financial companies, the attack on unions, the atomization of production in the form of microenterprise, outsourcing, and decentralization. As much as second-wave feminism wanted to politicize the private sphere, now the private has replaced the public, making it more susceptible to depoliticization, as much of the formerly public right is being privatized.

The first chapter of *Feminist Theory in Pursuit of the Public* presented the need for feminism to develop a theory of the public sphere to counter the privatization of everything that the constant return to an outdated private sphere evokes. With some of feminism's roots in liberalism, many of popular culture's renditions of feminism use some of the premises of the early second wave to build consensus around privatization policies. Without a theory of the public sphere, this chapter argues, feminism loses its investments in universalisms and autonomies, including its discourses of human emancipation, revolution, deliberation, open-ended learning, and a qualitatively different future. Also, without a theory of the public sphere, second-wave feminism is leaving the hard critique it performed on the private sphere open to appropriation for contrary interventions. The liberation of women in particular (but humanity in general), which second-wave feminism professed would come about with women's liberation from the private sphere, has been reversed: Now liberation takes the form—within discourses of "empowerment" and the like—of liberation not from the private sphere, as feminism would have it, but rather into the private sphere and away from the state, the public sector, and the public sphere, and women's traditional disassociation from the public sphere is being strewn about discursively and triumphantly as the moral core of privatization advocacy and market liberalization. This leaves women not liberated but ever more accessible to current regimes of exploitation, without recourse.

Feminist Theory in Pursuit of the Public went on to show how post-structuralism's project of abandoning or collapsing the public/private split has resulted, more often than not, in imaginings of the world as fully privatized. This tendency takes the form of the discarding of concepts and intersubjective debates as too general, conforming, imposing, rational, or external in favor of an injunction for the particular, contingent, empirical, real, concrete, or factual. It gives up on the Enlightenment and its master narratives, which it interprets as all equally teleological, abstract, or deterministic, in its preference for experience, immanence, affirmation, positivism, realism, ordinary language, and immediacy, thereby—most fundamentally—cutting out consideration of the differences between the "is" of the present and the "ought" that breaks the untenable present of exploitation from within and ensures the future's difference. The framing of feminism through experience and sensuousness as against the conceptual means the end of seeing history as a set of contradictions—as essences the stretch beyond each concretization, as the movement of general trends that explode up against their particular applications—and the beginning of seeing history as an infinite extension of the timeless present, no matter what kinds of horror that present propagates.

Turning to the philosophies of the Frankfurt School, *Feminist Theory in Pursuit of the Public* starts the work of rethematizing the public as other than an opposition to the private. From Habermas to Adorno and Marcuse, the Frankfurt School thinkers understood the private sphere of industrial capitalism as a symbolic structure that dissents from the present in its many manifestations: these thinkers all consider the private sphere as the space where public communication develops, the space of a socialization or educational process from where oppositional and autonomous public spheres can emerge. In other words, the communicational practices of the private sphere cannot be totally absorbed within the administrative state or its culture, but always leaves a resistant remainder that cannot be instrumentalized, and that this resistant remainder is always in danger of disappearing.

The Frankfurt School thinkers need to be considered as products of a particular historical moment, when production could still be thought about in national terms and industrialization had still to be eclipsed by transnational networks and circuits of production. They were responding to a moment when imperialism still in some sense meant that stronger states were overtaking and controlling weaker ones, when the politics of states were still dominant at least ideologically and seemed in control of arms production and distribution, rather than to a time like now when corporations demand direct access to labor and consumer markets beyond national borders, by skirting states, and when non-state actors seemed to be controlling conventional and some non-conventional weapons' markets and circulations. Yet, the Frankfurt School's insights into how working people would identify with the interests of the powerful, even against their own interests, set agendas for understanding what would become today's consumer society. They were also able to predict that consumption rather than production would become the strongest paradigm for constructing identities. Much of their warnings about this flattening out of concepts and collapse of opposites was part of a harsh critique of scientific recourse to positivism and factualism and the concurrent infiltration of realist, positivistic thinking into all walks of life, from politics (in the form of what we now call "biopolitics," or the condensing of "interest" into "population" or "identity") to education (which we see today in the imperative to measure things by test scores, to make decisions about school "success" or "failure" and teacher "merit" or "failure" based on test scores, and the consequent reduction of what can be taught in school to bits of knowledge that can be measured and quantified, like capital and commodities) and the humanities (in the now prevalent trends of historicism, the emphasis on field expertise defined for the most part in terms of period and regional or national origin, and the ethnographic or sociological turn).

Most important for the context of this study, the focus on nations, the context of the Cold War, and the reliance on the private/public divide of industrial labor gave the Frankfurt School a theoretical terminology for conceiving *an opposition*, an outside to a scientific thinking that forces the flattening out of the present and the disintegration of possibility into the solidity of what exists. This is what is missing in the theoretical terminology most prevalent in cultural and literary studies now. One must remember, too, that from post–World War II through the end of the Vietnam war, when most of the Frankfurt School texts analyzed in this book were written, the nation was starting to dissolve as the primary productive unit, and the private/public distinction was already being seriously challenged by the sexual revolution, as Marcuse points out, as well as by other cultural and economic trends, including feminism. So, the Frankfurt School's references to the private sphere were already antiquated, as were many of their other cultural references (for example, the references to silent cinema in "The Culture Industry"). In the readings of the Frankfurt School, the private sphere was already a reference to something gone, something past, and as such, it was a reference to temporalization and history: It opened the possibility of history in the present, as a break with the present.

Habermas imagines a public sphere out of the historicization of the private sphere and its socialization. In this, the public sphere becomes a site of transcendence, a place of autonomy, because it evolves from the private sphere that is immersed in the pedagogical practices of everyday life, in an argument that cannot resolve. As such, the public sphere is a private sphere that can infinitely expand because it is engaged with other subjects and learning processes, where decisions are always interrupted and reconceived within a spectrum of others' commitments, perspectives, worldviews, and involvements. Decisions are not based in identities, but neither do they disregard identities, as identities are reformed through arguing, and pluralism is not an excuse for cultural relativism or tolerance but rather an ongoing interaction of viewpoints that intersect, variously contradicting and agreeing, expanding through the knowledge of the other. Dialogue stands in the place of the general concept that is constantly reflecting on itself and revising itself in reference to its particular applications, and so dialogue must transcend its realization in the present. Habermas gives a sense of how the private sphere has moved through historical time that does not necessarily identify it with an autonomy *from* the public—or privatization—as it appears in the liberal tradition of political thinking and in free market liberalism, but rather frames it as the autonomy *of* the public, in pedagogical terms.

The effects and possibilities of such a Habermasian public sphere have become evident in situations of total destruction of the traditional public sphere in the state, which I have discussed in this book through analytical readings of Jean Said Makdisi's *Beirut Fragments* and Riverbend's *Baghdad Burning*. Where state and public institutions are devastated by extreme outbreaks of violence, corporate accumulation of profits and power, and global force, women, their work, and their civil societies seem to revert to seclusion in the private sphere, to be "re-privatized." Within the private sphere, however, basic elements of public life come to the fore, no longer under the shadow of entrenched power structures or solid state and institutional formations. Not based in the experience or knowledge of particularized identities, these basic elements of public life show women working in the seclusion of the private sphere, but communicating in ways that disrupt the traditional communications of the private sphere and connect with others through the unknown, or through a speculative sense of a radically different future. Rather than a return to a surpassed economic history of work privatization and domestication, this communication makes the private sphere into the possibility of an opening for the public. However, as stories are told of these violent eruptions or market expansions that obliterate the institutions of state, such private forms of public life are marginalized, or irrationalized. This situation needs to be reversed.

I am not nostalgically advocating here a return to the social relations that operated during an industrial era. Rather, I am concerned that the public sphere, as well as the personages called citizens who reside in it, have come to seem increasingly fantastical, unimaginable, impossible, quaint, passé, and out of range at a historical moment when their absence makes us most vulnerable, politically and economically. Yet, even as public functions are increasingly passing into private hands, even as the places where we are accustomed to seeing public interventions increasingly take shape within a logic of private life for private accumulation, there persists a sense of the public as a site of deliberation and communication that disrupts and transcends the present. As global privatization regimes continue to reference the private sphere of industrial production in order to wall off their markets from regulatory authority or public interventions, they also maintain the sense of a surviving public that is immanent within these references, and they keep telling its stories. Such stories provide slight but inextinguishable glimpses of a feminist public sphere still arriving.

Notes

Introduction

1. "This process included generalizing the morality attributed to middle-class women to all women, translating the discrepancy between what one now has and what one could acquire into a psychological narrative of personal development, and subsuming the economic rewards that capitalism seemed to promise into the emotional rewards that seemed available to every man in the castle of his home" (11).
2. Poovey, for example, "[Jane Eyre] compares [her 'restlessness'] specifically to the 'ferment' that feeds 'political rebellions' and she opposes it explicitly to the self-denial that caring for children requires" (146). Or, "The second face of Florence Nightingale bore a greater likeness to a politician or a soldier than a gentle mother; it was the image of a tough-minded administrator who 'encountered opposition but persevered'" (168). Amanda Anderson: "[T]here frequently appears within these accounts a privileged and anomalous figure or two who are granted deeper insights into the workings of power, and who seem not simply to instantiate modern power but to manipulate it not to inaugurate it" (53–54).
3. "The process, therefore, that clears the way for the capitalist system, can be none other than the process which takes away from the labourer the possession of his means of production; a process that transforms, on the one hand, the social means of subsistence and production into capital, on the other, the immediate producers into wage-labourers. The so-called primitive accumulation, therefore, is nothing else than the historical process of divorcing the producer from the means of production [...] The immediate producer, the labourer, could only dispose of his own person after he had ceased to be attached to the soil" (668–669).
4. "As soon as this process of transformation has sufficiently decomposed the old society from top to bottom, as soon as labourers are turned into proletarians, their means of labour into capital, as soon as the capitalist mode of production stands on its own feet, then the further socialisation of labour and further transformation of the land and other means of production into socially exploited and, therefore, common means of production, as well as the further expropriation of private proprietors, takes a new form" (714).

5. The widespread interest in teaching feminist theory as a necessary component of humanities and social science education and training, evident in the eighties and nineties, is now waning. I am making a distinction here between women's or gender studies and feminist theory. Women's and gender studies departments and programs seem to be thriving, expanding, hiring, and strengthening. Unlike feminism, women's studies tends to be empirical (with an accent on health or on anthropological/sociological fieldwork), whereas gender studies answers to the representational needs of men as well as women (often with a finger on the pulse of popular culture), is concerned with issues of identity, and often assumes gender as just one part of a wide cultural spectrum of identities. The empirical quality of much of this work tends to affirm existing realities by endlessly describing them, as well as describing them within a present that extends the same indefinitely. On the other hand, feminism is an edgy political and academic movement and is grounded in philosophical debate, language and linguistics issues, and historical/contextual analysis as they relate to social change and resistance. One person who was developing women's studies curricula told me that she did not like "feminist studies" or "feminist theory" as a rubric because "feminism excludes some women who wouldn't identify as feminist." I would say the reverse is even more prevalent, where "women's studies" excludes or marginalizes feminism, often at the expense of its own intellectual coherence.

6. New York governor Eliot Spitzer was caught engaging in sexual activities with a highly paid prostitute and was forced to resign. He was often praised during his political rise for his support of feminist issues, including bringing prostitution rings to prosecution. During his resignation speech, his wife appeared next to him, and there was a substantial amount of public commentary on the spectacle as a display of her private suffering.

CHAPTER 1   FEMINISM AND THE RETREAT FROM THE PUBLIC

1. Habermas has a similar definition: "'Private' designated the exclusion from the sphere of the state apparatus; for 'public' referred to the state that in the meantime had developed, under absolutism, into an entity having an objective existence over against the person of the ruler" (1989: 11).

2. Elizabeth Maddock Dillon makes a similar point. She writes, "[L]iberalism does not exclude women so much as it creates and reserves a discrete position for women within its structure. The position marked out for women—particularly white women—within liberalism is private and familial. Yet rather than simply standing as external to liberalism, this private position—and indeed, the entire notion of privacy and private property—must be seen as crucial to the structure and meaning of liberalism. This is why, for instance, sexual intimacy (coded as privacy) comes to be linked to freedom in the twentieth century" (3). Dillon does offer

a way of conceiving of women within liberal discourse other than in the weary tropes of exclusion, where it would seem that including women in public discourse would change public discourse and end inequality. However, her propensities to think exclusion and inclusion together pose other difficulties, for instance, that her model does not extend into the postliberal discourses of the present. Because exclusion and inclusion cannot be conceptually divided, Dillon's model cannot account for how the discourse of women's exclusion in privacy is concretized in ways that circumscribe "women's work" in a sphere of privacy that is unaccountable, unregulated, and beyond law. This is the version of women's privatization that corporate culture exploits.

3. Arlie Russell Hochschild sums up her analysis of Dowling's advice: "The idea of liberation and independence that early feminists applied to the right to vote, to learn, and to work, the cool moderns apply to the right to emotionally detach" (25). I would add that Dowling's vision implies social as well as emotional detachment.

4. Jacqueline Rose: "What distinguishes psychoanalysis from sociological accounts of gender [...] is that whereas for the latter, the internalization of norms is assumed roughly to work, the basic premise and indeed starting-point of psychoanalysis is that it does not. The unconscious constantly reveals the 'failure' of identity. Because there is no continuity of psychic life, so there is no stability of sexual identity, no position for women (or for men) which is ever simply achieved" (90–91).

5. For example, "Post-Freudian analysts [...] have all too often interpreted 'this great antithesis' between the sexes to mean an absolute distinction between men and women for whom, indeed, therefore, anatomy was the *only* destiny. Nature had made the sexes essentially different and in social life thus diverse they must go forth. Obviously, on the contrary, what Freud meant was that *both* sexes in their mental life reflected this great antithesis; that in the unconscious and preconscious of men and women alike was echoed the great problem of this original duality. Without distinction, both sexes are preoccupied with the great distinction: in different ways they both flee from its implications. Both men and women live out in their mental life the great difficulty that there are men and women. Only in their wildest dreams can they resolve the dilemma" (50).

6. "[F]emale subjectivity is considered to be innately maternal [...T]he modern feminist movement has identified with these experiences" (184–185).

7. "[This understanding] holds the minoritizing view that there is a distinct population of persons who 'really are' gay; at the same time, it hold the universalizing views that sexual desire is an unpredictably powerful solvent of stable identities; that apparently heterosexual persons and object choices are strongly marked by same-sex influences and desires, and vice versa for apparently homosexual ones; and that at least male heterosexual identity and modern masculinist culture may require for their maintenance the scapegoating crystallization of a same sex male desire that is widespread and in the first place internal" (85).

8. "Liberalism's rhetorical separations of state from economy, civil society, and the family never did describe the real, complex, interrelations of forms of collective life. The workings of the economy depended on the state for support and regulation; civil society was stratified by economic and political inequalities; the family was founded on the state-defined and regulated institutions of marriage; the economy provided the material base for state institutions and family life" (6).

9. "A hegemonic public has founded itself by a privatization of sex and the sexualization of private personhood" (559).

10. "We are trying to promote this world-making project, and a first step in doing so is to recognize that queer culture constitutes itself in many ways other than through the official publics of opinion culture and the state, or through the privatized forms normally associated with sexuality" (558).

11. Carole Pateman (1998): "In the United States in 1980 women occupied 70 percent of the jobs at all levels of government concerned with social services, which was a quarter of all female employment and about half of all professional jobs occupied by women" (243). Pateman also notes that women are the largest group of aid recipients: "Women are now the majority of recipients of many welfare benefits. In 1980 in the United States, for example, 64.8 per cent of the recipients of Medicare were women, while 70 per cent of housing subsidies went to women, either living alone or heading households; and by 1979, 80 per cent of the families receiving Aid to Families with Dependent Children (AFDC) were headed by women" (242).

12. "When this type of government defined a new arena of activity— call it 'the social'—and a new societal role—the welfare client—it included women among its original and paradigmatic subjects. Today [1989], in fact, women have become the principle subjects of the welfare state" (147).

13. As well as identifying the "private" as the structural place for women, and the "private" as an entry for the state into the family (as in aid to children), welfare policy also established the "private" as a situation where the regularized functioning of the rule of law—where particular applications of law could be bundled together and abstracted in general, repeatable, public principles—broke down and met its limits. As both David Garland and William E. Scheuerman have indicated, welfare was predicated on understated practices of singular application and legal exceptionalism—or "case studies" and social work—and applied in cases that fell outside the limits of legal standardization in industrial liberalism, or personalized. Garland: "The proper treatment of offenders required individualized, corrective measures carefully adapted to the specific case or the particular problem—not a uniform penalty tariff mechanically dispensed" (40). This leads to: "Crime control is 'beyond the state' inasmuch as the institutions of the criminal justice state are severely limited in their crime control capacities and cannot by themselves succeed in the

maintenance of 'law and order'" (123). Scheuerman: "The emergence of extensive state intervention in an unprecedented variety of spheres of social and economic activity has not only undermined the classical division between state and society presupposed by early liberal views of the rule of law but also broadened the scope of highly discretionary administrative and judicial decision making in many areas of state action. If a minimal demand of the ideal of the rule of law was always that government action should take a predictable form, contemporary liberal democracies probably do less well in living up to this standard than commentators suggest" (1). And then: "Insofar as existentially authentic politics is characterized precisely by its liberation from all normativities, the height of political action—sovereignty—needs to be defined in terms of the command of that moment or exception where normativities (or norm-based legalisms) are most irrelevant" (22). That is to say, with women entering more prominently into an embrace with the public sphere, as the state became a primary venue for women's work, state action and legal application were particularized and singularized sometimes according to individual needs. Rather than, as Freidan and others had predicted, the private disappearing as a framing device for certain types of labor, the public itself, in its increased feminization, could appear as excessive to regulatory regimes and the standardization of human outcomes predicted in the rule of law: The public was what was becoming increasingly unfathomable.

14. "Deregulation, privatization, and withdrawal of the state from many areas of social provision have been all too common" (3).

15. "Like Marxism in earlier times, with which, in this respect, it has many common features, this utopia [offered in neoliberal theory] generates a potent belief, a 'free trade faith', not only among those who life from it materially such as financiers, big businessmen, etc., but also those who derive from it their justifications for existing, such as the senior civil servants and politicians who deify the power of the markets in the name of economic efficiency, who demand the lifting of the administrative or political barriers that could hinder the owners of capital in their purely individual pursuit of maximum individual profit instituted as a model of rationality, who want independent central banks, who preach the subordination of the national states to the demands of economic freedom for the masters of the economy, with the suppression of all regulations on all markets, starting with the labour market, the forbidding of deficits and inflation, generalized privatization of public services, and the reduction of public and welfare spending [...] also and above all the destruction of all the collective institutions capable of standing up to the effects of the infernal machine—in the forefront of which is the state, the repository of all the universal ideas associated with the idea of the *public*" (1998: 100–102).

16. I analyzed Hernando de Soto's *The Other Path* and *The Mysteries of Capital* as incipient apologies for informalization and privatization in

the third world in my book *World, Class, Women: Global Literature, Education, and Feminism* (Routledge, 2004).

17. "10,000 Women," http://www.10000women.org. In relation to J.P. Morgan, see "J.P. Morgan Underscores Support for Microfinance at Women's World Banking Conference," June 12, 2009, http://www.jpmorgan.com/cm/cs?pagename=JPM_redesign/JPM_Content_C/Generic_Detail_Page_Template&cid=1159388295832&c=JPM_Content_C.

18. This phenomenon has been documented in much social science feminist literature. Most notably, anthropologist Maria Mies shows how "[w]hat the experts call 'flexibilization of labour', some of us have called the 'housewifization' of labour" (16) and that "capitalism had always needed [...] 'non-capitalist milieux and strata' for the extension of labour force, resources, and above all the extension of markets" (34). Grace Chang writes that "[t]he dismantling of public supports in the United States in general, and the denial of benefits and services to immigrants in particular, act in tandem with structural adjustment abroad to force migrant women into low-wage labor in the United States" (125). "In outwork or backyard production," Christa Wichterich writes of Nike and other textile work in Vietnam, Bangladesh, and Korea, "women toil under even more wretched conditions than in the factories: minimum wages, work safety and environmental protection can be more easily circumvented; the workers are isolated and hard for trade unions to reach; and there is no trace at all of health provision, maternity leave or other social protection. Here children can be used without anyone noticing, as can illegal immigrants. Informalization of the work process goes hand in hand with child labour" (16). Describing lace makers in India, Chandra Mohanty discusses how "[t]he polarization between men and women's work, where men actually defined themselves as exporters and businessmen who invested in women's labor, bolstered the social and ideological definition of women as housewives and their work as 'leisure time activity'" (149), and "[d]omestication works, in this case, because of the persistence and legitimacy of the ideology of the housewife, which defines women in terms of their place within the home, conjugal marriage, and heterosexuality. The opposition between definitions of the 'laborer' and of the 'housewife' anchors the invisibility [...] of work; in effect, it defines women as nonworkers" (150). Further, "[a]ll conflict around the question of work is thus accommodated within the context of the family. This is an important instance of the privatization of work and of the redefinition of the identity of women workers [...] as doing work that is a 'natural extension' of their familial duties" (158). J. K. Gibson-Graham celebrate that "[n]oncapitalism is found in the household, the place of woman, related to capitalism through service and complementarity. Noncapitalism is the before or the after of capitalism: it appears as a precapitalist mode of production (identified by its fate of inevitable supersession)" (7). Also, though less explicitly,

Zymunt Bauman notes that the weakening powers of the public sector have paved the way toward a self-help society. He describes an image of a society completely obsessed with mothering as a replacement for politics. For example, "The only way to suppress that horrifying truth is to slice the great, overwhelming fear into smaller and manageable bits—recast the big issue we can do nothing about into a set of little 'practical' tasks we can hope to be able to fulfill [...] Fat is but one issue of the large family of 'practical tasks' which the orphaned self may set itself just to sink and drown the horror of loneliness in the sea of small but time-consuming and mind-absorbing worries. But it is a well-chosen specimen, bringing into relief all the most important features of the whole family" (44–45).

19. For example, Sara Ruddick: "Many caretakers do 'resist,' even within the context of obedience, simply by continuing to care under appalling conditions of tyranny, poverty, and neglect. There are many examples of mothers [...] who resist collectively and *politically*, in the name of care. These women and men bequeath a history of resistance for feminist peacemakers and caregivers to extend and transform" (123). This is but one of many explanations for what certain trends in the feminist social sciences are calling "the politics of care."

20. Florida is a "right to work" state, which means not only the prohibition of the right to strike, but more important, that the union is not allowed to require that the people its contract represents pay dues. Historically, however, the union has found that defending the contract meant filing a grievance for any contract violation. In September we learned that not only did this make the union possibly liable for cases involving nonmembers, but also that we were the only local among our affiliates that had such a practice, and, indeed, our affiliates refused to give legal support in cases involving nonmembers if those cases reached the point of arbitration or beyond.

21. I wish to thank Tom Copella and the dean of Florida State University's film school, Frank Patterson, for inviting me to participate in a panel discussion about this film with Terry Coonan, Florida State University's director of the Human Rights Center, in August 2008.

22. "The most optimistic calculation is to figure that women a country's military admits a cone excluded or despised group, that institution is transformed and made more compatible with democratic culture. In this perhaps too-sanguine scenario, the outsider group campaigning to enter the military doesn't become militarized; rather, the newly diversified military becomes democratized" (16).

23. "Women are being used by militaries to solve their nagging problems of 'manpower' availability, quality, health, morale, and readiness" (44).

24. Karpinski should be applauded for her insistence that responsibility for the crimes at Abu Ghraib should move up the chain of command, including for her recent offer to testify against Donald Rumsfeld in the torture suit brought against him in France, and for her outspoken,

public condemnations of shadow prisons, interrogation techniques, and the U.S. departures from the Geneva Conventions.

CHAPTER 2   THE HABERMASIAN PUBLIC SPHERE: WOMEN'S WORK WITHIN THE CRITIQUE OF INSTRUMENTAL REASON

1. Habermas elaborates, "Proceduralized popular sovereignty and a political system tied in to the peripheral networks of the political public sphere go hand-in-hand with the image of a *decentered society*. This concept of democracy no longer needs to operate with the notion of a social whole centered in the state and imagined as a goal-operated subject writ large. Just as little does it represent the whole in a system of constitutional norms mechanically regulating the interplay of powers and interests in accordance with the market model" (1996: 27).

2. I return to this idea about the marginalization of the public sphere in chapter 5.

3. As Maeve Cooke explains, "Habermas himself reminds us that feminist theory has especially good reason to wish to bear in mind the dialectical relationship between public and private autonomy, for women's equal right to an autonomous private life depends on a strengthening of their position in the political public sphere" (190).

4. Elizabeth Maddock Dillon sees this structure of temporality in Habermas as what gives him a step up on other liberal and social contract theorists. For her, Habermas does not restrict himself to a narrative version of the liberal citizen's acquisition of freedom, with its "emergence of the liberal subject from out of the private into the public" (27). Rather, Habermas suggests to her the possibility that the private sphere and the public sphere are coarticulated: "Habermas's historical model locates the intimate sphere as the site of production of a new form of subjectivity that is the prerequisite of public sphere activity. In emphasizing the importance of the intimate sphere in its co-relation with the public sphere, Habermas proposes a model of liberal identity that is not, I would argue, wholly linear [...T]he interiority created in the conjugal family only seems to come to fruition—to 'attain clarity about itself'—in the public sphere. Indeed, public communication seems to concern interiority itself, suggesting that interiority may be less the predicate of rational communication than its result" (28).

5. This multiplying of the lifeworld's meanings led to the debates in moral theory and feminist ethics about conventional and postconventional morality, following Carol Gilligan's intervention. Habermas makes a distinction between ethics—a sometimes inarticulable set of standards and procedures for living together based in familiar communal values, relationships among people, and proximity—and justice—an

autonomous normativity that, collectively decided, coordinates action. For Habermas, the morality of justice needs to be translated back into the everyday that it has left behind in the ethical forms of life. Feminists like Seyla Benhabib have criticized Habermas for making the barrier between conventional and postconventional too rigid, while other critics, like Charles Wright, disagree: "[I]t is also possible," he contests, "for conventional moral consciousness to incorporate highly abstract and relatively recently institutionalized postconventional norms of justice" (55).

6. Habermas defines this term here: "It is characteristic of the development of modern states that they change over from the sacred foundations of legitimation to foundation of a common will, communicatively shaped and discursively clarified in the political public sphere...Against the background of this conversion of the state over to a secular basis of legitimation, the development of the contract from a ritual formalism into the most important instrument of bourgeois private law suggests the idea of a 'linguistification' of a basic religious consensus that has been set communicatively aflow" (1987: 81–82).

7. As Maeve Cooke has stressed, one of the reasons Habermas's theory has been important to feminists is that "it emphasizes the importance of capacities for critical reflection, for assuming responsibility for the coherence of one's identity and life history, and for value-directed judgement and action—capacities that many feminists see as indispensable ingredients of a normative conception of self-identity. These capacities are ones that have a close connection with the ideal of autonomy as it has developed within the evaluative framework of modern Western societies" (187).

8. Habermas is, of course, citing Hannah Arendt, who was Heidegger's student, disciple, and lover. "According to Greek thought," Arendt explains the *vita activa* that becomes the action of politics, "the human capacity for political organization is not only different from but stands in direct opposition to that natural association whose center is the home" (*Human Condition*, 24). But this idea of the political gets left out in modernity: "The distinction between a private and a public sphere of life corresponds to the household and the political realms, which have existed as distinct, separate entities at least since the rise of the ancient city-state; but the emergence of the social realm, which is neither private nor public, strictly speaking, is a relatively new phenomenon whose origin coincided with the emergence of the modern age and which found its political form in the nation-state [...W]e see the body of peoples and political communities in the image of a family whose everyday affairs have to be taken care of by a gigantic nation-wide administration of housekeeping" (*Human Condition*, 28).

9. "Being-already-in-a-world, however, as Being-alongside-the-ready-to-hand-within-the-world, means equiprimordially that one is ahead of oneself" (1962: 369).

10. Not necessarily in conjunction with Weber, Adorno, and the legacy of the Frankfurt School, but certainly similarly distrustful of the Enlightenment's accent on cognitive and scientific rationality, feminism had also developed a critique of instrumental reason as a form of the domination of nature, and of its conceptual thought processes and identity thinking as a blockage to the autonomy and difference that many feminists also extolled in their politics. "Those wonderful hysterics [...]," laugh Cixous and Clément, ecstatic over the revolutionary potential of insanity for its attack on instrumental reason. "[T]hey were dazzling [...] It is you, Dora, you, who cannot be tamed" (1975: 95).

11. "Affective labor is better understood by beginning from what feminist analyses of 'women's work' have called 'labor in the bodily mode' [...] Here one might recognize once again that the instrumental action of economic production has been united with the communicative action of human relations" (293). And again in reference to affective labor, here called biopower: "Biopower becomes an agent of production when the entire context of reproduction is subsumed under capitalist rule, that is, when reproduction and the vital relationships that constitute it themselves become directly productive" (364).

12. "It became clear [to feminists researching housework starting in the 1980s] that women's unpaid caring and nurturing work in the household was subsidizing not only the male wage but also capital accumulation. Moreover, by defining women as housewives, a process which I then called '*housewifization*', not only did women's unpaid work in the household become invisible, unrecorded in GDP, and 'naturalized'—that is, treated as a 'free good'—but also her waged work was considered to be only supplementary to that of her husband, the so-called breadwinner, and thus devalued. The construction of woman as mother, wife and housewife was the trick by which 50 per cent of human labour was defined as a free resource. It was female labour. As [feminist research] demonstrated not just that housework and housewifization were models for women's labour, but that transnational capital, in its effort to break the dominance of trade unions and to 'flexibilize' labour, would eventually also housewifize male labour: that is to say, men would be forced to accept labour relations which so far had been typical for women only. This means labour relations outside the protection of labour laws, not covered by trade unions and collective bargaining, not based on a proper contract—more or less invisible, part of the 'shadow economy'" (ix). See also Chandra Mohanty's *Feminism Without Borders*, which picks up on Mies's analysis to describe neoliberal labor situations in India's lace-making companies and assembly lines in Silicon Valley: "[Mies] is able to analyze the 'ideology of the housewife,' the notion of a woman sitting in the house, as providing the necessary subjective and sociocultural elements for the creation and maintenance of a production system that contributes to the increasing pauperization of women and keeps them totally atomized and disorganized as workers" (31–32).

13. For example, Johanna Meehan: "Habermas' insistence that there is no subject prior to socialization opens up a way to understand that there is not first an androgynous infant and then a child who at age two or three becomes a girl in pink or a boy in blue. In his account the process of socialization is the process that produces identity in the first place. A conceptualization of subjectivity resulting from taking up social roles mediated by language, can be of use to feminists who argue that one of the most fundamental distinctions demonstrating social role competence and, in many languages, rudimentary linguistic competence, is the understanding of the distinction between male and female and the ability to perform gender consonant with the social meanings of its signifiers" (41).

14. David Ingram outlines Habermas's four main differences with Heidegger as "cognitive reductionism, antirationalism, romanticism, and cultural idealism" (81n): Heidegger distinguishes art from expression and depersonalizes it; Heidegger grounds art in "presubjective artistic tradition, or Being"; Heidegger links art to religious revelation; Heidegger treats art "as the primary motor force underlying history" (81n). Instead of seeing art as prereflective and buried in the earth as an "*ontological destiny*" as Heidegger does, says Ingram, Habermas finds that "it illuminates by critically exposing reification and suppressed possibilities for utopian fulfillment" (81n). However, Ingram then concedes that Habermas later acknowledged that his aesthetic is much more proximate to the illuminating power of art that Heidegger ascribes and Benjamin adopts.

15. I discuss feminism's pastness as part of the pastness of the public sphere in chapter one. I return to this Heideggerian idea of temporality in chapter five, where the public sphere reveals the future in the private sphere's pastness.

16. In the splitting between the private and the public on which Habermas's whole network of systems–lifeworld exchanges depends, the only other lifeworld mechanism that manages to escape from systems colonization is the mass media. On this topic, Habermas takes sides with Benjamin over Adorno, who believes that the mass media is but another system's colonization of the lifeworld. For Habermas, in contrast, the mass media is a representative new form of social integration that shores itself up by freeing communication. Like Habermas, Benjamin interpreted mass communications—in his case in the form of the cinema—as a redemptive moment, an access to the lost "aura" that Benjamin sees as the wonder of art. For Benjamin, the "aura" takes its power not only from the sacred, but also from tradition and community, and from the place and singularity of the art object's origin. The technologies of mass reproduction at first destroyed the "aura" (like systems do to the lifeworld), but eventually the "aura" would be restored as these technologies allowed for a connection between subjects in the position of viewing. Like the Habermasian differentiation between systems and lifeworld in modernity,

the disappearance of the "aura" in the age of mechanical reproduction signals "the liquidation of the traditional value" (220), a "tremendous shattering of tradition" (220), and a dispersal of the community coherence and authentic context in which the object was made to be viewed. Older ways of seeing would mix with newer technologies so that historical images and associations burst into the present. Particularly, cinema would allow for a "deeper apperception" in that it provided identification, simultaneously and distractedly, with multiple points of view in time as well as space, or, as Benjamin puts it, "we calmly and adventurously go traveling" (236). Benjamin calls this "entirely new structural formations of the subject" (236), and Habermas would agree.

17. There have been too many criticisms of this claim to cite the particulars. Suffice it to say that Habermas lumps together these philosophers as "straw men" on whom he can place all the ideas he dislikes about "post-Enlightenment" philosophy. That is, if Enlightenment promised freedom in the autonomy of reason, and if that very same autonomy of reason had no recourse besides to objectify consciousness or turn consciousness into a tool of accumulation, and if lifeforms were as a consequence disenchanted, then—Habermas says these thinkers believe—Enlightenment needs to be forsaken, rejected, or negated. He concludes that such philosophers never prove the end of the Enlightenment tradition, and so he can retrieve and continue on in what he is calling the Enlightenment tradition. He reduces all that he dislikes about these "post-Enlightenment" or postmodern philosophers to the idea of the instrumentalization of reason. The problem is that the instrumentalization of reason is most fervent and pervasive in such thinkers as Marx (in terms of money) and Weber (in terms of administrative power), who are Enlightenment or modernist thinkers. In other words, Habermas pushes the problems of Enlightenment onto the post-Enlightenment in order to extract from the Enlightenment isolated but redeemable concepts. At the same time, he borrows key philosophical innovations from some of those he lambastes for the mistakes of modernity—most relevantly his questioning of foundations, sovereignty, and the subject—and borrows many of their tools—like the linguistification of the social, a wariness of philosophies of transcendence, and the fragmentation of reason. His ultimate task is to find "*other* paths leading out of the philosophy of the subject" based in domination besides the "flight into the immediacy of mystical ecstasy" (1987a: 137) that he attributes to these postmodern writers. Habermas does not include a critique of feminist theory in *The Philosophical Discourses of Modernity*, though feminist theory would certainly share some of the features of these "post-Enlightenment" philosophies, particularly in its foregrounding of the irrational, the preconceptual, and the aesthetic.

18. "[T]he authority of the holy is gradually replaced by the authority of an achieved consensus. This means the freeing of communicative action from sacrally protected normative contexts" (1987: 77).

19. The example Habermas gives of the lifeworld in action is during a break at work, when the workers ask the newest employee to go on a beer run. In this situation, the familiar is disclosed: A span of cultural knowledge—"what we can count on" (1987: 135); "a totality of what is taken for granted" (1987: 132)—that the new employee shares with the crew surfaces in order for the action to be coordinated; for example, the hierarchy of seniority, the location of the neighborhood beer joints, the demands of the job, the time that travel will take, the routine.

20. "The individual is not master of the cultural interpretations in light of which he understands his motives and aims, his interests and value orientations" (1987: 96).

21. "When an assignment to some particular 'towards-this' has been thus circumspectively aroused, we catch sight of the 'towards-this' itself, and along with it everything connected with the work—the whole 'workshop'—as that wherein concern always dwells. The context of equipment is lit up, not as something never seen before, but as a totality constantly sighted beforehand in circumspection. With this totality, however, the world announces itself" (105).

22. Habermas is critical of Heidegger because he "adopts this pragmatist motif for an analysis of being-in-the-world that is insensitive to the phenomena of sociation" and does not heed "cooperative interrelations" (1987: 44).

23. Habermas criticizes Heidegger for the vagueness caused by the lack of linguistic or communicative structure to the question of Being: "Heidegger flees [...] to the luminous heights of an esoteric, special discourse, which absolves itself of the restrictions of discursive speech generally and is immunized by vagueness against any specific objections" (1987a: 183).

24. "[A] collective consciousness or a group identity" (1987: 45).

25. As Habermas explains, what "makes it necessary that we place 'their' standards in relation to 'ours,' so that in the case of a contradiction we either revise our preconceptions or relativize 'their' standards of rationality against 'ours'" (1984: 238–239).

26. In part, Habermas is here again employing Heideggerian notions of time as operative through the privatization and re-privatization of women's work. Heidegger: "[B]y taking *the question of Being as our clue*, we are to *destroy* the traditional content of ancient ontology until we arrive at those primordial experiences in which we achieved our first ways of determining the nature of Being—the ways that have guided us ever since" (1962: 44).

27. Heidegger: "Being-towards-death is the anticipation of a potentiality-for-Being of that entity whose kind of Being is anticipation itself. In the anticipatory revealing of this potentiality-for-Being, *Dasein* discloses itself to itself as regards its uttermost possibility. But to project itself on its own most potentiality-for-Being means to be able to understand itself in the Being of the entity so revealed—namely, to exist" (307).

28. Marie Fleming: "[T]he public sphere's concept of humanity draws its inspiration from the 'illusion of freedom' in the bourgeois family. Habermas' mistake occurs early on in his argument, just after he traces the bourgeois concept of humanity to a feeling of 'human closeness in the intimate sphere of the patriarchal conjugal family. He is now confronted with two 'realities'—the fundamental inequality of internal relations of the bourgeois family and the illusion harbored by the family that family members were all free and equal 'human beings.' But he is drawn to the normative power of the family's 'illusion of freedom,' and he puts the 'reality' of gender inequality to one side" (1997: 224).

29. Marie Fleming: "Habermas has seriously underestimated the challenge of contemporary feminism, and he is mistaken in thinking that he can simply stand by the 'larger outline' of his earlier analysis [...] I argue that his model of the internal dynamic of the public sphere not only is unable to point the way to gender freedom, but that it actually presupposed gender exclusion" (1995: 119).

30. Joan Landes: "By Habermas' own account, then, the oppositional bourgeois public sphere only partially achieved its stated goals of equality and participation. But he sees this as an imitation of actually existing society, not of the model of a universal public according to which pre-existing social inequalities are bracketed" (1995: 97).

31. "Appeals to opinion, truth, and reason and virulent attacks on style were constituents of a backlash against the privilege of public women in the absolutist publish spheres of court and salon" (1988: 49).

32. For Kant, the seeming "as though" implies a connection between subjects: "Consequently there must be attached to the judgment of taste, with the consciousness of an abstraction in it from all interest, a claim to validity for everyone without the universality that pertains to objects, i.e., it must be combined with a claim to subjective universality" (*Critique*, 97).

33. Because it cannot be limited to one sense and its particular experience, but combines them all, "common sense," says Rancière, "is a delimitation of spaces and times, of the visible and the invisible, of speech and noise, that simultaneously determines the place and the stakes of politics as a form of experience. Politics revolves around what is seen and what can be said about it, around who has the ability to see and the talent to speak" (13). Common sensibility can be "perceived and thought of as forms of art *and* as forms that inscribe a sense of community" (14).

34. Critics of Kant have also identified the beautiful as feminized or subordinated. Terry Eagleton, for example, has said (perhaps ridiculously): "The beautiful representation, like the body of the mother, is an idealized material form safely defused of sensuality and desire, with which, in a free play of the faculties, the subject can happily sport" (91). In more serious engagements, feminists have read the beautiful as the feminine counterpart to the masculine sublime. This reading of the relationship of beauty with the sublime conforms with Kant's own interpretation thirty years before *The Critique*, in the precritical work *Observations*

on the Feeling of the Beautiful and Sublime (1760), where he writes, for example, "The fair sex has just as much understanding as the male, but it is a *beautiful understanding*, whereas ours should be a *deep understanding*, an expression that signifies identity with the sublime" (78). "Her philosophy," he goes on, "is not to reason, but to sense" (79). Though women have "unconstrained charms" (78), they are not "capable of principles" (81), Kant says, hoping not to offend, whereas men can indulge in "deep mediation" and "long-sustained reflection," "laborious learning," and "painful pondering" (78). Feminists have construed this precritical observation as extending into the critical work, especially in that moral reason, in this early approach, is dependent on the combination or marriage between these aesthetic categories. For Cornelia Klinger, for example, the beautiful in Kant is immersed in nature, whereas the sublime virtues are what underlie the moral autonomy and mastery over nature on which Enlightenment maturity relies for Kant; they "are independent of a benevolent providence; they are not given by nature as a kind of instinct but result from human freedom and are an accomplishment of reason" (197), notes Klinger.

35. This is exactly what Seyla Benhabib faults him for: "Instead of asking what I as a single rational moral agent can intend or will to be a universal maxim for all without contradiction, the communicative ethicist asks: what principles of action can we all recognize or agree to as being valid if we engage in practical discourse or a mutual search for justification?" (1992: 28). Benhabib prefers a weaker version of universalism by agreement that would be open-ended in its recognition of "concrete human beings whose capacity to express this standpoint we ought to enhance" (1992: 31).

36. "The beautiful interests empirically only in society; and if the drive to society is admitted to be natural to human beings, while the suitability and the tendency toward it, i.e., sociability, are admitted to be necessary for human beings as creatures destined for society, and thus as a property belonging to humanity, then it cannot fail that taste should be regarded as a faculty for judging everything by means of which one can communicate even his feeling to everyone else, and hence as a means for promoting what is demanded by an inclination natural to everyone" (*Critique*, 176–177).

37. As Paul Guyer interprets it, "[T]he universal validity of our response to a beautiful object can neither be deduced from any concept of the object nor grounded on any information about the actual feelings of others, Kant believes, and so it can be based only on an *a priori* assumption of similarity between our own responses and those of others" (1).

38. "The agreeable is that which pleases the senses in sensation [...] All satisfaction (it is said or thought) is itself sensation (of a pleasure). Hence everything that pleases, just because it pleases, is agreeable (and, according to its different degrees or relations to other agreeable sensations, graceful, lovely, enchanting, enjoyable, etc)" (*Critique*, 91).

39. "With regard to the agreeable, everyone is content that his judgment which he grounds on private feeling, and in which he says of an object that it pleases him, be restricted merely to his own person" (*Critique*, 97).

40. In chapter 3, I address this idea more extensively as a problem of post-structuralist thinking more generally.

41. "In contrast to the detachment and disinterestedness which aesthetic theory regards as the only way of recognizing the work of art for what it is, i.e., autonomous, *selbständig*, the 'popular aesthetic' ignores or refuses the refusal of 'facile' involvement and 'vulgar' enjoyment" (4).

42. Kant talks about the difficulty of this process only in terms of art, not in terms of nature. Students of art are prone to imitation, and only with "severe criticism" can they be broken of this habit and learn instead to stimulate the imagination (*Critique*, 229).

43. Robert Kaufman: "The as if imparts a fundamentally aporetic character to the entire process of aesthetic judgment. However much the subject feels as if there are grounds for universal agreement with his or her 'disinterested' judgment of beauty, he or she simultaneously knows that, in empirical fact, such a presumption cannot possibly be met" (694).

44. "Argumentation makes possible behavior that counts as rational in a specific sense, namely learning from explicit mistakes. Whereas the openness of rational expressions to criticism and to grounding merely *points* to the possibility of argumentation, learning processes—through which we acquire theoretical knowledge and moral insight, extend and renew our evaluative language, and overcome self-deceptions and difficulties in comprehension—themselves *rely on* argumentation" (1981: 22).

45. This interpretation of the aesthetic as original also translates into Kant's explanation of genius. Genius is "the exemplary originality of the natural endowment of a subject for the free use of his cognitive faculties" (*Critique*, 195). There can be no rules or precedents to it, nor can it serve as an example to others. Genius can "express what is unnameable" and make it "universally communicable" (*Critique*, 195). Students can learn to imitate the genius, and can form institutions and schools where the methodologies can be taught, but these latecomers are operating in accordance with established rules, but "nature gave the rule through genius" alone (*Critique*, 196).

46. "The idea that societies are capable of democratic self-control and self-realization has until now been credibly realized only in the context of the nation-state" (2001: 61). Or: "Only the transformed consciousness of citizens, as it imposes itself in areas of domestic policy, can pressure global actors to change their own self-understanding sufficiently to begin to see themselves as members of an international community who are compelled to cooperate with one another, and hence take one another's interests into account" (2001: 55). Nancy Fraser has criticized Habermas on this account: "If the interlocutors do not constitute a

demos," Fraser speculates, "how can their collective opinion be translated into binding laws and administrative policies? If, moreover, they
are not fellow citizens, putatively equal in participation rights, status,
and voice, then how can the opinion they generate be considered legitimate? How, in sum, can the critical criteria of efficacy and legitimacy
be meaningfully applied to transnational public opinion in a postwe-
staphalian world" (2009: 88).

47. I return to this idea extensively in chapter 5.

CHAPTER 3   *BEIRUT FRAGMENTS*:
THE CRUMBLING PUBLIC SPHERE,
LANGUAGE PRIVATIZATION, AND THE
"RE-PRIVATIZATION" OF WOMEN'S WORK

1. Current attacks on the public sphere include policies that undermine
   education globally on a broad scale at all levels, from cuts in funding,
   teachers, classes, and programs, to commercialization, corporatization,
   privatization, discipline, and so on. Many scholars in educational cultural
   theory have pointed to this link between the public sphere and education. Most notably, see Henry A. Giroux. For example, his book *Against
   the Terror of Neoliberalism* shows the specific connection between the
   neoliberal takeover of civil society in the form of deliberating, debat-
   ing citizens on the one hand, and, on the other, pedagogical practice:
   "Part of the task of developing a new understanding of the social and
   a new model of democratic politics rests with the demand to make the
   political more pedagogical while resisting at every turn the neoliberal-
   ization of public and higher education" (179). And, "Democracy in this
   view is not limited to the struggle over economic resources and power;
   indeed, it also includes the creation of public spheres where individuals
   can be educated as political agents equipped with the skills, capacities,
   and knowledge the need to perform as autonomous political agents"
   (3). See also Kenneth J. Saltman: "Public schools play a unique role in a
   democratic society as a place for the public debate and deliberation over
   social values and priorities [...] Public schools stand as one of the few
   places left where citizens can learn about and talk about noncommercial
   social and individual values and imagine hopeful futures of democratic
   participation in which individual and cooperative opportunities can be
   realized and human suffering, poverty, and discrimination can be overcome through collective public action" (10).

2. The dating is arguable. The historical accounting that gives the war a
   fourteen-year interval of course does not include its resurgence in 2006.
   The official dating starts in 1975 and ends in 1990, with an estimated
   130,000 to 250,000 dead. Syria, Israel, the United States, the Palestinian
   Liberation Organization (PLO), and the Arab League were all involved
   in different periods of the war. Though most versions explain the cause

of the war as a clash between the Maronite Christian minority—with its guarantee of the seat of the presidency as a compromise of the Lebanese state with the French at the time of France's withdrawal in 1943—and the growing Arab majority, further underrepresented because of the influx of Palestinians following the founding of the State of Israel in 1948. However, the causes of the war were multiple, as were the parties involved, and the coalitions and conflicts varied as the war progressed.

3. This connection between fallen buildings and the death of civil society seems to be a recurring trope in descriptions of the Lebanese civil war. For example, in his own memoir, British journalist Robert Fisk uses metaphors of burned-out buildings as a backdrop for talking about the end of the myth of Lebanon as a place of national renewal, cosmopolitan integration, and happy consumerism: "The canyons of ruins," he notes of his trip to Beirut as early as 1976, "the heaps of pancaked houses, formed a front line as static as the valleys and mountains to the east of the city [...] Here the buildings were disfigured almost beyond recognition; some had fallen into the street while others leaned outwards, a hopeless thoroughfare of broken concrete, stones, weeds and pillaged furniture across which had been built a low barricade made of chairs, doors and broken tables" (49–50). Later on, he interprets the ruins as necessary to the Beirutis, since they supplied a reference point in the absence of any other symbols or institutions of social integration or common beliefs. The ruins replaced the "thought that an identity consisted beyond the civil conflict" (52). Ken Seigneurie interprets ruins in Lebanese war novels as signifying a skepticism towards modernist projects of progress and humanism. The novels tend to employ ruins to reference traditions of Arab literature where the narrative time is stopped in the face of a resurgent memory of human dignity and histories that have become irretrievably lost: "In these novels the ruins motif sets in motion the mental processes that condition the conviction that human life is possessed of innate dignity regardless of how history and war may compromise it" (2008: 53).

4. "But the old buildings—the villas, the municipal structures, the law school, all with their great colonnaded arches, their louvered shutters, and their red-tiled roofs, their old gardens with cypress trees and cedars, oaks, and pines, with honeysuckle and jasmine, bougainvillea, and oleander—ah, the old buildings! One after another they fell pretty to the war and now stand wounded, holes in the red roofs, shutters askew, balconies fallen, arched windows now without colored glass, like old women without teeth" (70).

5. "There was no doubt in my mind that the Israelis wished to destroy not just an organization or just an army but to stamp something out entirely: principally, the idea of Palestine in the minds of Palestinians and their supporters" (163).

6. Bauman goes on: "The most powerful powers float or flow, and the most decisive decisions are taken in a space remote from the *agora* or

even from the politically institutionalized public space; for the political institutions of the day, they are truly out of bounds and out of control [...T]he real power will stay at a safe distance from politics and the politics will stay powerless to do what politics is expected to do: to demand from all and any form of human togetherness to justify itself in terms of human freedom to think and to act—and to ask them to leave the stage if they refuse or fail to do so" (1999: 5–6).

7. Harvey continues, "Furthermore, if markets do not exist (in areas such as land, water, education, health care, social security, or environmental pollution) then they must be created, by state action if necessary. But beyond these tasks the state should not venture. State interventions in markets (once created) must be kept to a bare minimum [...] There has everywhere been an emphatic turn towards neoliberalism in political-economic practices and thinking since the 1970s. Deregulation, privatization, and withdrawal of the state from many areas of social provision have been all too common" (2–3).

8. "Pressmen from everywhere filed their reports about large parts of Asian and Africa," she goes on, "as well as the Arab world, from their listening post here. Students and their teachers from the many Beirut universities sat for hours in animated and passionate discussion of national and regional issues" (79).

9. Habermas famously defined the public sphere as "the sphere of private people come together as a public [...] to engage them in a debate over the general rules governing relations in the basically privatized but publicly relevant sphere of commodity exchange and social labor" (1989: 27). Constituted in part by the freeing up of the claims to referential validity in the community acceptance of sacred authority, the public sphere is a historical development of Western modernity that ideally—as autonomous from the state and the economy but contingent all the same—has the function of critiquing both.

10. "If one has to imagine someone else's pain on the model of one's own, this is none too easy a thing to do; for I have to imagine pain which I *do not feel* on the model of the pain which I *do feel*" (§302).

11. Literariness, for Habermas, in contrast to realism, is the occasion in which "the rhetorical means of representation depart from communicative routine and take on a life of their own" (1987: 203). In response, Derrida explains, "[O]ne must realize that the limits between the two are more complex (for example, I don't believe they are *genres,* as you suggest) and especially that these limits are less natural, ahistorical, or given than people say or think" (1997: 217).

12. "Two centuries after the American and the French revolutions, the entry of women into the public sphere is far from complete, the gender division of labor in the family is still not the object of moral and political reflection, and women and their concerns are still invisible in contemporary theories of justice and community [...] A theory of universalist morality or of the public sphere cannot simply 'ignore' women and be

subsequently 'corrected' by their reinsertion into the picture from which they were missing. Women's absence points to some categorical [*sic*] distortions within these theories; that is to say, because they exclude women these theories are systematically skewed. The exclusion of women and their point of view is not just a political omission and a moral blind spot but constitutes an epistemological deficit as well" (13).

13. Saul A. Kripke disputes that meaning is governed by preset community-enforced rules that are internalized. Kripke asks, if I can only be given a finite number of examples, how do I know that addition can apply up the scale to infinite examples, how do I know that the experience of the past would extend into the future, or how do I know that my private or singular experience is translatable to others? How then, inquires Kripke, do we follow rules to such a degree that we can expect others to say 125 in answer to "what is $68 + 57$?" even though, in the finitude of examples given, it is impossible to know that "+" means addition into all future occurrences of "+," even in instances that seem unfamiliar? "We all suppose," Kripke interprets Wittgenstein to mean, "that our language expresses concepts—'pain', 'plus', 'red'—in such a way that, once I 'grasp' the concept, all future applications are determined" (107).

14. Sometimes Wittgenstein himself seems to imply this. For example, "When someone whom I am afraid of orders me to continue the series, I act quickly, with perfect certainty, and the lack of reasons does not trouble me" (§212). Or, "Following a rule is analogous to obeying an order" (§206).

15. For example, "Here the term 'language-*game*' is meant to bring into prominence that the *speaking* of language is part of an activity, or of a life-form" (§23). "The common behaviour of mankind is the system of reference by means of which we interpret an unknown language" (§206). "It is what human beings *say* that is true or false; and they agree in the *language* they use. That is not agreement in opinions but in form of life" (§241).

16. Michael A. Peters, Nicholas C. Burbules, and Paul Smeyers offer a reading of Wittgenstein from the perspective of what it contributes to our knowledge of pedagogical practice in the field of social and educational theory. Much of their interpretation focuses on what can be gained in Wittgenstein to construct a type of teaching that counters the "narrow-minded and normalizing conceptions of standardized testing and of teaching to the test" (6); for example, "indirection" (7), "irreducibility plurality" (7), "confessional" (8), use of figurative language (8), "image-less thought" and Gestalt psychology (4), teaching through "involvement in an ongoing activity or practice" (9), "seeing connections and intermediate causes" (37), use of the visual (83), use of the therapeutic (102), learning through doing (3), or changing a problem by "changing the way in which we look at a problem" (11). Some of these—for example "use of the visual" and "Gestalt psychology"—may seem rather loose readings of Wittgenstein. In addition, the authors reduce the

complexity of use that Wittgenstein describes in detail to a set of class-room procedures. Though they are concerned with classroom methods rather than the broader political issues I take on here, they do give quite an extensive literary review of critics who have been particularly interested in how Wittgenstein as a philosopher was influenced by his career as a teacher (Ray Monk, Fania Pascal, Rush Rhees, Stephan Toulmin, Hans Sluga), his participation in the Australian school-reform movement (William Bartley), or his contact with children (Eugene Hargrove, Paul Engelmann).

17. For example, "When a child learns this language, it has to learn the series of 'numerals a, b, c, . . . by heart. And it has to learn their use. Will this training include ostensive teaching of the words? Well, people will, for example, point to slabs and count: 'a, b, c slabs'. Something more like the ostensive teaching of the words 'block', 'pillar', etc. would be the ostensive teaching of numerals that serve not to count but to refer to groups of objects that can be taken in at a glance. Children do learn the use of the first five or six cardinal numerals in this way" (§9). In this section, Wittgenstein is demonstrating the teaching of teaching. Such socialization is a dominant form of presentation throughout, with two or three figures responding to assertions with agreement or disagreement. Stanley Cavell has called this an exchange between a "voice of temptation" and a "voice of correction" (71), while Kripke calls the questioning voice the challenge of the skeptic and compares its position to Hume's skepticism on causality.

18. Immediately before the "private language" part of the text when the "rules of the game" presentation is drawing to a close, the pedagogical voice broadens into the voice of expectation of a broader community: " 'So you are saying that human agreement decides what is true and what is false?' It is what human beings *say* that is true and false; and they agree in the *language* they use" (§241), the student confirms.

19. "[L]anguage functions as a medium not only of reaching understanding and transmitting cultural knowledge, but of socialization and of social integration as well" (1987: 24).

20. The example that Habermas uses is of a member of a tribe who shouts "Attack!" when she sees approaching enemies, expecting her co-tribalists to respond appropriately and set up a defense against the aggression. Habermas asks in what situation the co-tribalists might respond in an unexpected way and fail to lend assistance. For example, a failure to communicate could result from a failure to recognize the one approaching as to be following the rule in reading the symbol of aggression correctly. Even though the tribal member had internalized the working rules of the community as a member of the tribe, the rules would need to be confirmed or unconfirmed in a test of application to which other members would have to concede. Habermas concludes: "Wittgenstein emphasized the internal connection that holds between the competence to follow rules and the ability to respond with a 'yes' or

'no' to the question whether a symbol has been used correctly, that is, according to the rules. The two competencies are equally constitutive of rule-consciousness" (1987: 22). Habermas thus demonstrates that the very survival of the community depends on the members' (unconscious) abilities to read and interpret signs that allow them to follow the rules, but, paradoxically, also to reach agreement with others on whether or not the interpretation is appropriate within a situational context.

The example itself is revealing. Wittgenstein starts out with proto-capitalist scenarios rather than resorting to the anthropological record and "the primitive." His first explanation of ordinary language in *Philosophical Investigations* described a scene where someone goes into a shop and asks the shopkeeper for "five red apples" (§1). Immediately after, Wittgenstein follows up at a construction site, where one worker is training a second worker by calling out the name of the different materials and pointing to them: "block," "pillar," "slab," "beam," until the second worker learns to bring the right one (§2). Wittgenstein attests that this commonplace—where we learn language through pointing, or that each word designates a picture of something—is "a primitive idea of the way language functions" (§2), and compares it to the way children learn (§5), but also to the way language is learned in tribes (§6). Common to late-nineteenth-century/early twentieth-century scientific and sociological theories of recapitulation, this recourse to "the primitive" in Wittgenstein is both where learning goes wrong due to philosophical nonsense—"When we do philosophy we are like savages, primitive people, who hear the expression of civilized men, put a false interpretation on them, and then draw the queerest conclusions from it" (§195)—and where expression is at its most natural and basic, what both words and philosophy distort: "words are connected with the primitive, the natural, expressions of sensations and used in their place. A child has hurt himself and he cries; and then adults talk to him and teach him exclamations and, later, sentences. They teach the child new pain-behavior" (§244). Be that as it may, Habermas's choice to place his example of ordinary language learning within a projection backward into primitive society—rather than within ideal situations of consumption and production that Wittgenstein alternatively selects as contemporary or recognizable in the contemporary world—is an effect of Habermas's temporal challenge, where he wants to locate the public sphere in the bourgeois age while inserting it as part of the human condition, always imminent.

21. An example might be in the section where Wittgenstein questions if it is possible for dogs to talk to themselves: "But do I also say in my own case that I am saying something to myself, because I am behaving in such-and-such a way?" he asks, and the other voice responds, "I do *not* say it from observation of my behaviour. But it only makes sense because I do behave in this way" (§357). Because of the use of the first person here, it is not clear whether the person answering is just answering his own question, or if there is an external exchange happening.

22. "Don't you understand the call 'Slab!' if you act upon it in such-and-such a way?" (§6). Using a construction site to explain how we might go about knowing a language game, Wittgenstein here questions why pointing at things is not the way we learn language, but rather we learn language as we apply it to social interactions that become familiar as the background hierarchies of coordinated use in production. "In the practice of the use of language," Wittgenstein resumes, "one party calls out the words, the other acts on them" (§7).

23. Habermas: "In this respect the transition from gesture-mediated to symbolically mediated interaction also means the constitution of rule-governed behavior, of behavior that can be explained in terms of an orientation to meaning conventions" (1987: 16).

24. Yet, the meaning of words cannot be fully determined by rules: "when we follow the rules, things do not turn out as we had assumed. That we are therefore as it were entangled in our own rules" (§125). Therefore, as Stanley Cavell maintains, "That everyday language does not, in fact or in essence, depend upon such a structure and conception of rules, and yet that the absence of such a structure in no way impairs its functioning, is what the picture of language drawn in [Wittgenstein's] later philosophy is all about" (48). "[H]ow *can* previous experience be a ground for assuming that such-and-such will occur later on?" (§480) Wittgenstein wonders. "I said that the application of a word is not everywhere bounded by rules" (§84). The application of rules must always go astray. As Wittgenstein puts it: "This was our paradox: no course of action could be determined by a rule, because any course of action can be made out to accord with the rule. The answer was: if *any* action can be made out to accord with the rule, then it can also be made out to conflict with it" (§201).

25. "[T]he development of the modern faith in the 'autonomy of the aesthetic,'" she notes, "begins when aesthetics is severed from ethics" (2006: 90).

26. "This urge is the effect of the spatial picture of language. If that picture loses its hold on us, the deconstruction comes to seem less urgent. The belief in the beyond of discourse as well as the further belief that entities beyond discourse are always struggling and straining to disrupt it, always threatening to make our language nonsensical or meaningless, leads to an obsession with boundaries, borderlines, and limits, which will be proclaimed as the place where 'representation' or 'intelligibility' breaks down, where meaninglessness and chaos begin" (2004: 861). Moi is worried that representing meaning through pictures means that words that are not nouns fall outside of sense-codes as preestablished determinants or metaphysical destabilizers (2004: 861–864): "We are, then, asked to believe that in the outer darkness beyond representation dwell the shadows of potentially meaningfully entities [...] That they are there is proved by the fact that they exert pressure on ordinary, organized symbolic language, sometimes breaking it down entirely" (2004: 864).

27. "I have come to the conclusion that no amount of rethinking of the concepts of sex and gender will produce a good theory of the body or subjectivity. The distinction between sex and gender is simply irrelevant to the task of producing a concrete historical understanding of what it means to be a woman (or a man) in a given society" (1999: 4–5).

28. "The widespread tendency to criticize anyone who thinks that biological facts exist for their 'essentialism' or 'biologism' is best understood as a *recoil* from the thought that biological facts can ground social values" (1999: 41). Moi takes poststructuralist feminists to task for "a pronounced tendency to believe that if we accept that there are biological facts, then they somehow will become the ground for social norms" (1999: 38).

29. Feminism has had an at best wary relationship with the category of experience. On the one hand, "experience" can give representations within historical narrative to aspects whose importance was previously denied or ignored; on the other hand, "experience" lends itself to positivism or other philosophical perspectives that assume the transparency or permanence of the real. Moi uses "experience" in a way that takes the former seriously by turning "experience" around existentialist themes while avoiding the metaphysical propensities of the latter. For an example of a feminist who sets out the problem of the feminist turn toward experience as defining identity, see Joan Scott: "This kind of communication has long been the mission of historians documenting the lives of those omitted or overlooked in accounts of the past. It has produced a wealth of new evidence previously ignored about these others and has drawn attention to dimensions of human life and activity usually deemed unworthy of mention in conventional histories. It has also occasioned a crisis for orthodox history, by multiplying not only stories, but subjects, and by insisting that histories are written from fundamentally different—indeed irreconcilable perspectives or standpoints, no one of which is complete or completely 'true.' [...T]hese histories have provided evidence for a world of alternative values and practices whose existence gives the lie to hegemonic constructions of social worlds" (24). However, she adds in warning, "[These histories also] take as self-evident the identities of those whose experience is being documented and thus naturalize their difference. They locate resistance outside its discursive construction, and reify agency as an inherent attribute of individuals" (25). It could be argued that Scott is one of the poststructuralists that Moi is contesting, since Scott argues in this essay that experience is just as constructed as discourse, similarly to the way Moi presents the poststructuralist attitude toward sex and gender as noted above: "To put it another way, the evidence of experience, whether conceived through a metaphor of visibility or in any other way that takes meaning as transparent, reproduces rather than contests given ideological systems—those that assume that the facts of history speak for themselves and, in the case of histories of gender, those that rest on notions of a natural or established opposition between sexual practices and social conventions" (25).

30. "Used in different situations by different speakers, the word 'woman' takes on very different implications. If we want to combat sexism and heterosexism, we should examine what work words are made to do in different speech acts, not leap to the conclusion that some word must mean the same oppressive thing every time it occurs, or that words oppress us simply by having determinate meanings, regardless of what those meanings are" (1999: 44–45).

31. Heidegger's idea of "world" that Moi is here referencing has been much talked about, and I do not need to rehearse those debates here. In short, the "world" for Heidegger is when an entire system of relationships between users of things and things gets "undisclosed" or revealed when I use a piece of equipment—the world, like the workshop or the environment, is a network of usages and relationships: "The work that we chiefly encounter in our concernful dealings—the work that is to be found when one is 'at work' on something—has a usability which belongs to it essentially; in this usability it lets us encounter already the 'towards-which' for which *it* is usable. A work that someone has ordered is only by reason of its use and the assignment-context of entities which is discovered by using it" (99). The world is not subjective, nor is it empirical or in common—it connects to both "the 'public' we-world" and "one's 'own' closest (domestic) environment" (Heidegger, 93)—but is always described from the perspectives of activities that belong to it and from which it cannot separate either in whole or in part. The world is what we deal with and structures what we are in our everyday concern of being in it.

32. "[T]here are situations in which we do not want to be defined by our sexed and raced bodies, situations in which we wish that body to be no more than the insignificant background of our main activity" (1999: 204). Certainly, if I come across something like a mountain crag, I could climb it or admire it, and my body could acquire a meaning or identity in this activity that might change in a subsequent activity. However, social entities like gender and sex might not allow me quite so much leeway in deciding what to do with them each time I come across them. I cannot just decide, for example, whether to have an abortion if I come across a pregnancy in my body: The pregnancy, and my gender and sex in relation to it, have acquired meaning through the many different approaches to pregnancy that have saturated law, politics, conventions, and ideology.

33. Moi continually insists that her call for existentialism is not as a "radical voluntarist" (1999: 198), that her existentialism does not mean that women "can just throw off the sexist yoke and realize themselves" (198) and can still acknowledge that "institutions and ideology [...] oppress women" (199).

34. In an interview with Jeffrey Williams in *The Minnesota Review*, Toril Moi elaborates: "I'm interested in how the words we use have all kinds of possibilities. That's why the first essay in *What is a Woman?* is about recuperating the word 'woman' for ordinary use, not handing it over

to the essentialists. New contexts, new speakers, new listeners give new meaning. An individual can never determine the meaning of a word—its usage—but you can analyze different instances and find that sometimes people use the word 'woman' perfectly adequately and other times completely offensively."

35. Chapter heading for Makdisi's second chapter, p. 33.

36. Habermas defines this term here: "It is characteristic of the development of modern states that they change over from the sacred foundations of legitimation to foundation on a common will, communicatively shaped and discursively clarified in the political public sphere [...] Against the background of this conversion of the state over to a secular basis of legitimation, the development of the contract from a ritual formalism into the most important instrument of bourgeois private law suggests the idea of a 'linguistification' of a basic religious consensus that has been set communicatively aflow" (1987: 81–82).

37. Many outside of Iran were surprised, I believed, by the vibrancy of Iranian civil society—even against the unleashed and aggressive forces of oppression—that was demonstrated to us via YouTube, Facebook, and Twitter in response to the alleged theft of the 2009 presidential elections. In fact, one might wonder why U.S. civil society did not respond with so much vitality in the aftermath of the 2000 presidential elections that many still believe were stolen. As Katha Pollitt said in *The Nation*: "Who knew that our arch-enemy, member in good standing of the Axis of Evil, had all these hip young people, these tech-savvy Tweeters, these ordinary citizens eager to go into the streets day after day and risk beatings, arrests and death at the hands of the feared Basij? Who knew it had so many women who, however devout they may or may not be, don't want to be denied ordinary human freedoms in the name of religion, thank you very much?"

38. Upon withdrawal of the French colonial administration in 1943 (and in order to appease the Christian Maronites who were opposed to this withdrawal), the Lebanese state was set up to distribute power proportionally between different religious sects according to preset guidelines. Each sect was granted a fixed amount of parliamentary seats and designated cabinet posts based on a 1932 census, when Christians were clearly the dominant majority. After 1948, however, the influx of Palestinian refugees changed the population ratios while the power structure remained the same. Although Palestinian Christians were often granted citizenship, Palestinian Muslims were denied. Who would stand in for populations in this representational power-share was decided according to a confessional system that designated denominations. Robert Fisk infers that the endurance of this system for so long, even after similar models had collapsed in Ireland and Cyprus, is a difficult to explain and unjustifiable miracle (66).

39. I elaborate on this point in chapter 5.

40. "It is only participation in the practice of *politically autonomous* law-making that makes it possible for the addressees of law to have a correct understanding of the legal order as created by themselves" (1996: 121).

CHAPTER 4 ADORNO FACES FEMINISM: INTERIORITY, OR MODERN POWER AND THE LIQUIDATION OF PRIVATE LIFE

1. Fredric Jameson disagrees with Habermas's assessment: "But Habermas is wrong to conclude that Adorno's implacable critique of reason [...] paints him into the corner of irrationalism and leaves him no implicit recourse but the now familiar poststructural one of *l'acéphale*, cutting off the intolerable, hyperintellectual head of the formerly rational being. He thinks so only because he cannot himself allow for the possibility or the reality of some new genuinely dialectical thinking that would offer a different kind of solution in a situation in which the limits and failures—indeed the destructive effects—of non-dialectical 'Western' reason are well known" (24). J. M. Bernstein, too, thinks Habermas misstates Adorno's commitment to Enlightenment: Adorno, he writes, "unswervingly affirmed the values of Enlightenment, and believes that modernity suffered from a deficit rather than a surplus of reason and rationality. Because one of the central places in which Adorno works through his critique of modern rationalism is in his writings on art and aesthetics, it is widely believed that his project is to displace reason with aesthetic praxis and judgement. This is a massive misunderstanding and distortion of his thought. Adorno believes that scientific and bureaucratic rationalism are, in their claim to totality, irrational in themselves, and hence that the meaning deficit caused by the disenchantment of the world is equally a rationality deficit. Only an expanded conception of reason which derives from a reinscription of conceptuality can lead to a restoration of ethical meaning" (2001: 4). There are numerous indications that Jameson and Bernstein are right about this. For example, in the beginning of *Negative Dialectics*, Adorno specifies: "No theory today escapes the marketplace [...] But neither need dialectics be muted by such a rebuke, or by the concomitant charge of its superfluity" (4–5). In his lectures on Kant, Adorno traces reason into a series of divergent yet unified procedures—synthetic a priori judgments, empirical judgments, metaphysical judgments, and practical judgments—that both cohere with and contradict one another, that are identical and nonidentical at the same time. The play between them constitutes "a game played by reason with itself" (*Kant's Critique*, 65), and "it aims to employ the tools of reason to judge the adequacy of reason itself" (*Kant's Critique*, 66).

2. Russell Berman writes convincingly against this charge. Instead, he suggests, "[d]espite the ultimate rupture between Adorno and parts of the student movement, understanding Adorno's politics requires

recognizing the extent of his sympathy for student radicalism. He saw the students as targets of the same hostility once directed against Jews, and therefore the violence they incurred only confirmed his own doubts regarding the depth of democratic institutions in Germany" (127). In his *Introduction to Sociology* lectures to students in 1968, Adorno divides the student movement into two tendencies. The first, which he identifies as emancipatory, opposes university reforms where, he says, thought is "led by the nose" (57)—that is, where students are taught to adapt to or integrate within the administered society—or that criticize the university for not doing enough "of the total leveling of standards through the production of performers for useful work" (58), turning the university into a "people factory" (58). Rather, he values the part of the student movement that approaches society as though "while all particulars depend upon it, it cannot be logically abstracted from them" (59); that is, the ones that rebel because the university is "too much of a factory" (59).

3. Adorno characterized this as an historical concern. He agreed with Marxist philosophies that said theory and practice had a fundamentally dialectical relationship, but saw that the division between them was increasingly reified in a bureaucratic society. He therefore saw praxis as increasingly divorced from thought. In answer to the classic question "what should we do?" Adorno responds: "But the reality is that the more uncertain practical action has become, the less we actually know what we should do, and the less we find the good life guaranteed to our haste in snatching at it. This impatience can very easily become linked with a certain resentment towards thinking in general, with a tendency to denounce theory as such" (*Problems of Moral Philosophy*, 3).

4. Adorno uses the term "the social" rather than the public. "The social" takes the structural place where Habermas will later theorize the public.

5. Just as "[philosophy]," as Adorno famously begins *Negative Dialectics*, "lives on" (3), Adorno admits in the end that survival involves a guilt that "is irreconcilable with living," that "compels us to philosophize" (364)—to live on. The irreconcilability of philosophizing leads Adorno in turn to the conclusion that education and psychology are the principle public institutions of social and political action. "[E]ducation must transform itself into sociology, that is, it must teach about the societal play of forces that operates beneath the surface of political forms" ("Education after Auschwitz," 203).

6. "[T]he question whether history is in fact rational is a question of how it treats the individuals who have been caught up in the flow of events. We can really talk about the rationality of history only if it succeeds increasingly in satisfying the needs and interests of individuals" (*History and Freedom*, 41).

7. "[T]he commodity character which spread increasingly with the unfolding bourgeois society, and especially the growing difficulty of utilizing capital, gave rise to a situation in which the public realm itself has been

manipulated and finally monopolized, and has transformed itself, as a commodity, as something produced and treated for the purpose of sale, into the exact opposite of what its concept really implies" (*Introduction to Sociology*, 148).

8. He goes on, "[T]he demand for a fully public realm was first directed at feudal society, in the name of a natural reason virtually common to all people, as a condition of the democracy of people who have come of age [...] If the present-day phenomena of the public are studied without also considering what was intended by the concept of the public and in what ways and, above all, under what compulsions this concept has internally transformed itself, one arrives at the entirely otiose, conceptless stocktaking which informs the activity now generally referred to as communication research" (*Introduction to Sociology*, 147–148).

9. "The contradiction thus constituted between the concept of the public and that which it has become is, in its turn, an essential component of a critical theory of the public; and if the historical moment in this is disregarded, anything like a critique of the public realm, and the conditions determining it today, is quite impossible" (*Introduction to Sociology*, 148).

10. "[I]n being made absolute, in losing its genesis, the fact appears as something natural, and therefore as something which in principle [...] is unalterable. To this extent the elimination of the historical dimension is an important instrument for sanctioning and justifying whatever happens currently to be the case" (*Introduction to Sociology*, 149).

11. "[T]he individual is a crucial phenomenon of history. After all, we might just as well assert that history is the history of the rise and fall of the individual" (*History*, 87).

12. "The universal that compresses the particular until it splinters, like a torture instrument," Adorno observes, "is working against itself, for its substance is the life of the particular; without the particular, the universal declines to an abstract, separate, eradicable form" (*Negative*, 346).

13. "The pressure exerted by the prevailing universal upon everything particular, upon the individual people and the individual institutions, has a tendency to destroy the particular and the individual together with their power of resistance" ("Education after Auschwitz," 193).

14. Bozzetti: "[T]here can be no rigid concept of non-identity for Adorno, not only because it hinges on identity but because it can only be pursued within a dialectical movement. It must therefore be critical of itself" (294).

15. "To the degree to which it remains, the ethical has retreated into forms of practice that are most remote from and least necessary for capital reproduction—private existence" (2001: 41).

16. "The isolated individual, the pure subject of self-preservation, embodies in absolute opposition to society its innermost principle" ("Sociology and Psychology," 77).

17. Against formulations of the social such as Talcott Parsons's, Adorno does not believe that the social can be thought as the sum of those individuals that compose it, nor as an exterior force to which individuals

connect. Rather, the particular individuals necessarily do not correspond, all together, to their generalized form, but are conflicted with it, even terrified by it, as well as conflicted with each other. "While remaining products of the totality, individuals, as such products, no less necessarily enter into conflict with the totality" ("Sociology and Psychology," 72). The relation of the individual to the social parallels the relation of the ego, as the substance of individuality, to the unconscious, as the register of social order.

18. "Private rationalization, the self-deception of the subject, is not identical with the objective untruth of public ideology [...] The phenomenon of rationalization, that is, the mechanisms whereby objective truth can be made to enter the service of subjective untruth [...] betrays not merely neurosis but a false society" ("Sociology and Psychology—II," 82).

19. Ideology "no longer has an independent existence and can no longer claim a truth of its own" (*Negative*, 268).

20. In fact, in *Dialectic of Enlightenment*, Horkheimer and Adorno make a clear-cut distinction between the consumerist individual and the individual philosophical consciousness that they develop: "Amusement under late capitalism is the prolongation of work. It is sought after as an escape from the mechanized work process, and to recruit strength in order to be able to cope with it again. But at the same time mechanization has such power over a man's leisure and happiness, and so profoundly determines the manufacture of amusement goods, that his experiences are inevitably after-images of the work process itself. The ostensible content is merely a faded foreground; what sinks in is the automatic succession of standardized operations. What happens at work, in the factory, or in the office can only be escaped from by approximation to it in one's leisure time" (137). In fact, the interlacing of consumerism into productive processes through "work" rather than "labor" allows Adorno to envision those productive processes as heading toward privatization: Factory work, for instance, is just an extension of spectatorship; automation assumes the form of isolation.

21. J. M. Bernstein would disagree with this view. The distortions caused in the private, individual subject by modern disremption, as a consequence of disenchantment, means that there can be "no safe or privileged subject positions" (2001: 19).

22. Russell Berman has attributed this rhetorical shift of Marxist terminology to Adorno's personal experience of exile. Because German citizens living in the United States were under FBI surveillance, Horkheimer and Adorno chose to mask their espousal of Marxist theory under "the model of aesthetic education, inherited from Kant and Schiller, which located opportunities for social progress in the aesthetic rather than in the political sphere" (114). In addition, the substitution of "work" for labor made Adorno's critique of the subject—and contingently, of the

private—both part of the human condition, that is, expressible through classical epic on the one hand, and on the other, particular to the historical moment of industrial capitalism.

23. Though Gibson offers insights into how Adorno's formative concepts grow out of his idiosyncratic or even wrongful interpretations of antecedent texts, one might still side with Adorno in asserting that total systemic transformation is unlikely to come out of a confrontation between the superexploitation of a single, manufacturing class of working-class people, a profit regime, and a technology that has advanced to a point where it can no longer be said to be an agent of progress.

24. Adorno's method for revising Marx by substituting "work" for "labor," Gibson alleges, entails reading the means of production within the terms of what Adorno called an exchange society. Adorno needs the prevalence of exchange in order to configure a modern world where the private individual risks being lost because consciousness has been saturated in identity thinking, where working people have become abstractable, exchangeable units that reflect the totality of existing society, the interests of the ruling classes, ideology, or power, rather than embodying the sense of a different future potential—or a science stuck in positivism—where human experience is abstracted into comparable categories that correspond with preexisting general concepts, producing a "hypostasis of social facts" (*Introduction to Sociology*, 78). Adorno filters Marx's category of labor through Weber's theory of the bureaucratic rationalization of work.

25. For Jessica Benjamin, Horkheimer and Adorno's announcement of the family's decline amounts to nostalgia for stability, which pits paternal authority against the growing helplessness of modern experience, and the only recourse of damaged life is in rebuilding it: "internalization of authority is the best or only basis for the later rejection of authority" (1978: 38).

26. Sometimes feminists are reluctant to embrace Adorno's thought at all, even when that is the specific mission. The issue of *Differences: A Journal of Feminist Cultural Studies*, which purports to be reopening the question of feminist theory's relationship to the Frankfurt School, is very wary and sparse in doing just this in relation to Adorno. The introduction to the volume, in fact, scolds recent feminist scholarship for shying away from the Frankfurt School, as this shying away suggests that it has "abandoned radicalism" in favor of "resignification" (Brown, 2). The first two articles that deal with Adorno, however, oddly marginalize Adorno's work for the most part. Rebecca Combay's contribution, "Adorno avec Sade," launches off of Adorno's misreading of Sade as nothing but "the tedious administration of routine piled upon routine" (8), and from there uses Lacan to say that Sade expresses rather a break from reason. Meanwhile, Elisabeth Bonfen does a superficial reading of "The Culture Industry" in order to frame a discussion of the mediation of the Iraq war through images of Lindy England and Jessica

Lynch. In this, she reduces what she assimilates from Adorno to the not very enlightening thesis that "political realities today are more than ever interlocked with the production of popular narratives and images that are treated as commodities" (21). Both of these papers use different methods to divide Adorno from the real critique that feminism needs to perform. Neither of these two approaches is interested in looking to Adorno for a new perspective on feminist theory, of borrowing from Adorno, or of seeing Adorno as engaged in issues that would be of importance to the continuation of feminism in an age of advanced capitalism. Rather, they seem to want to separate Adorno out, or to imply that feminism should be engaged in a critique of advanced capitalism only through an analysis of "images of" women in the media (not, that is, through Adorno's formative concern with the division of labor). This "images of" approach is not one you need Adorno to make, nor would Adorno necessarily be the best choice. I am not really denouncing these analyses, which I do find compelling, but rather suggesting that the contemporary feminist engagement with Adorno seems not to be about Adorno. Judith Butler is an exception to this, as I discuss below.

27. According to the same "myth" (as Lee calls it), Adorno then left the classroom and died of anguish four months later. Lee doubts this story's veracity, but goes on to show that the story itself exhibits some of the fundamental features of Adorno's philosophy of the body.

28. The relationship between Adorno and poststructuralism/postmodern theory has been troubled. I would agree with Martin Jay that situating Adorno within this movement would require oversimplifications: "It would be mistaken, of course, to reduce the legacy of Critical Theory *tout court* to a prolegomenon to postmodernism, however we may define that vexed term. Habermas's spirited defense of the uncompleted project of modernity, Lowenthal's last warnings against 'irrational and neomythological' concepts like 'post-histoire,' and Adorno's insistence on the distinction between high and low art and partisanship for modernists such as Beckett, Kafka and Schoenberg against the leveling impact of the Culture Industry, all make it plain that in many important ways the Frankfurt School resists wholesale inclusion among the forebears of postmodernism [...] And yet, in certain respects, the general theoretical trajectory of at least several members of the School's first generation can be said to have prepared the ground for the postmodern turn [...]" (1996: xvii). Rita Felski, on the other hand, argues that Adorno cannot be embraced by feminists precisely because he could not emerge from modernism and has nothing about him that speaks to the much more postmodern aesthetic with which feminism identifies: "[T]he Frankfurt School's categories of analysis cannot simply be taken over unmodified into a feminist aesthetic theory. The privileging of a modernist aesthetic as a site of freedom within Critical Theory is crucially dependent upon a prior diagnosis of the modern world as a totally administered society with no possibility of genuine opposition or dissent. If, however, this

originating premise is rejected, the dichotomy of authentic art versus degraded mass culture loses much of its rhetorical force" (163). Felski believes that feminism depends on both realism and popular art, which Adorno rejects as under the thumb of the culture industry. She therefore abandons both modernism and Adorno as essentially nonfeminist.

29. For example, as Hardt and Negri explain it in *Empire*: "The passage to Empire and its process of globalization offer new possibilities to the forces of liberation [...] Our political task, we will argue, is not simply to resist these processes but to reorganize them and redirect them toward new ends. The creative forces of the multitude that sustain Empire are also capable of autonomously constructing a counter-Empire, an alternative political organization of global flows and exchanges" (xv). The "multitude" and the "common" are what appear when Empire pushes itself to extremes, augmenting itself to the point when its own forms of domination produce excess.

30. Moi proposes that giving up on the sexed body as simply another discursive form does not necessarily serve feminism's purposes, and would mean that women's bodies and the multiple meanings produced in them are irrelevant to a commitment to justice. Borrowing from an existentialist version of Heidegger where the body discovers the world that it is inside, as I explore in chapter 3, Moi wants to return to a feminized body that does not enforce norms or determination and therefore has various particular definitions that it embodies as contexts and situations. That is, whereas Moi's sense of the body is conceptless, the poststrucuralism she criticizes is stuck in and determined by the concept.

31. Frederic Jameson explains, "the Frankfurt School's pioneering use of Freud applied the latter's categories as a kind of supplementary social psychology (repression and the damaged subject as indices and results of the exchange process and the dynamics of capitalism) but never as any centrally organizing concept" (26).

32. What Horkheimer here sees as the continued process of the family's obsolescence resulting from women's increasing employment in factories does not for him suggest the demise of the family as a symbolic form that is inconsistent with a society of exchange. Rather, "[t]he more the family as an essential economic unit loses ground in Western civilization, the more society emphasizes its conventional forms" (385).

33. After a careful reading, Hull concludes that for Butler, "there is no *analytically* distinct material realm" (26). Though "the world cannot be reduced to our thought of it [...], the most we can ascribe to the material is that it is a demand for signification. In sum, Butler wants to maintain a distinction between language and materiality, yet she insists that materiality 'cannot be said to exist' apart from language" (26).

34. "My analysis of Butler's understanding of sex and gender does not entail a critique of her politics. Butler's important work has given an intellectual voice to gay and lesbian critics. Her critique of heterosexism and homophobia has inspired thousands, and for good reason. Writing as I

am in a country where gays and lesbians are shot, tortured, and beaten to death by rabidly homophobic terrorists, I fully realize the importance of Butler's political task" (1999: 45).

35. The activist group the Yes Men seem in some sense to be enacting performativity in the way Butler describes. For example, in their movie *The Yes Men Fix the World,* they show how they created a Web site, DowEthics.com, which made them look as though they were supposed to be spokespersons for Dow Chemical. BBC (the British Broadcasting Company) World Television called them and asked them to appear on their program to talk about the Bhopal disaster, when in 1984 a plant owned by Union Carbide (a company bought by Dow in 2001) released a toxic gas that killed 5,000 people, with 15,000 more dying afterward of toxicity and 120,000 Bhopalis subsequently requiring medical care (see http://theyesmen.org/dowtext/). Appearing on BBC as faux Dow executive "Jude Finesterra," Andy Bichlbaum, one of the Yes Men, announced, on the twentieth anniversary (2004) of Bhopal tragedy, that Dow Chemical was taking full responsibility for the tragedy and would compensate the victims adequately, as well as carry out a full-scale cleanup and demand the extradition of those responsible in order to prosecute them. However, the political moment of the Yes Men's performance did not seem to be their "performance" of the Dow executive that would destabilize the corporate identity by exposing their identity as nothing more than a performance. Rather, the political moment was when the true Dow spokespersons disclaimed the Yes Men's appearance, said that they would not take responsibility for the disaster or pay compensation, and that they were really the "psychopathic monster" that everybody thought they were. Though sharing some of Butler's views on parody and resignification, the moment of politics here is the *reclaiming* of a *true* identity. More needs to be said about this.

36. In the next chapter, I discuss a case study of the preservation of the disappearing private sphere as the condition of possibility for a public-sphere narrative unwinding.

37. The reason that Foucault assumes this perspective on modern power is that he is reenvisioning the relationship between knowledge and power begun by Kant. According to Foucault, when Kant asks the question, "What is Enlightenment?" he institutes a division between Enlightenment and critique that Foucault thinks creates an obstacle to identifying the connections "between mechanisms of coercion and elements of knowledge" (1997: 59); that is, how reason itself, with its liberating promise of autonomy, could also take shape as an excess of power or a method of control, a development of state power in the form of techniques of knowledge. Enlightenment is found in the Kantian imperative "Dare to know!" where knowledge is an escape from tutelage, an outside, an act of courage. Critique, on the other hand, "is the idea we have of our knowledge and its limits" (1977: 49). This separation conceals the way that knowledge itself cannot be dissociated

from its constraints, that knowledge and power are the same, that the rationality of opposition—of "how not to be governed like that"—is continuous with the rationality that constitutes power. Though praising the Frankfurt School and attributing his own thinking to its legacy, Foucault goes on to distinguish his approach from that of Habermas, whose project is concerned with separating legitimate and illegitimate knowledge. Rather, Foucault says, his own intention is to start from the point where knowledge is acceptable and examine this neutralization—of what constitutes the acceptability of, for example, the prison system or the mental health system.

38. Ideological State Apparatuses are forms of state power that operate predominantly through ruling-class ideology rather than through repressive mechanisms that also belong to the ruling class. Like Foucault's discourses or sites of power, they are "multiple, distinct, 'relatively autonomous' and capable of providing an objective field to contradictions which express, in forms which may be limited or extreme, the effects of the clashes between the capitalist class struggle and the proletarian class struggle, as well as their subordinate forms" (141–142).

39. "If sexuality is culturally constructed within existing power relations, then the postulation of a normative sexuality that is 'before,' 'outside,' or 'beyond,' power is a cultural impossibility" (1990: 30).

40. "Habermas made the operation of critique quite problematic when he suggested that a move beyond critical theory was required if we are to seek recourse to norms in making evaluative judgments about social conditions and social goals. The perspective of critique, in his view, is able to call foundations into question, denaturalize social and political hierarchy, and even establish perspectives by which a certain distance on the naturalized world can be had. But none of these activities can tell us in what direction we ought to move, nor can they tell us whether the activities in which we engage are realizing certain kinds of normatively justified goals [...]. In making this kind of criticism of critique, Habermas became curiously uncritical about the very sense of normativity he deployed" (2002: 213–214). Habermas does not suggest a move beyond critical theory, but rather a move beyond an instrumentalist critique of instrumental reason. In addition, in Habermas the public sphere is precedural, and so the content of norms is not preestablished, but rather established through a coming-to-agreement that is only ever contingently resolved. Normativity in Habermas is not preconstituted, but rather structural; that is, the allusion to a normativity—the possibility of an intersubjective consensus or a lifeworld context—is what makes speech acts possible and what makes them make sense, forming the conditions of a public sphere. Butler's understanding of Habermas here seems to reverse the horse and the carriage in order to make Habermas (and the public sphere) even more Kantian than he is.

41. "The figure of the interior soul understood as 'within' the body signified through its inscription *on* the body, even though its primary mode of signification is through its very absence, its potent invisibility. The effect of a structuring inner space is produced through the signification of a body as a vital and sacred enclosure. The soul is precisely what the body lacks; hence, the body presents itself as signifying lack. That lack which *is* the body signifies the soul as that which cannot show. In this sense, then, the soul is a surface signification that contests and displaces the inner/outer distinction itself, a figure of interior psychic space inscribed *on* the body as a social signification that perpetually renounces itself as such" (1990: 135).

42. "For Adorno, the very operation of judgment serves to separate the critic from the social world at hand, a move which deratifies the results of its own operation, constituting a 'withdrawal of praxis'" (Butler, 2002: 213).

CHAPTER 5 *BAGHDAD BURNING*: CYBORG MEETS THE NEGATIVE

1. Andrew Feenberg has criticized Marcuse for too easily collapsing scientific thinking into a form of governance. Marcuse, says Feenberg, "fails to make explicit the different temporalities implied by his treatment of technology as subject to political control in contrast to science which is only loosely influenced by the environment" (253). Feenberg is arguing that Marcuse was confused by his Marxist reading of technology, where technology can be developed in the interests of capital in a capitalist society but would ultimately shed off these interests—or in some way have a transcendent usage—as the same technology entered the productive sphere of communism. In the post-Bush years, however, it is increasingly difficult to pose such a separation between political interests and scientific experience.

2. "[W]hen technics becomes the universal form of material production, it circumscribes an entire culture; it projects a historical totality—a 'world'" (1964: 154).

3. "Thought is always more and other than individual thinking; it I start thinking of individual persons in a specific situation, I find them in a supra-individual context of which they partake, and I think in general concepts. All objects of thought are universals. But it is equally true that the supra-individual meaning, the universality of a concept, is never merely a formal one; it is constituted in the interrelationship between the (thinking and acting) subjects and their world" (1964: 138–139).

4. "I'm female, Iraqi, and 24. I survived the war. That's all you need to know. It's all that matters these days anyway" (2005: 5), she begins the blog.

5. Instead, during the course of her writing, she witnesses her own further seclusion, the violent escalation of a Sunni/Shiite standoff, the entrenchment of the U.S. military, and a growing right-wing hardcore

clerical religious militancy that imposes sharia law and surveillance on women.

6. The famed president of the Iraqi National Congress (INC), who is most noted for assuring George W. Bush and his administration that Saddam Hussein was harboring weapons of mass destruction and that the Iraqi people would greet American troops as liberators. He was placed on the Iraqi governing council, and for a brief time in 2005 was prime minister and acting oil minister of Iraq. In 2007, Prime Minister Nouri al Maliki appointed him to head the Iraqi services committee coordinating reconstruction of the public infrastructure. Riverbend's account occurs before Ahmed Chalabi's fallout with U.S. authorities when they discovered in 2004 that he was selling U.S. state secrets to the Iranians. As late as 2007, General David Petraeus was singing Chalabi's praises as the person who would restore the connection between Iraq's government and its citizens, and so was vital to the "surge" efforts.

7. "Being out in the streets is like being caught in a tornado. You have to be alert and ready for anything every moment" (2005: 40).

8. "Women's rights aren't a primary concern for anyone, anymore. People actually laugh when someone brings up the topic. 'Let's keep Iraq united first...' is often the response when I comment about the prospect of Iranian-style Shari'a" (2006: 131).

9. "The Myth: Iraqis, prior to occupation, lived in little beige tents set up on the sides of little dirt roads all over Baghdad. The men and boys would ride to school on their camels, donkeys, and goats [...] Girls and women sat at home, in black burkas, making bread and taking care of 10–12 children. The Truth: Iraqis lived in houses with running water and electricity. Thousands of them own computers. Millions own VCRs and VCDs [Video Compact Discs]. Iraq has sophisticated bridges, recreational centers, clubs, restaurants, shops, universities, schools, etc. Iraqis love fast cars [...] and the Tigris is full of little motor boats that are used for everything from fishing to water-skiing" (2005: 34).

10. "I prefer a network ideological image, suggesting the profusion of spaces and identities and the permeability of boundaries in the personal body and in the body politic" (1991: 170).

11. This may be true of the version of dialectics developed by Marcuse, who—following Marx—does think that man can ultimately reveal and realize his essence in some future, though what would count as this realization is not quite so specific (he criticizes Hegel for locating it in the bourgeois state). It is not true, however, of all dialectical philosophies. As I presented in the last chapter, Adorno, for example, thinks that such reconciliation is the petrification of thought, and he attributes this to a Hegelian dialectic, which he also believes denies an ultimate resolution.

12. "If it was ever possible ideologically to characterize women's lives by the distinction of public and private domains—suggested by images

of the division of working-class life into factor and home, of bourgeois life into market and home, and of gender existence into personal and political realms—it is now a totally misleading ideology, even to show how both terms of these dichotomies construct each other in practice and in theory" (170).

13. "Pharmacia is also a common noun signifying the administration of the *pharmakon*, the drug: the medicine and/or poison. 'Poisoning' was not the least usual meaning of 'pharmacia' [...] This *pharmakon*, this 'medicine,' this philter, which acts as both remedy and poison, already introduces itself into the body of the discourse with all its ambivalence" (1981: 70). For Derrida, the pharmakon—as writing—is the "basis of oppositions as such" (1981: 103) since it sets up the opposing quality as an externality, but then turns out not to be "governed by these oppositions," but rather "opens up their very possibility without letting itself be comprehended by them" (1981: 103). Like *Dasein*, it composes the "difference between inside and outside" (1981: 103) of which, constituting, it plays no part. Like the cyborg, the pharmakon cannot therefore be "subsumed under concepts whose contours it draws" or "assigned a site within what it situates" (1981: 103).

14. "I would like to sketch a picture of possible unity, a picture indebted to socialist and feminist principles of design. The frame for my sketch is set by the extent and importance of rearrangements in world-wide social relations tied to science and technology. I argue for a politics rooted in claims about fundamental changes in the nature of class, race, and gender in an emerging system of world order analogous in its novelty and scope to that created by industrial capitalism; we are living through a movement from an organic, industrial society to a polymorphous, information system" (161).

15. "[W]*ith* this thing, for instance, which is ready-to-hand, and which we accordingly call a 'hammer', there is an involvement with hammering; with hammering, there is an involvement in making something fast; with making something fast, there is an involvement in protection against bad weather; and this protection 'is' for the sake of proving shelter for *Dasein*—that is to say, for the sake of a possibility of *Dasein's* Being. Whenever something ready-to-hand has an involvement with it, *what* involvement this is, has in each case been outlined in advance in terms of the totality of such involvements. In a workshop, for example, the totality of involvements which is constitutive for the ready-to-hand in its readiness-to-hand, is 'earlier' than any single item of equipment" (1962: 116).

16. For Marcuse, positivism's relegation of ghosts to philosophy is a tactic of scientific thinking to project its own mystifications onto its outside. Rational thinking is what erects mystificatory ghosts in the name of rationality, for example, in the promises of its advertisements and the magical celebrity of its politicians.

17. Through remembering the erotics of polymorphous perversity that were objectified under an archaic psychic structure, says Floyd, "Marcuse dialectically embraced the psychoanalytic configuration of unrepressed homosexuality as a direct threat to the progress of civilization" (107). Though Marcuse ultimately allowed "Freud's original association of Eros with the biological 'life instincts' to stand," he also critiqued "the *injunction* to procreate under the regime of the performance principle" (119).

18. C. Fred Alford: "To make eros historical, so that it might be liberated by changes in technology, labor, and society, is to risk its emancipator potential, which rests in its immunity to social influences" (1994: 135).

19. For a reading of the complexities of this argument, see C. Fred Alford; for example, "Marcuse embraces much of the Enlightenment ideal of science, although he does so in a convoluted fashion under the influence of the critique of the dialectic of Enlightenment. Ironically, it is science as an instrument of the domination of nature that he ultimately finds most liberating. The Enlightenment ideal of science that he embraces is that of the utopian popularizers of science, such as Francis Bacon and Thomas More. To be sure, he does not share their optimism, so characteristic of the Enlightenment, in the potential of scientific reason to 'migrate' throughout society and so make other social institutions more rational. Rather, it is Bacon's and More's embrace of science as the vehicle of man's liberation from the bondage of sickness, toil, and scarcity that he adopts" (1985: 67).

20. "With the affirmation of the inwardness of subjectivity, the individual steps out of the network of exchange relationships and exchange values, withdraws from the reality of bourgeois society, and enters another dimension of existence. Indeed, this escape from reality led to an experience which could (and did) become a powerful force in *invalidating* the actually prevailing bourgeois values, namely, by shifting the locus of the individual's realization from the domain of the performance principle and the profit motive to that of the inner resources of the human being: passion, imagination, conscience" (1978: 4–5).

21. The private sphere would disappear along with the pleasure principle, but not completely, as "life under the performance principle still retained a sphere of private non-conformity" (1955: 97).

22. "[T]he man who is enclosed in his inner freedom has so much freedom over all outer things that the becomes free *from* them—he doesn't even *have* them any more, he has no control over them. Man no longer *needs* things and 'works'—not because he already has them, or has control over them, but because in his self-sufficient inner freedom he doesn't need them at all" (1972: 13).

23. "[T]he universality of the state is, as it were, privatized: it is reduced to a combination of private persons" (1972: 54).

24. Haug believes that feminism steered itself in the wrong direction by trying to dislodge the public/private split, even in a technological age,

because many of its concerns—from reproduction to health care, oppression in the home, and inequality—continue to depend on an analysis of the private sphere in its present form.

25. For example, she sets the record straight on Abu Ghraib, disparaging American "shock" in responding to the lurid photographs as though they were a singular event rather than a continuation in time: "You've seen the troops break down doors and terrify women and children...curse, scream, push, pull and throw people to the ground with a boot over their head. You've seen troops shoot civilians in cold blood. You've seen them bomb cities and towns. You've seen them burn cars and humans using tanks and helicopters. Is this latest debacle so very shocking or appalling?" (2005: 263).

26. Mark Kimmitt, Assistant secretary of state for political-military affairs under George W. Bush.

27. This connection between the new technologies and communication with the dead has been a standard topos in the scholarly literature on new media. Many of these perspectives follow on a Heideggerian sense of decenteredness, a "Being-towards-Death" that individualizes and objectivizes in the same motion. Avital Ronnell, for example, addresses how Alexander Graham Bell's partner, Thomas A. Watson, as being a spirit medium before inventing the telephone: "As thing, the telephone will have to be despooked without, however, scratching its essential ghostly aspect. Thus Watson always presents the telephone as something that speaks, as if by occult force [...] He was already himself attuned to the ghost within" (246). Alexander Graham Bell himself modeled the telephone on a dead human ear that one of his scientist friends had donated to him. The dead specimen started to stand in for Bell's attempts to connect with his mother, Ma Bell: "Now, when mourning is broached by an idealization and interiorization of the mother's image, which implies her loss and the withdrawal of the maternal, the telephone maintains this line of disconnection while dissimilating loss" (341). For Ronell, ghostliness becomes the apparition of the disembodiment that translocational mediation demands. Others see the ghostliness of the new media technologies as participating in a postmodernist euphoria, a birth by the image. Scott Bukatman contests that virtual reality is tied up with the advent of the image as pure image or simulation; that is, without a previous referent or representation and "no relation to reality whatever" (98), as the "word made flesh" (97). As he defines identities in cyberspace, or "terminal identities": "an unmistakable doubled articulation in which we find both the end of the subject and a new subjectivity constructed at the computer station or television screen" (9). On the flip side, the link between new media technologies and death can lead to conclusions that are less than celebratory. Hubert Dreyfus points out that the disembodied, "desituated, detached spectator" (76) status of the Internet user—who transcends space—takes its form from the detached, non-concrete world of

the public sphere. Following Kierkegaard, he calls this "despair" (83): "But, in using [the Internet], we have to remember that our culture has already fallen twice for the Platonic/Christian temptation to try to get rid of our vulnerable bodies, and has ended in nihilism. This time around, we must resist this temptation and affirm our bodies, not in spite of their finitude and vulnerability, but because, without our bodies, as Nietzsche saw, we would be literally nothing" (106–107).

WORKS CITED

Abromeit, John. "Herbert Marcuse's Critical Encounter With Martin Heidegger 1927–33." In *Herbert Marcuse: A Critical Reader*. Ed. John Abromeit and W. Mark Cobb. New York and London: Routledge, 2004. pp. 131–151.

Abu-Lughod, Lila. "Do Muslim Women Really Need Saving? Anthropological Reflections on Cultural Relativism and Its Others." *American Anthropologist* 104, 3 (2002): 783–790.

Adorno, Theodor W. *Aesthetic Theory.* Ed. Gretel Adorno and Rolf Tiedemann. Trans. Robert Hullot-Kentor. Minneapolis: University of Minnesota Press, 1997.

———. "Education after Auschwitz." *Critical Models: Interventions and Catchwords.* Trans. Henry W. Pickford. New York: Columbia University Press, 1998. pp. 191–204.

———. *Hegel: Three Studies.* Trans. Shierry Weber Nicholsen. Cambridge, MA and London, UK: MIT Press, 1993.

———. *History and Freedom: Lectures 1964–1965.* Ed. Rolf Tiedemann. Trans. Rodney Livingstone. Malden, MA and Cambridge, UK: Polity, 2006.

———. *Introduction to Sociology.* Ed. Christoph Gödde. Trans. Edmund Jephcott. Stanford, CA: Stanford University Press, 2000.

———. *Kant's Critique of Pure Reason.* Ed. Rolf Tiedmann. Trans. Rodney Livingstone. Stanford, CA: Stanford University Press, 2001.

———. *Kierkegaard: Construction of the Aesthetic.* Ed. and Trans. Robert Hullot-Kentor. Minneapolis and London: University of Minnesota Press, 1989.

———. *Minima Moralia: Reflections from Damaged Life.* Trans. E. F. N. Jones. London and New York: Verso, 1951.

———. *Negative Dialectics.* Trans. E. B. Ashton. London and New York: Routledge, 1973.

———. *Problems of Moral Philosophy.* Ed. Thomas Schröder. Trans. Rodney Livingstone. Stanford, CA: Stanford University Press, 2001.

———. "Reconciliation under Duress." In *Aesthetics and Politics: The Key Texts of the Classic Debate within German Marxism.* Ed. and Trans. Ronald Taylor. London and New York: Verso, 1977. pp. 151–176.

———. "Sociology and Psychology." *New Left Review* 46 (Nov.–Dec., 1967): 67–80.

Adorno, Theodor W. "Sociology and Psychology—II." Trans. Irving N. Wohlfarth. *New Left Review* 47 (1968): 79–97.

Aghacy, Samira. "Domestic Spaces in Lebanese War Fiction: Entrapment or Liberation?" In *Crisis and Memory: The Representation of Space in Modern Levantine Narrative.* Ed. Ken Seigneurie. Wiesbaden: Reichert, 2003. pp. 83–99.

Alford, C. Fred. "Marx, Marcuse, and Psychoanalysis: Do They Still Fit After All These Years." In *Marcuse: From the New Left to the Next Left.* Ed. John Bokina and Timothy J. Lukes. Lawrence: University Press of Kansas, 1994. pp. 131–146.

———. *Science and the Revenge of Nature: Marcuse & Habermas.* Tampa and Gainesville: University Presses of Florida, 1985.

Allen, Amy. *The Politics of Our Selves: Power, Autonomy, and Gender in Contemporary Critical Theory.* New York: Columbia University Press, 2008.

Althusser, Louis. "Ideology and Ideological State Apparatuses (Notes Towards an Investigation)." In *Lenin and Philosophy and Other Essays.* Trans. Ben Brewster. London: New Left Books, 1971. pp. 123–173.

Anderson, Amanda. *The Way We Argue Now: A Study in the Cultures of Theory.* Princeton, NJ and Oxford: Princeton University Press, 2006.

Arendt, Hannah. *The Human Condition.* 2nd Edition. Chicago and London: University of Chicago Press, 1958.

Arendt, Hannah. *Lectures on Kant's Political Philosophy.* Ed. Ronald Beiner. Chicago: University of Chicago Press, 1992.

Aronowitz, Stanley. "The Unknown Herbert Marcuse." *Social Text* 58 (Spring 1999): 133–154.

Bauman, Zygmunt. *In Search of Politics.* Stanford, CA: Stanford University Press, 1999.

Beauvoir, Simone de. *The Second Sex.* Ed. and Trans. H. M. Parshley. New York: Vintage Books, 1952.

Benhabib, Seyla. "Feminism and Postmodernism: An Uneasy Alliance." In *Feminist Contentions: A Philosophical Exchange.* Ed. Seyla Benhabib, Judith Butler, Drucilla Cornell, and Nancy Fraser. New York and London: Routledge, 1995. pp. 17–34.

———. "Models of Public Space: Hannah Arendt, the Liberal Tradition, and Jürgen Habermas." *Habermas and the Public Sphere.* Ed. Craig Calhoun. Cambridge, MA and London: MIT Press, 1992. pp. 73–98.

———. *Situating the Self: Gender, Community, and Postmodernism in Contemporary Ethics.* New York and London: Routledge, 2002.

Benjamin, Jessica. "Authority and the Family Revisited: or, A World without Fathers?" *New German Critique* 13 (Winter 1978): 35–57.

———. "The End of Internalization: Adorno's Social Psychology." *Telos* 32 (Summer 1977): 42–64.

Benjamin, Walter. "The Work of Art in the Age of Mechanical Reproduction." In *Illuminations: Essays and Reflections.* Ed. Hannah Arendt. Trans. Harry Zohn. New York: Schocken Books, 1968. pp. 217–252.

Bergeron, Suzanne. "Political Economy Discourses of Globalization and Feminist Politics." *Signs* 26, 4 (Summer 2001): 983–1006.

Berlant, Lauren. *The Queen of America Goes to Washington City: Essays on Sex and Citizenship.* Durham, NC and London: Duke University Press, 1997.

Berlant, Lauren, and Michael Warner. "Sex in Public." *Critical Inquiry* 24, 2 (Winter, 1998): 547–566.

Berman, Russell. "Adorno's Politics." *Adorno: A Critical Reader.* Malden, MA and Oxford, UK: Blackwell, 2002. pp. 110–131.

Bernstein, J. M. *Adorno: Disenchantment and Ethics.* Cambridge, UK and New York: Cambridge University Press, 2001.

———. *The Fate of Art: Aesthetic Alienation from Kant to Derrida and Adorno.* University Park: Pennsylvania State University Press, 1992.

Bourdieu, Pierre. *Acts of Resistance: Against the Tyranny of the Market.* Trans. Richard Nice. New York: New Press, 1998.

———. *Distinction: A Social Critique of the Judgement of Taste.* Trans. Richard Nice. Cambridge, MA: Harvard University Press, 1984.

Bozetti, Mauro. "Hegel on Trial: Adorno's Critique of Philosophical Systems." *Adorno: A Critical Reader.* Malden, MA and Oxford, UK: Blackwell, 2002. pp. 292–311.

Bronfen, Elisabeth. "Reality Check: Image Affects and Cultural Memory." *differences: A Journal of Feminist Cultural Studies* 17, 1 (2006): 20–46.

Brown, Wendy. *Edgework: Critical Essays on Knowledge and Politics.* Princeton, NJ and Oxford: Princeton University Press, 2005.

———. "Feminist Theory and the Frankfurt School: Introduction." *differences: A Journal of Feminist Cultural Studies* 17, 1 (2006): 1–5.

———. *States of Injury: Power and Freedom in Late Modernity.* Princeton, NJ: Princeton University Press, 1995.

Buck-Morss, Susan. *The Origin of Negative Dialectics: Theodor W. Adorno, Walter Benjamin, and the Frankfurt Institute.* New York: Free Press, 1977.

Bukatman, Scott. *Terminal Identity: The Virtual Subject in Postmodern Science Fiction.* Durham, NC and London: Duke University Press, 1993.

Butler, Judith. "Contingent Foundations: Feminism and the Question of 'Postmodernism.'" In *Feminist Contentions: A Philosophical Exchange.* Ed. Seyla Benhabib, Judith Butler, Drucilla Cornell, and Nancy Fraser. New York and London: Routledge, 1995. pp. 35–54.

———. "Critique, Dissent, Disciplinarity." *Critical Inquiry* 35 (Summer 2009): 773–795.

———. *Gender Trouble: Feminism and the Subversion of Identity.* New York and London: Routledge, 1990.

———. *Giving an Account of Oneself.* New York: Fordham University Press, 2005.

Butler, Judith. *The Psychic Life of Power: Theories in Subjection.* Stanford, CA: Stanford University Press, 1997.

———. *Undoing Gender.* New York and London: Routledge, 2004.

Butler, Judith. "What Is Critique? An Essay on Foucault's Virtue." In *The Political*. Ed. David Ingram. Malden, MA and Oxford: Blackwell, 2002. pp. 212–226.

Cavell, Stanley. *Must We Mean What We Say?* Updated Edition. Ithaca, NY: Cornell University Press, 2002.

Cerullo, Margaret. "Marcuse and Feminism." *New German Critique* 18 (Autumn, 1979): 21–23.

Chang, Grace. *Disposable Domestics: Immigrant Women Workers in the Global Economy*. Cambridge, MA: South End Press, 2000.

Cixous, Hélène and Catherine Clément. *The Newly Born Woman*. Trans. Betsy Wing. Minneapolis and Oxford, UK: University of Minnesota Press, 1986.

Clarren, Rebecca. "Paradise Lost: Greed, Sex Slavery, Forced Abortions and Right-Wing Moralists." *Ms.* (Spring 2006): 35–41.

Cohen, Jean L. "Democracy, Difference, and the Right of Privacy." In *Democracy and Difference: Contesting the Boundaries of the Political*. Ed. Seyla Benhabib. Princeton, NJ: Princeton University Press, 1996. pp. 187–217.

———. "Personal Autonomy and the Law: Sexual Harassment, Privacy, and the Dilemmas of Regulating 'Intimacy.'" In *Privacies: Philosophical Evaluations*. Ed. Beate Rössler. Stanford, CA: Stanford University Press, 2004. pp. 73–97.

Comay, Rebecca. "Adorno avec Sade…" *differences: A Journal of Feminist Cultural Studies* 17, 1 (2006): 6–19.

Cooke, Maeve. "Habermas, Feminism and the Question of Autonomy." In *Habermas: A Critical Reader*. Ed. Peter Dews. Oxford, UK and Malden, MA: Blackwell, 1999. pp. 178–210.

Cooke, Miriam. *Women Claim Islam: Creating Islamic Feminism through Literature*. New York: Routledge, 2001.

Coole, Diana. "Habermas and the Question of Alterity." In *Habermas and the Unfinished Project of Modernity: Critical Essays on* The Philosophical Discourse of Modernity. Ed. Maurizion Passerin d'Entrèves and Seyla Benhabib. Cambridge, MA: MIT Press, 1997. pp. 221–244.

Dahlberg, Lincoln. "The Habermasian Public Sphere: Taking Difference Seriously?" *Theory and Society* 34, 2 (April, 2005): 111–136.

Davis, Angela Y. "Marcuse's Legacies." In *Herbert Marcuse: A Critical Reader*. Ed. John Abromeit and W. Mark Cobb. New York and London: Routledge, 2004. pp. 43–50.

Derrida, Jacques. *Dissemination*. Trans. Barbara Johnson. Chicago and London: University of Chicago Press, 1981.

———. "Is There a Philosophical Language?" In *Points…Interviews, 1974–1994*. Trans. Peggy Kamuf. Ed. Elisabeth Weber. Stanford, CA: Stanford University Press, 1995. pp. 216–227.

Dillon, Elizabeth Maddock. *The Gender of Freedom: Fictions of Liberalism and the Literary Public Sphere*. Stanford, CA: Stanford University Press, 2004.

Douglas, Mary. *How Institutions Think*. Syracuse, NY: Syracuse University Press, 1986.

Dowling, Colette. *The Cinderella Complex: Women's Hidden Fear of Independence*. New York: Pocket Books, 1981.

Dreyfus, Hubert L. *On the Internet*. London and New York: Routledge, 2001.

Duggan, Lisa. *The Twilight of Equality? Neoliberalism, Cultural Politics, and the Attack on Democracy*. Boston: Beacon Press, 2003.

Eagleton, Terry. *The Ideology of the Aesthetic*. Oxford, UK and Malden, MA: Blackwell, 1990.

Eickelman, Dale F. and Jon W. Anderson. "Redefining Muslim Publics." In *New Media in the Muslim World: The Emerging Public Sphere. 2nd Edition*. Ed. Dale F. Eickelman and Jon W. Anderson. Bloomington and Indiana, IN: Indiana University Press, 1999, 2003.

Elshtain. Jean Bethke. "Kant, Politics, & Persons: The Implications of His Moral Philosophy." *Polity* 14, 2 (Winter 1981): 205–221.

Elyachar, Julia. *Markets of Dispossession: NGOS, Economic Development, and the State in Cairo*. Durham, NC and London: Duke University Press, 2005.

Enloe, Cynthia. *Maneuvers: The International Politics of Militarizing Women's Lives*. Berkeley: University of California Press, 2000.

Feenberg, Andrew. "The Bias of Technology." *Marcuse: Critical Theory and the Promise of Utopia*. Ed. Robert Pippin, Andrew Feenberg, and Charles P. Webel. South Hadley, MA: Bergin and Garvey, 1988.

Felski, Rita. *Beyond Feminist Aesthetics: Feminist Literature and Social Change*. Cambridge, MA: Harvard University Press, 1989.

Firestone, Sulamith. *The Dialectic of Sex: The Case for a Feminist Revolution*. New York: Farrar, Straus and Giroux, 1970.

Fisk, Robert. *Pity the Nation: The Abduction of Lebanon*. New York: Thunder's Mouth Press/Nation Books, 1990.

Fleming, Marie. *Emancipation and Illusion: Rationality and Gender in Habermas's Theory of Modernity*. University Park, PA: Pennsylvania State University Press, 1997.

———. "Women and the 'Public Use of Reason.'" In *Feminists Read Habermas*. New York and London: Routledge, 1995. pp. 117–138.

Floyd, Kevin. "Rethinking Reification: Marcus, Psychoanalysis, and Gay Liberation." *Social Text 66*, 19, 1 (Spring 2001): 103–128.

Foucault, Michel. *The History of Sexuality: An Introduction, Volume I*. Trans. Robert Hurley. New York: Vintage Books, 1978.

———. *The Politics of Truth*. Trans. Lysa Hochroth and Catherine Porter. Ed. Sylvère. Los Angeles, CA: Semiotext(e), 1997, 2007.

———. *Security, Territory, Population. Lectures at the Collège de France 1977–1978*. Ed. Michel Senellart. Trans. Graham Burchell. New York: Palgrave Macmillan, 2007.

Fraser, Nancy. "Feminism, Capitalism and the Cunning of History." *New Left Review* 56 (March/April 2009): 97–117.

Fraser, Nancy. "Rethinking the Public Sphere: A Contribution to the Critique of Actually Existing Democracy." In *Habermas and the Public Sphere*. Ed. Craig Calhoun. Cambridge, MA and London: MIT Press, 1992. pp. 109–142.

———. *Scales of Justice: Reimagining Political Space in a Globalizing World*. New York: Columbia University Press, 2009.

———. *Unruly Practices: Power, Discourse and Gender in Contemporary Social Theory*. Minneapolis: University of Minnesota Press, 1989.

Gal, Susan. "A Semiotics of the Public/Private Distinction." In *Going Public: Feminism and the Shifting Boundaries of the Private Sphere*. Ed. Joan W. Scott and Debra Keates. Urbana and Champaign: University of Illinois Press, 2004.

Gallop, Jane. *Anecdotal Theory*. Durham and London: Duke University Press, 2002.

Garland, David. *The Culture of Control: Crime and Social Order in Contemporary Society*. Chicago and Oxford, England: University of Chicago Press, 2001.

Gibson-Graham, J. K. *The End of Capitalism (As We Knew It): A Feminist Critique of Political Economy*. Malden, MA and Oxford: Blackwell, 1996.

Gibson, Nigel. "Rethinking an Old Saw: Dialectical Negativity, Utopia, and *Negative Dialectic* in Adorno's Hegelian Marxism." In *Adorno: A Critical Reader*. Ed. Nigel C. Gibson and Andrew Rubin. Malden, MA and Oxford, UK: Blackwell, 2002. pp. 257–291.

Giroux, Henry A. *Against the Terror of Neoliberalism: Politics Beyond the Age of Greed*. Boulder and London: Paradigm, 2008.

Guyer, Paul. *Kant and the Claims of Taste*. Cambridge: Cambridge University Press, 1997.

Habermas, Jürgen. *Between Facts and Norms: Contributions to a Discourse Theory of Law and Democracy*. Trans. William Rehg. Cambridge, MA: MIT Press, 1996.

———. "Further Reflections on the Public Sphere." In *Habermas and the Public Sphere*. Ed. Craig Calhoun. Cambridge, MA and London: MIT Press, 1992. pp. 421–461.

———. "Habermas: Questions and Counter-Questions." *Praxis International* 4, 3 (1984): 229–249.

———. *The Philosophical Discourse of Modernity: Twelve Lectures*. Trans. Frederick G. Lawrence. Cambridge, MA: MIT Press, 1987.

———. *The Postnational Constellation: Political Essays*. Ed. and Trans. Max Pensky. Cambridge, MA: MIT Press, 2001.

———. *The Structural Transformation of the Public Sphere: An Inquiry into a Category of Bourgeois Society*. Trans. Thomas Burger with Frederick Lawrence. Cambridge, MA: MIT Press, 1989.

———. *The Theory of Communicative Action, Volume One: Reason and the Rationalization of Society*. Trans. Thomas McCarthy. Boston: Beacon Press, 1981.

Habermas, Jürgen. *The Theory of Communicative Action, Volume Two: Lifeworld and System: A Critique of Functionalist Reason.* Trans. Thomas McCarthy. Boston: Beacon Press, 1987.

———. "Three Normative Models of Democracy." In *Democracy and Difference: Contesting the Boundaries of the Political.* Ed. Seyla Benhabib. Princeton, NJ: Princeton University Press, 1996. pp. 21–30.

Haraway, Donna J. *Simians, Cyborgs, and Women: The Reinvention of Nature.* New York: Routledge, 1991.

———. *Modest_Witness@Second_Millennium. FemaleMan_Meets_ OncoMouse^{TM}: Feminism and Technoscience.* New York and London: Routledge, 1997.

———. *When Species Meet.* Minneapolis, MN and London: University of Minnesota Press, 2008.

Hardt, Michael, and Antonio Negri. *Empire.* Cambridge, MA and London, UK: Harvard University Press, 2000.

Harvey, David. *A Brief History of Neoliberalism.* Oxford, UK and New York: Oxford University Press, 2005.

Hassan, Salah D. "Unstated: Narrating War in Lebanon." *PMLA* 123, 4 (October 2008): 1621–1629.

Haug, Frigga. *Beyond Female Masochism: Memory- Work and Politics.* Trans. Rodney Livingstone. London and New York: Verso, 1992.

Heberle, Renée. "Introduction: Feminism and Negative Dialectics." *Feminist Interpretations of Theodor Adorno.* Ed. Renée Heberle. University Park: Pennsylvania State University Press, 2006. pp. 1–20.

Heidegger, Martin. *Being and Time.* Trans. John Macquarrie and Edward Robinson. New York: Harper and Row, 1962.

———. "The Question Concerning Technology." In *The Question Concerning Technology and Other Essays.* Trans. William Lovitt. New York: Harper Torchbooks, 1977. pp. 3–35.

Hewitt, Andrew. "A Feminine Dialectic of Enlightenment? Horkheimer and Adorno Revisited." In *Feminist Interpretations of Theodor Adorno.* Ed. Renée Heberle. University Park: Pennsylvania State University Press, 2006. pp. 69–96.

Hochschild, Arlie Russell. *The Commercialization of Intimate Life: Notes from Home and Work.* Berkeley: University of California Press, 2003.

Hohendahl, Peter U. "The Dialectic of Enlightenment Revisited: Habermas' Critique of the Frankfurt School." *New German Critique* 35 (Spring–Summer, 1985): 3–26.

Honig, Bonnie. "Dead Rights, Live Futures: A Reply to Habermas's 'Constitutional Democracy.'" *Political Theory* 29, 6 (2001): 792–805.

Horkheimer, Max, and Theodor W. Adorno. *Dialectic of Enlightenment.* Trans. John Cumming. New York: Continuum, 1991.

Horkheimer, Max, with Theodor W. Adorno. "Authoritarianism and the Family." *The Family: Its Function and Destiny.* Ed. Ruth Nanda Anshen. New York: Harper, 1949.

Horowitz, Gad. "Psychoanalytic Feminism in the Wake of Marcuse." In *Marcuse: From the New Left to the Next Left*. Ed. John Bokina and Timothy J. Lukes. Lawrence: University Press of Kansas, 1994. pp. 118–130.

Hull, Carrie L. "The Need in Thinking: Materiality in Theodor W. Adorno and Judith Butler." *Radical Philosophy* 84 (July/August 1997): 22–35.

Ingram, David. "Habermas on Aesthetics and Rationality: Completing the Project of Enlightenment." *New German Critique* 53 (Spring–Summer, 1991): 67–103.

Jameson, Fredric. *Late Marxism: Adorno or the Persistence of the Dialectic.* London and New York: Verso, 1990.

Jay, Martin. "Habermas and Modernism." In *Habermas and Modernity*. Ed. Richard J. Bernstein. Cambridge, MA: MIT Press, 1985. pp. 125–139.

———. "Preface to the 1996 Edition." 1996. In *The Dialectical Imagination: A History of the Frankfurt School and the Institute for Social Research, 1923–1950*. Berkeley, Los Angeles, and London: University of California Press, 1973. pp. xi–xxi.

Kant, Immanuel. *Critique of the Power of Judgment*. Ed. Paul Guyer. Trans. Paul Guyer and Eric Matthews. Cambridge: Cambridge University Press, 2000.

———. *Observations on the Feeling of the Beautiful and Sublime*. Trans. John T. Goldthwait. Berkeley: University of California Press, 1960.

Karpinski, Janis, with Strasser, Steven. *One Woman's Army: The Commanding General of Abu Ghraib Tells Her Story.* New York: Hyperion, 2005.

Kaufman, Robert. "Red Kant, or The Persistence of the Third Critique in Adorno and Jameson." *Critical Inquiry* 26, 4 (Summer 2000): 682–707.

Kellner, Douglas. *Herbert Marcuse and the Crisis of Marxism.* Berkeley and Los Angeles, University of California Press, 1984.

———. "Marcuse and the Quest for Radical Subjectivity." In *Herbert Marcuse: A Critical Reader*. Ed. John Abromeit and W. Mark Cobb. New York and London: Routledge, 2004. pp. 81–99.

Klinger, Cornelia. "The Concepts of the Sublime and the Beautiful in Kant and Lyotard." In *Feminist Interpretations of Immanuel Kant*. Ed. Robin May Schott. University Park: The Pennsylvania State University Press, 1997.

Kripke, Saul A. *Wittgenstein on Rules and Private Language: An Elementary Exposition.* Oxford, UK: Basil Blackwell, 1982.

Kristeva, Julia. "Women's Time." In *French Feminism Reader*. Ed. Kelly Oliver. Lanham, MD: Rowman and Littlefield, 2000.

Landes, Joan B. "Introduction." In *Feminism, the Public and the Private*. Ed. Joan B. Landes. Oxford and New York: Oxford University Press, 1998. pp. 1–20.

———. *Women and the Public Sphere in the Age of the French Revolution.* Ithaca, NY: Cornell University Press, 1988.

Lee, Lisa Yun. "The Bared-Breasts Incident." *Feminist Interpretations of Theodor Adorno*. Ed. Renée Heberle. University Park: Pennsylvania State University Press, 2006. pp. 113–139.

Lukács, Georg. *The Meaning of Contemporary Realism,* Trans. John and Necke Mander (London: Merlin Press, 1962).

Makdisi, Jean Said. *Beirut Fragments: A War Memoir.* New York: Persea Books, 1990.

Manalansan, Martin F. IV. "Race, Violence, and Neoliberal Spatial Politics in the Global City." *Social Text* 23, 3–4 (Fall-Winter 2005): 141–155.

Marcuse, Herbert. *The Aesthetic Dimension: Toward a Critique of Marxist Aesthetics.* Boston: Beacon Press, 1978.

———. *Counterrevolution and Revolt.* Boston: Beacon Press, 1972.

———. *Eros and Civilization: A Philosophical Inquiry into Freud.* Boston: Beacon Press, 1955, 1966.

———. "Marxism and Feminism." *differences: A Journal of Feminist Cultural Studies* 17, 1 (Spring 2006): 147–157.

———. *One-Dimensional Man: Studies in the Ideology of Advanced Industrial Society.* Boston: Beacon Press, 1964.

———. *Reason and Revolution: Hegel and the Rise of Social Theory.* 2nd Edition. London and New York: Routledge, 2000.

———. *A Study on Authority.* Trans. Joris De Bres. London and New York: Verso, 1972.

Martin, Randy. *An Empire of Indifference: American War and the Financial Logic of Risk Management.* Durham, NC and London: Duke University Press, 2007.

Marx, John. "The Feminization of Globalization." *Cultural Critique* 63 (Spring 2006): 1–32.

Marx, Karl. *Capital: A Critique of Political Economy. Volume I: The Process of Capitalist Accumulation.* Ed. Frederick Engels. Trans. Samuel Moore and Edward Aveling. New York: International Publishers, 1967,

Meehan, Johanna. "Feminism and Habermas' Discourse Ethics." *Philosophy & Social Criticism* 26, 3 (2000): 39–52.

Mies, Maria. *Patriarchy & Accumulation on a World Scale: Women in the International Division of Labour.* London and New York: Zed Books, 1986, 1998.

Mieszkowski, Jan. *The Labors of Imagination: Aesthetics and Political Economy from Kant to Althusser.* New York: Fordham University Press, 2006.

Mill, John Stuart. *On Liberty with the Subjection of Women and Chapters on Socialism.* Ed. Stefan Collini. Cambridge, UK and New York: Cambridge University Press, 1989.

Mitchell, Juliet. *Psychoanalysis and Feminism.* New York: Pantheon Books, 1974.

Moghadam, Valentine M. "Global Feminism, Citizenship, and the State: Negotiating Women's Rights in the Middle East and North Africa." In *Migrations and Mobilities: Citizenship, Borders, and Gender.* Ed. Seyla Benhabib and Judith Resnik. New York and London: New York University Press, 2009. pp. 255–275.

Mohanty, Chandra Talpade. *Feminism without Borders: Decolonizing Theory, Practicing Solidarity.* Durham, NC and London: Duke University Press, 2003.

Moi, Toril. "From Femininity to Finitude: Freud, Lacan, and Feminism, Again." *Signs: Journal of Women in Culture and Society* 29, 3 (2004): 841–878.

———. *Henrik Ibsen and the Birth of Modernism: Art, Theater, Philosophy.* Oxford, UK and New York: Oxford University Press, 2006.

———. "What Can Literature Do? Simone de Beauvoir as Literary Theorist." *PMLA* 124, 1 (2009):189–198.

———. *What Is a Woman? And Other Essays.* Oxford, UK and New York: Oxford University Press, 1999.

———. *What Is a Woman?* Oxford, UK and New York: Oxford University Press, 1999.

Najmbad, Afsaneh. "(Un)veiling Feminism." *Social Text* 64, 18 (Fall 2000): 29–45.

Nicholsen, Shierry Weber. "The Persistence of Passionate Subjectivity: Eros and Other in Marcuse, by Way of Adorno." In *Marcuse: From the New Left to the Next Left.* Ed. John Bokina and Timothy J. Lukes. Lawrence: University Press of Kansas, 1994. pp. 149–169.

Nouraie-Simone, Fereshteh. "Wings of Freedom: Iranian Women, Identity, and Cyberspace." In *On Shifting Ground: Muslim Women in the Global Era.* Ed. Fereshteh Nouraie-Simone. New York: The Feminist Press at the City University of New York, 2005. pp. 61–79.

Ong, Aihwa. "A Bio-Cartography: Maids, Neo-Slavery, and NGOs." In *Migrations and Mobilities: Citizenship, Borders, and Gender.* Ed. Seyla Benhabib and Judith Resnik. New York and London: New York University Press, 2009. pp. 157–186.

Pateman, Carole. "The Patriarchal Welfare State." *Feminism, the Public & the Private.* Oxford and New York: Oxford University Press, 1998.

———. *The Sexual Contract.* Stanford, CA: Stanford University Press, 1988.

Peters, Michael A., Nicholas C. Burbules, and Paul Smeyers. *Showing and Doing: Wittgenstein as a Pedagogical Philosopher.* Boulder, CO and London: Paradigm, 2008.

Pollitt, Katha. "Muslim Women's Rights, Continued." *The Nation* (24 June 2009).

Poovey, Mary. *Uneven Development: The Ideological Work of Gender in Mid-Victorian England.* Chicago: University of Chicago Press, 1988.

Rancière, Jacques. *The Politics of Aesthetics.* Trans. Gabriel Rockhill. New York and London: Continuum, 2004.

Ridgeway, James. "Introduction." In *Baghdad Burning: Girl Blog From Iraq.* Ed. Riverbend. New York: The Feminist Press at the City University of New York, 2005. pp. xi–xxiii.

Riverbend. *Baghdad Burning: Girl Blog from Iraq.* New York: The Feminist Press at the City University of New York, 2005.

———. *Baghdad Burning II: More Girl Blog from Iraq.* New York: The Feminist Press at the City University of New York, 2006.

Ronell, Avital. *The Telephone Book: Technology, Schizophrenia, Electric Speech.* Lincoln, NE and London: University of Nebraska Press, 1989.

Rosaldo, Michelle Zimbalist. "Women, Culture, and Society: A Theoretical Overview." In *Woman Culture & Society.* Ed. Michelle Zimbalist Rosaldo and Louise Lamphere. Stanford: Stanford University Press, 1974. pp.17–42.

Rose, Jacqueline. *Sexuality in the Field of Vision.* London and New York: Verso, 1986,

Rössler, Beate. "Gender and Privacy: A Critique of the Liberal Tradition." Trans. Jack Ben-Levi. *Privacies: Philosophical Evaluations.* Ed. Beate Rössler. Stanford, CA: Stanford University Press, 2004.

Rubin, Gayle. "The Traffic in Women: Notes on the 'Political Economy' of Sex." In *Towards an Anthropology of Women.* Ed. Rayna R. Reiter. New York: Monthly Review Press, 1976. Pp. 157–210.

Ruddick, Sara. "Notes Toward a Feminist Peace Politics." In *Gendering War Talk.* Ed. Miriam Cooke and Angela Woollacott. Princeton, NJ: Princeton University Press, 1993.

Ryan, Mary. "Gender and Public Access: Women's Politics in Nineteenth-Century America." In *Habermas and the Public Sphere.* Ed. Craig Calhoun. Cambridge, MA and London, England: MIT Press, 1992. pp. 259–288.

Said, Edward. *Culture and Imperialism.* New York: Vintage Books, 1993.

———. *Out of Place: A Memoir.* New York: Vintage Books, 1999.

Saltman, Kenneth J. *The Edison Schools: Corporate Schooling and the Assault on Public Education.* New York and London: Routledge, 2005.

Sassen, Saskia. *Globalization and Its Discontents: Essays on the New Mobility of People and Money.* New York: New Press, 1998.

Scheuerman, William E. *Between the Norm and the Exception: The Frankfurt School and the Rule of Law.* Cambridge, MA and London, England: MIT Press, 1994.

Scott, Joan W. "Experience." In *Feminists Theorize the Political.* Ed. Judith Butler and Joan W. Scott. New York and London: Routledge, 1992.

Sedgwick, Eve Kosofsky. *Epistemology of the Closet.* Berkeley and Los Angeles: University of California Press, 1990.

Seigneurie, Ken. "Anointing the Rubble: Ruins in the Lebanese War Novel." *Comparative Studies of South Asia, Africa and the Middle East* 28: 1 (2008): 50–60.

———. "Introduction: A Survival Aesthetic for Ongoing War." In *Crisis and Memory: The Representation of Space in Modern Levantine Narrative.* Ed. Ken Seigneurie. Wiesbaden: Reichert, 2003. pp. 11–32.

Sinno, Nadine. "Deconstruction the Myth of Liberation @ Riverbendblog. com." In *Feminism and War: Confronting U.S. Imperialism.* Ed. Robin L. Riley, Chandra Talpade Mohanty, and Minne Bruce Pratt. London and New York: Zed Books, 2008.

Tavernise, Sabrina. "Afghan Enclave Seen as Model to Rebuild, and Rebuff Taliban." *New York Times* (November 13, 2009): http://www.nytimes.com/2009/11/13/world/asia/13jurm.html?_r=1&scp=1&sq=Afghan%20Enclave&st=cse.

Taylor, Charles. "To Follow a Rule..." *Bourdieu: Critical Perspectives.* Ed. Edward Lipuma, Moishe Postone, and Craig J. Calhoun. Chicago: University of Chicago Press, 1993. pp. 45–60.

Warner, Michael. *Publics and Counterpublics.* New York: Zone Books, 2005.

Wellmer, Albrecht. "Reason, Utopia, and the *Dialectic of Enlightenment.*" In *Habermas and Modernity.* Ed. Richard J. Bernstein. Cambridge, MA: MIT Press, 1985.pp. 35–66.

Wichterich, Christa. *The Globalized Woman: Reports from a Future of Inequality.* Trans. Patrick Camiller. London and New York: Zed Books, 2000.

Wilke, Sabine and Heidi Schlipphacke. "Construction of a Gendered Subject: A Feminist Reading of Adorno's *Aesthetic Theory.*" In *The Semblance of Subjectivity: Essays in Adorno's Aesthetic Theory.* Ed. Tom Huhn and Lambert Zuidervaart. Cambridge, MA and London: MIT Press, 1997. pp. 287–308.

Williams, Jeffrey. "What Is an Intellectual Woman? An Interview with Toril Moi." *Minnesota Review* 67 (Fall 2006): http://www.theminnesotareview.org/journal/ns67/interview_moi.shtml#.

Wittgenstein, Ludwig. *Philosophical Investigations: The German Text, with a Revised English Translation, 50th Anniversary Commemorative Edition.* Trans. G. E. M. Anscombe. Malden, MA and Oxford, UK: Blackwell, 1953, 1958, 2001.

Wollstonecraft, Mary. *A Vindication of the Rights of Woman: An Authoritative Text, Backgrounds, The Wollstonecraft Debate, Criticism. Second Edition.* Ed. Carol H. Poston. New York and London: W. W. Norton, 1988/1975.

Wright, Charles. "Particularity and Perspective Taking: On Feminism and Habermas's Discourse Theory of Morality." *Hypatia* 19, 4 (Fall 2004): 49–77.

Wright, Melissa W. *Disposable Women and Other Myths of Global Capitalism.* New York and London: Routledge, 2006.

Yamani, Mai. "The Challenge of Globalization in Saudi Arabia." In *On Shifting Ground: Muslim Women in the Global Era.* Ed. Fereshteh Nouraie-Simone. New York: The Feminist Press at the City University of New York, 2005. pp. 80–87.

Yes Men. "Routledge Just Says 'Yes' To Dow: The Collaboration of a Progressive Academic Press and a Large Chemical Corporation." Access: December 31, 2009.

Young, Iris Marion. *Throwing Like a Girl and Other Essays in Feminist Philosophy and Social Theory.* Bloomington and Indianapolis: Indiana University Press, 1990.

Zernike, Kate. "Postfeminism and Other Fairy Tales." *New York Times, Week in Review* (Sunday, March 16, 2008): 1, 8.

INDEX

CPSIA information can be obtained at www.ICGtesting.com
Printed in the USA
BVOW011621210911

271777BV00002B/1/P